QUEEN OF THE WEST

QUEEN OF THE WEST

A DOCUMENTARY HISTORY

OF SAN ANTONIO, 1718–1900

RICHARD BRUCE WINDERS

Schreiner University • Kerrville, TX
325-660-1752 • www.mcwhiney.org

Copyright 2021, State House Press
All rights reserved

Cataloging-in-Publication Data

Names: Winders, Richard Bruce, 1953 -, author.
Title: Queen of the west: a documentary history of San Antonio, 1718-1990 / Richard Bruce Winders.
Description: First edition. | Kerrville, TX: State House Press, 2021. | Includes bibliographical references, illustrations, maps, and index.
Identifiers; ISBN 9781649670038 (cloth); ISBN 9781649670045 (e-book)
Subjects: LCSH: San Antonio (Tex.) – History. | San Antonio (Tex.) – History – Sources.
Classification: F394.S2 (print) | DCC 976.4

No part of this book may be reproduced in any form unless with written permission from State House Press, except for brief passages by reviewers.

First edition 2021

Cover and page design by Allen Griffith of Eye 4 Design

Distributed by Texas A&M University Press Consortium
800-826-8911
www.tamupress.com

Contents

1	INTRODUCTION

PART 1: SPANISH TEXAS

7	Claiming San Antonio for Spain, 1718
11	Regulating Life at a Mission
18	The Canary Islanders Travel to Texas
22	Dispute Between the Villa and the Missions, 1739–1741
41	San Antonio as Seen by Governor Winthuysen, ca. 1744
44	1772 Presidial Regulations Resulting from Rubí's 1766–68 Inspection Tour
48	Royal Decree on Wild Cattle and Horses, 1778
55	Change Comes to the Missions, ca. 1792
62	Description of Texas in 1803
65	Zebulon Pike Visits San Antonio de Béxar in 1807
70	Rebels & Royalists Bring Devastation to San Antonio de Béxar, 1813

PART 2: MEXICAN TEXAS

83	Stephen F. Austin Arrives in San Antonio in 1821
85	Mexican Border Commission Views San Antonio, 1828
94	San Antonio de Béxar in 1828 by J. C. Clopper
102	City Ordinances for San Antonio de Béxar, 1829
114	Benjamin Lundy Visits San Antonio, 1833
122	Col. Juan Almonte's Report: Department of Bexar in 1834
125	Samuel A. Maverick's Account of the Siege of Béxar, 1835
137	Importance of San Antonio de Béxar in the Texas Revolution

140   Eulalia Yorba: An Eye Witness Account of the Battle of the Alamo
145   Juan Seguin to the Residents of Béxar, 1836

PART 3: REPUBLIC OF TEXAS

149   Mary A. Maverick Moves to San Antonio, 1838
154   Mary A. Maverick's Account of the Council House Fight, 1840
159   Christmas Time in San Antonio, 1840
161   Republic of Texas Recognizes Catholic Church's Property Rights, 1841
163   General Rafael Vázquez Captures San Antonio, March 1842
165   General Adrian Woll Captures San Antonio, September 1842
169   Frederic Benjamin Page: A "Suthron's" View of San Antonio ca. 1845

PART 4: EARLY STATEHOOD

179   San Antonio in 1846 by Josiah Gregg
182   A Kentucky Volunteer in San Antonio, 1846
187   A German Scientist Attends a Fandango, 1847
192   Recommendation to Use Parts of the Alamo as Military Depot, 1847
196   San Antonio As Reported in *The Alamo Star*, 1854
218   U.S. Inspector General's Inspection Report, 1856
221   Frederick Law Olmstead on San Antonio, ca. 1857
227   Inspector General Report for San Antonio in 1861

PART 5: SAN ANTONIO IN THE CIVIL WAR

235   General Twiggs Surrenders San Antonio to the State of Texas, 1861
241   Federal Surrender of San Antonio from a Texan's View, 1861
245   Life in San Antonio during the Civil War

PART 6: SAN ANTONIO COMES OF AGE

251   A U.S. Cavalryman's View of San Antonio, 1866
256   Sidney Lanier Visits San Antonio, 1873
267   Description of San Antonio in the Late Nineteenth Century by a Resident
278   President William McKinley Visits San Antonio, 1901
281   The San Antonio International Fair, ca. 1901

285   **ENDNOTES**
289   **SOURCES CITED**
293   **INDEX**

Acknowledgements

Few endeavors in life are truly solitary efforts. Perhaps this notion is no more evident than in the field of history. Although authors' conclusions may their own, they all relied on a trail left by others that directed them along their own investigations of the past. I certainly benefited from the work of others in my career and in the production of this collection of documents. I owe a debt of gratitude to all whose work appears in this volume.

I would like to think Judge Nelson Wolfe, Betty Bouche, and the Béxar County Historical Commission for making this work possible. Judge Wolfe contacted me shortly after I left the Alamo and offered me the opportunity to serve as a historical consultant for the BCHC. Queen of the West is the result of a project I pitched to Betty and she encouraged me to proceed on it. It would not have been possible without the support they all gave me.

I owe another debt of gratitude to Don and Louise Yena. Noted collectors of Spanish and Western artifacts, this generous couple has graciously allowed me to view and examine tangible pieces of Texas' history. Don, a well-known Western artist, offered to provide the cover art for the more when I gave him and Louise an early copy of the manuscript to read. The vignettes he created perfectly illustrate the story told by these documents. Thanks, too, to John Goodspeed, who provided photographs of the original oil painting to the press.

QUEEN OF THE WEST

Introduction

What a different appearance SAN ANTONIO now presents, she is now making rapid strides in everything that pertains to the advancement of civilization, there are many beautiful buildings going up in our city, both private and mercantile. This spirit of endeavor is diffusing itself among the people and we now have very good schools, but we need a College, and when we get it, we will have every facility for education. And we may look to the time when SAN ANTONIO will be the QUEEN of the WEST.

The Alamo Star
May 13, 1854

I moved to San Antonio in 1996 when I was asked by the Daughters of the Republic of Texas to serve as the Alamo's curator and its first professional historian. I left that position in 2019, long after the Texas Legislature transferred custodianship of the site to the Texas General Land Office. My twenty-three years at the Alamo gave me a unique perspective on the Alamo's history and the equally unique history of San Antonio. It has been an education that I could not have obtained anywhere else.

My primary task, as I viewed it, was to find a way to explain to visitors why the site matters. I started by endeavoring to understand the elements of the traditional Alamo story. How did this story come to be? Where and when did these elements become part of the narrative? This led me to start examining the evidence, some of it old and some of it recently uncovered. My work convinced me that it is still important to honor the traditional story because it is deeply rooted in the hearts and minds of Texans, Americans, and indeed, people of all nationalities. However, it has also become equally important to place the Alamo story in a context that treated it as a real historical event.

That might sound strange but I encountered many visitors, nonresidents and residents alike, whose knowledge of the Alamo mainly came from popular culture. The common perception was that the Alamo was an abandoned mission in the middle of nowhere. With this in mind, visitors wondered why the Texans bothered to defend something that was essentially worthless. It seemed to them that the Alamo's garrison had needlessly thrown their lives away for no reason other than empty posturing. What explanation could make the defense of the old mission reasonable and justifiable?

By studying the evidence, I determined that the Battle of the Alamo was not really about the Alamo but about the town of San Antonio de Béxar. However, the town almost never figures into the traditional story in any significant manner. When I would tell visitors that the battle was actually over control of the town, their responds was often, "What town?" I decided that any interpretation of the Alamo story had to include the history of San Antonio in order to ensure that visitors understood the context of the battle. Additionally, I believed it was important for visitors to see the battle as an event that both involved and affected the community in which the Alamo was located.

We developed a philosophy at the Alamo that contends that all history is connected. While many who study history tend to break it into distinct episodes, I see it as a continuous stream where one phase flows into the next. Tracing continuity is as important as chronicling change. I found that especially true in learning about San Antonio's history. To give one example of continuity, its Spanish missions are still an important part of the city's identity even though they have been closed for more than two hundred years. Moreover, the descendants of the people who founded the town and turned it into a modern city are still among its residents. Continuity helps give San Antonio its unique identity.

In short, the story of San Antonio centers on how a frontier outpost became a thriving modern city. The process took place from its founding in 1718 through the end of the nineteenth century. The original purpose of establishing the mission, presidio, and villa was to build a stable community that would contribute to the settlement of frontier. Like all frontiers, dangers and hardships had to be overcome. That was true for all who lived here from 1718 through the end of the frontier era. For me, one of the threads of continuity is how the Spanish, Mexicans, Texians, Texans, and Americans all faced the same problems presented by frontier life and often responded with the same solutions. As an example, the Spanish employed Flying Companies for frontier defense while Texans fielded Texas Rangers. Spanish vaqueros and Texan cowboys both herded Texas cattle at different periods. And through it all people of many different ethnicities and nationalities became Béxareños.

This volume does not claim to be a history of San Antonio. It is a collection of documents and sources that I have found useful in understanding how and why the city developed as it did. To me, the history comes alive through the documents' various authors. I focused on the period from 1718 to 1900 because it was during these years that San Antonio transformed from a frontier outpost to model Edwardian city. My intention is to make these documents available to both visitors and residents so that they can begin to understand the rich story that is San Antonio. As such, I hope that this volume provides a starting place for the reader and not a final destination. I encourage readers who are interested to consult the sources from which these documents were drawn in order to view comments other editors have made. An important tool in gaining historical knowledge is the ability to follow trails left by others.

Dr. Richard Bruce Winders
Alamo Curator & Historian, 1996–2019
Béxar County Historical Commission Consultant, 2019–2021

PART 1: SPANISH TEXAS

Claiming San Antonio for Spain, 1718

INTRODUCTION TO DOCUMENT

By the mid-1600s Spanish advancement northeastward from Mexico City had reached the modern Mexican states of Tamaulipas, Nuevo Leon, and Coahuila but had not yet extended beyond the Rio Grande. News of a French settlement on the coast somewhere on Matagorda Bay forced Spanish officials to act decisively if they were to uphold Spain's claim to Texas. Although relieved by the news that a Spanish expedition had found the remains of La Salle's failed attempt to establish a French foothold, officials realized that the time had come to physically occupy what had become contested territory. Several outposts manned by missionaries and soldiers sprang up along the Texas-Louisiana border. Officials decided that they needed to establish a interior line to support both support these isolated settlements as well as establish Spanish power and culture between Louisiana and the Rio Grande. Several previous expeditions had recommended the headwaters of the San Antonio River as the best location for a mission, presidio, and civil town.

In February 1718, Martín de Alacrón, the recently appointed governor of the Province of Texas, led an expedition to plant Spain's footprint on what would become San Antonio. He was accompanied by "seventy-two persons, including three religious, six soldiers with their families, muleteers, and servants of the

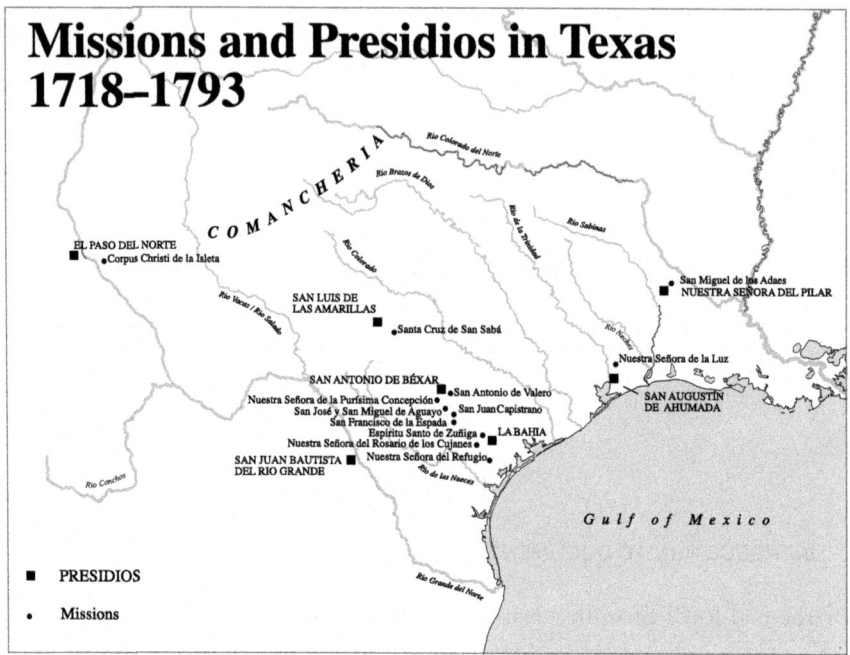

governor." He took with him "six droves of mules laden with supplies, cattle, sheep, and goats, chickens, and more than five hundred and fifty horses, more or less." The expedition crossed the Rio Grande on February 16 and arrived at the future site of San Antonio on April 25, 1718, a journey lasting about sixty-five days.

DOCUMENT[1]

On the 25th [April 1718] we arrived at about noon at the first spring of San Antonio which is about six leagues [18 miles] distant. The road is rough until arriving at the creek which they call De Léon, which is about three leagues [9 miles] from the Medina. Near it is another with running water, which they say runs abundantly further downstream. The rest of the road is very level. This place in which we find ourselves is pretty because of the trees that it has at its spring. The water is sweet and very fine. Where the two springs meet the stream is about two varas wide [5 feet]

The Texas cattle industry had its origins in the mission ranches surrounding Béxar.
Daughters of the Republic of Texas Collection at Texas A&M University-San Antonio.

and is more than a vara and a half deep [4 feet]. It is swift, very easy to extract, and leaves the stream to irrigate good and sufficient lands. The trees which the wood contains consist of pecans, mulberries, elms, and poplars, and there are also many grapevines, one of which is larger than the one on the Frío River.

From this day until the sixth of May, several excursions were made to examine the land, and nothing of special interest was found, except that above the ford of the San Antonio River, about a fourth of a league [3/4 mile], near the spring, a place to draw water was found. From this place the entire river may be drawn out with ease. It will involve a good deal of work, since the lands are a league and a half distant [4.5 miles]. The water rises to the top of the ground, and the entire work is a matter of using a plow. The lands are extensive and level. They form a kind of pasture enclosed on one side by the river and on the other by some hills, not very high. The water is sufficient for maintaining a populous villa and two or three missions. The governor took possession of all this land on the 5th of May, fixing the royal standard on it as a symbol of possession. After the holy sacrifice of the mass had first been celebrated. The mission of the reverend father, Fray Antonio de San Buenaventura y Olivares, is near the first spring, half a league [1.5 miles] from the high ground and adjoining a small thicket of live oaks, where at present he is building a hut.

Regulating Life at a Mission

INTRODUCTION TO DOCUMENT

Spain, a Catholic nation, entered its quest for new kingdoms in the Americas at the culmination of two religious conflicts. The first, the Reconquista had just resulted in the victory over the Islamic forces that had occupied the Iberian peninsula for centuries. The second, the Protestant Reformation, gave rise to a split within the Church where reformers, or Protestants, broke away from the Catholic Church and Roman control. These conflicts would help shape Spanish actions for years to come.

To be Spanish was to be Catholic. Thus, defending the faith was seen as a prime duty of not just the Church but the state as well. Missionary endeavors, which followed in the wake of the conquistadors' campaigns and the wars of religion at home in Europe, were initially funded in part out of the royal war chest. This joint venture by the Catholic Church and Spanish state worked together to plant Spanish culture in new territories claimed for the King.

The Church's interest was in saving souls by introducing Christianity among native population. To accomplish this on the frontier, the Church established settlements called missions which served as Indian pueblos. The physical structure of the mission benefited the Church because it furthered the process of religious conversion by (1) separating converts from the unconverted, (2) collecting the converts in a central location for management & education, and (3) providing the comforts that should be afforded Christians. Once converted, natives who accepted the faith could no longer live in the wild as heathens so attempts were made to bring them back to the mission lest their souls be lost by being separated from God.

The Spanish state's interest was in safeguarding and expanding its territory and resources. The physical structure of the mission benefited the state because it furthered the process of secular conversion by (1) staking out territory claimed by the Spanish king by providing sites for defense and diplomacy, (2) serving as home to a loyal Spanish population where before there had been none, and (3) becoming the nucleus of a permanent Spanish community.

The goal of any mission was to create a loyal and self-sufficient village of Indian converts trained in Spanish culture and governance. Missions can be best be understood as a type of seminary where the converts received instruction not only in religion but on-the-job-training to become Spanish subjects. Missionaries followed guidelines in regulating life at their missions.

DOCUMENT[2]

Article 1. On all feast days, whether of two crosses [first-class feast], which binds the Indians, or of one cross [second-class], Mass is offered and all should attend. There is this difference: on the eve of a first-class feast, the bells are rung at noon, in the evening and before Mass; but on second-class feasts, the bells are not rung at noon, but only in the evening and before Mass.

Article 2. On all Saturdays of the year it is also customary to say Mass and the bell is rung just before it. If it can be a high Mass [sung Mass] and someone is available to officiate, it should be the Mass of the Immaculate Conception whenever possible.

Article 7. With regards to the prayers which the Indians are to say during the week, the following is to be observed: on all days of catechizing and on Fridays the bell is rung at sunset. When the people have assembled the *Doctrina* is recited. On Mondays and Wednesdays Fr. Casaño's catechism is said aloud. When a boy asks a question, all answer. When this is finished, all recite the Act of Contrition. Then the missionary ascends to pulpit and begins to explain as he sees fit. On

Tuesdays and Thursdays they recite the prayers, beginning with our Father and continuing on to the Sacraments and general confession. On Friday they pray the Way of the Cross inside the church, and one of them leads the prayers. During Lent the Missionary is the one who leads the Way of the Cross in church and prays before the stations portraying the mysteries. A boy carries the lamp so that the missionary can read the prayers. On all these days services are concluded with the singing of the "Salve" in verse form, as is customary. On Saturday before the setting of the sun, the bells are rung briefly and as soon as the people gather, they begin to pray the Rosary and finish with singing the "Alabado." On feast days which are obligatory for the Indians, they are dispensed from reciting the *Doctrina* and praying the Way of the Cross, but not praying the Rosary on Saturdays. It is up to the missionary to dispense from prayers on other days, according to the events that take place. Ordinarily this happens on the feast days of St. John the Baptist, St. Peter, St. James, and St. Ann, which are the days when the Indians go horseback riding.

Article 13. The evening before the principal feast of the Most Holy Virgin, namely the Immaculate Conception, the Rosary is said in procession in the plaza and the Indians sing the mysteries. In the meantime, firecrackers are set and lights are lit in front of the friary. If so desired, the oil lamps are used, and candles are given to the Indian women to illuminate their homes. When the Rosary is ended, the missionary sings the Litany, and the services end with the usual "Salve."

Article 20. The musicians who perform in church usually are those who specialize in this. The missionary must supply them with musical instruments and repair them when this is needed. From time to time he sees to it that a boy learns how to play, so that there is always one who can play.

Article 25. Every Sunday after Mass as the people leave the church, the missionary gives the fiscal two bundles of tobacco to be distributed to the adults, men and women. This is to be done in the doorway or some other place where the missionary can oversee it. What is left is returned to the missionary. He gives to those who request tobacco during the week, observing the rule, however, not to give until

Wednesday. If he gives before Wednesday when they know they will still have some, they squander what is given to them on Sunday, bartering with the people at the presidio for any trifle. Only two or three leaves of tobacco should be given to them during the week to last until Sunday.

Article 26. Every Monday all the women come for their ration of corn which is given them by the fiscal. He gets the key for the granary from its usual place in the missionary's cell. The amount of corn given to each woman varies with the season; when an abundance of corn is harvested, the married women are given four *almudes* of unshucked corn, and two and a half or three *almudes* to the widow. [One *almude* equaled about 4.5 liters.] When there is little corn, only three *almudes* are given to the married women and two to widows. When shelled corn is available, two *almudes* are given. In order that the missionary may regulate the corn and decide whether the supply is large or small, he must keep in mind that regularly 400 *fanegas* are needed each year to maintain the Indians, taking into account the number of persons in the pueblo and the *fanegas* the missionary can give out either as payment for salaries or for selling purposes.

Article 29. The Indian women frequently ask for things, importuning the missionary for sweets, lard, beans, chili, and a thousand other things. If the missionary is so lenient as to give them what they all ask for, he will have nothing left in the treasury. Therefore, he must act according to what he has on hand, according to the season of the year and other prevailing conditions.

Article 37. By this time the looms should be in operation, making blankets, which the missionary will distribute according as the weaver binds off the material, unless he prefers waiting until all are woven, so that they may be given out at the same time. However, this causes confusion. There should be a narrow cloth for small blankets for the children. The missionary draws up a list of all men, women, and children, and checks their names as they receive their items. This same list serves as a guide in all other rationing of clothing.

Article 45. In order that the missionary may know what he is to include in the annual report for what is needed in the church for divine worship, and to provide for the friary, for the natives' clothing and to keep the servants supplied, he scans the reports of the past years. Experience teaches him to know what is needed to provide for the mission.

Article 54. Each year during the month of October or November, the missionary sees to it that all who can go are sent to herd the cattle in the mission pasture and brand the unbranded cattle. He informs the other missions and the dwellers of the presidio in due time, so that they may separate their cattle from the rest. He cooperates with them in like manner when it is their turn to brand.

Article 60. When the time for planting nears, the irrigation ditches are cleaned, stopping the water where the river enters. The missionary also sees to it that the bridges and the dam are repaired, when needed.

Article 61. When the irrigation ditches are cleaned, the natives will mend the gaps in the fences around the field and repair what is in poor condition. If the weather requires urgency, some can be appointed for this work, while others begin to plow the land, if opportune, or burn the cane which remains from the past harvest. Thus the missionary sees to it that the field is tilled, so that in May, which is the best time of the year, corn can be planted. If this is not possible, then in June.

Article 62. While some do repair work, others are busy preparing the soil for the planting of cotton, fruit, chile, the seedings having already been prepared. The beans are planted in June and there is a designated area for them in the field, or wherever the missionary directs. He also must provide for irrigating in due time, and for the hoeing and weeding. If the cotton has to be replanted, ever effort should be made to have a good crop that year.

Article 63. If the missionary sees that the corn from the last harvest is not enough for the Indians of the mission, he will have it sown early in February or March to have on hand a sufficient supply.

Article 64. During the time of preparing the soil, the women were accustomed to helping the men, doing as much as possible. However, this was stopped for a good reason, due to misconduct, which, prescinding from other matters, resulted in the men's not working fully because they paid too much attention to the women. Also, and this is more important, the women should be home grinding grain and preparing the meals for their husbands and not be going through the fields and doing men's work. During the harvest time it is permitted (only when necessity demands it because of the scarcity of men) for the women who are not infirm or rearing children or expecting a child, to go and help after they have prepared a meal and brought it to their husbands. They can help gather the crop, and care must be taken so that the men do not slow down in their work. Every effort is to be made that as much as possible is gathered in and put away each day. The women and children who are in the mission take the corn from the carts to the granary with the fiscal directing operations.

Article 65. When the harvest is all gathered in, the Indians are accustomed to draw the last cart decorated with banners and ribbons, with bands or straps, and go to the superintendent, governor, and alcalde [of the mission] and sing the "Alabado" with accompanying music. This ends in church. They then go to the missionary's cell to enjoy a refreshment which is usually a bottle of wine. All this rejoicing is had when the harvest is abundant, but when it is small, one can hardly then celebrate.

Article 79. The missionary should see to it also that the small children speak Spanish in order to meet the demands of various decrees, and because of the facility it promotes for both the missionary to understand what they are saying and for the Indians to understand him. The missionary has worked so hard on this that it is a pleasure to listen to the Indian children, even the tiniest ones speaking Spanish. In general, the men and women speak it now, except the newly arrived Indians, for the missionary spares no effort in helping them to learn the language.

Article 80. From time to time the missionary should journey to the coast and bring back the fugitives, who regularly leave the mission trying at the same time to gain some recruits, if possible, so that more conversions are realized and the mission does not come to an end because of the lack of natives. While the missionary is on this errand, the supernumerary is taking his place at the mission, as has been decided by the commandant general and our superiors.

Article 81. Dealing and communications between the Indians and Spaniards are not only allowed but are commanded by the commandant general. Nonetheless, the missionary must expel from the mission those Spaniards who come only to take from the Indians all that they can, gambling with them and exchanging trifles for utensils and practicing evil. This cannot be tolerated, and the missionary should not permit them at the mission. If he asks them not to return and they persist in doing so, he is to order them tied to a stake and whipped. Thus they learn by experience.

Supplement to Articles 23 & 24. . . . . The [new] missionary will experience in his communication and dealings with the Indians that some are good and some are bad, as is the case in the whole wide world.

Likewise, it is good to let him know that while he is getting acquainted with each one, some men and women will not fail to come to him with stories and lies, making disparaging remarks about the former missionary, telling what he gave or did not give, what this one did, and a thousand other things. Nonetheless, the missionary's prudence will keep him from believing such tales. He will always conduct himself as his state in life and religion require. May he excuse all the shortcomings he sees in this instruction which was given only to help him and for his convenience. It is the hope that this may be of assistance to him, especially in matters about which he is doubtful. May all this be for the greater honor and glory of God our Lord, and his most holy Mother, the Virgin Mary.

The Canary Islanders Travel to Texas

INTRODUCTION TO DOCUMENT

Spain planned to settle its northern borderlands by using three separate corporate entities: mission, presidio, and civil town. Besides saving souls, the mission's role was to introduce the local native population to Spanish culture. The presidio's role was to support and defend the mission and deter foreign encroachment into Spanish territory. A civil town, populated with ethnic Spaniards was intended to reinforce the Iberian nature of the newly growing community. In May 1718, the Marqués de San Miguel de Auguyo, acting on the behalf of Viceroy, formally established these three institutions near the headwaters of the San Antonio River: Mission San Antonio de Valero, Presidio de Béxar, and the Villa de Béxar. Of the three the villa failed to take hold because most civilians who came with Auguyo's expedition lived at the presidio for protection.

In 1719, Auguyo recommended that 400 additional settlers from the Spanish Canary Islands be recruited and sent to the newly established outpost on the San Antonio River. Although only fifty-six Islanders eventually agreed to be transported to Texas, by 1730 the group had landed at Vera Cruz. Their journey took them westward from the coast to Mexico City, where they then turned northward to complete their long trek to Texas. While in Saltillo, the Islanders were counted and resupplied before being sent on their last leg of their trip.

Mission San Antonio de Valero was never completed before it was secularized in 1793. Daughters of the Republic of Texas Collection at Texas A&M University-San Antonio.

In addition to royal officials covering the transportation and providing supplies, tools, and utensils to the Islanders, the immigrants were designated *hidalgos*, the lowest title given to nobility. Once they reached San Antonio they were allowed to establish a new villa, called the Villa de San Fernando, as well as organize a civil government.

DOCUMENT[3]

In the town of Santiago del Saltillo de la Nueva Vizcaia [Coahuila], on the twenty-ninth of January, 1731, appeared for me the Notary Public and undersigned witnesses:

Juan Leal Gorza, Juan Leal the boy, Antonio Santos, Salvador Rodriguez, Josephe Cabrera, Manuel de Niz, Francisco Arocha, Vicente Alvarez, Juan Delgado, Mariano Melano, Juan Curbelo, and Phelipe Perez, Josephe Antonio, Martin Lorenzo, Ignacio Lorenzo. These last four comprise one family. They are sixteen families, although the Derrotero counted but fifteen. It was resolved here by Captain Don Mathias de Aguirre, at the request of the above named parties, to adjust (or regulate) for sixteen families, numbering altogether fifty-six persons, and these families declared that having presented and represented in writing to Captain Mathias de Aguirre that they came without provisions of any kind and were with neither mules or horses, as stated to his Honor (or to his Worship) and proved by the fact that the horses they had exchanged were unable to continue the journey, and the mules had been returned to their owners; that in order that they might continue the journey to Presidio of San Antonio de Vejar that they be given what was most convenient and necessary, namely: Eighty-six horses, as stated in detail in the account of repartition that was made to each one of the families; also, seventy-seven mules loaded with provisions for their maintenance during the journey from this town to San Antonio; also, twenty-six mules moreover to carry biscuit, meat and everything needed and necessary; also, four mules employed to carry four panier loads (cargas de arganas), making in all the number alluded to, seventy-seven mules. Also, sixteen yokes of oxen. But His Excellency ordered Captain Don Mathias de Aguirre to give only fifteen yokes, yet there was added one yoke for the four single men who made up a family, adding to the said yoke the necessary ploughshare, an axe and pickaxe. In the same manner they declared having received from said Captain sixteen metates, with their grinding stones, as His Excellency had ordered the said Captain. And they said that the said Captain had delivered faithfully and without fault in the said Presidio de San Antonio de Bejar the sixteen yoke of oxen. All of which contained in aforesaid arrived as expressed (or stated). They confessed and acknowledged to having received conformably all the above-mentioned, remaining satisfied, renouncing the laws of the delivered (las leyes de la entrega) and the proof of the receipt contained in them. Leaving the payment of the amount to the will and convenience of His Excellency the Viceroy, Governor and Captain General of this new Spain, which amount the said Don Mathias de Aguirre will give in detail to the officials of the Royal Treasury in the City of Mexico, and to his Attorney, in order that he may be paid the sum that would be equivalent to the above named conformity with that which His Excellency would be pleased to determine and order to be executed, and in order that all agreed upon remain as expressed in the above named contents, they signed it, the witnesses being

Joseph Ramon Ramos, Diego de los Santos and Augustin de Imenarrieta, present, and neighbors of this said town, and who signed it at the request of those who could not sign, and those that could sign for themselves before me, the present Notary, I certify

Juan Leal Goraz, Francisco Arocha, Biscente Alvarez, Francisco Antonio Santo, Juan Delgado, at the request of Juan Curbeleo, Manuel de Niz, Juan Leal the boy, Josephe Cabrera, Salvador Rodriguez, Josephe Padron, and the four that comprised the extra family; and for the widows Maria Rodriguez and Maria Meleano. (Witnesses) Diego de los Santos, Josephe Ramon Ramos, Augustin Imenarrieta. Before me,

Juan Sanchez de Tagle,
Royal Notary Public and of the Corporation

Dispute Between the Villa and the Missions, 1739–1741

INTRODUCTION TO DOCUMENT

In the span of twenty years the headwaters of the San Antonio River had become home to several separate corporate entities, each with its own government. The missions represented the Church and its Indian charges, the presidio represented royal authority, and the villa represented the Canary Islanders and other civilian residents of the town. While all were supposed to advance the interest of Spain, their own interests often caused them to clash. At stake was who had the authority to control local resources such as land, water, and labor.

Friction arose between the area's original settlers and the more recent arrivals from the Canary Islands. Part of the problem can be traced to the fact that the Canary Islanders had been awarded the title of *hidalgo*, the lowest level of nobility, as part their agreement for agreeing to relocate to the Texas frontier. Proud of their position in the emerging local society, they expected the older residents to defer to them. Church officials mounted a vigorous defense against demands such as allowing the missions to hire out their Indian converts as day laborers to work in the fields of the Canary Islanders. These two documents, the first which lays out the grievances of the Canary Islanders and the second which is the response on behalf of the missions, reveal the important issues that occupied the competing communities. The statements identified as errors in the petition submitted for the Canary Islanders are addressed by the Church in the second.

The Church's response to Error No. 8 provides the reason for Mission Valero's transfer to the east bank of the San Antonio River.

DOCUMENT [NO. 1][4]

Royal Presidio of San Antonio de Béjar, March 15, 1741.
Petition of the Canary Islanders—1739

Don Vicente Travieso, high constable, and Don Juan Leal, magistrate of the council, the tribunal and administration of the Villa of San Fernando in the Province of Tejas, come before Your Excellency to see to it that the right prevails and to say that the citizens and first settlers of this villa (error 1), ever since they left the Canary Islands to come to this kingdom (error 2) by the decree of His Majesty, have experience notable discomforts and hardships, especially in this new settlement they have formed. Various and moderate assistance has been given by His Excellency and also by the Marqués de Casafuerte, as can be seen in the three dispatches I present with all due solemnity; the one was orders to be issued by His Excellency and the other two by the Marquez de Casafuerte. But still these most devout measures have not been sufficient to alleviate the miseries and hardships, for the kind influence of His Excellency is some 500 leagues away [1500 miles] (error 3). And so they have felt notable hardships in matters spiritual (error 4) and temporal. In order that Your Excellency may lend assistance, I ask for a better solution to each problem.

The first hardship which these miserable people is the lack of a church in which mass can be said and divine services held. They must, therefore, attend services in a room of the presidio (error 5), and during the rainy season this cannot be done because of the heavy rains. Mass is then said in the room of the guard, which is an open porch. Both places are unbecoming for the celebration of the august Mystery. Some citizens, who want a decent church, have agreed to contribute towards building a church, in so far as their meager means allow. This is clear from the testimony given by the governor of this province, which I duly present. But they have been unable to contribute what they promised because of their great needs (as will be shown later). Would Your Excellency be so kind as to give orders to proceed with the building of a church and assign from the royal treasury the amount Your Excellency would be please to grant, and to appoint a person to look after the accounts. The citizens (error 6) are ready to help with their personal labor.

Likewise, may I mention to Your Excellency that these miserable settlers have no means whatsoever to maintain themselves, because this province has no trade or anything which can give them work, unless it be farming their land, which they cultivate with their own hands. Even by this one occupation that that they have (error 7), they cannot obtain a life's sustenance, because there is no place to sell the corn they harvest (error 8). If they go outside the province, besides the danger from savages, their expenses soar so high, that there is nothing left. On the other hand, if they want to sell to the presidios, the captains do not want to buy, even though the Marquéz de Casafuerte has given regulation for the captains to buy at the price of three pesos (error 9) to supply the presidios. The reason why the captains do not buy from the Islanders is the fact that the missionaries sell corn at two pesos (error 10), since they have no expense in harvesting it. The Indians of the missions are obliged to work for the missionaries and cultivate the fields, but the settlers are unable to get the Indians for work in their fields even though they pay them. In view of this, would Your Excellency order those captains, especially Captain Don Gabreil Costales (error 11) to buy the corn they need from these citizens who are ready to sell at two pesos, which is a very moderate price.

Also, may parties feel the disadvantage of not being able to obtain from the missionaries permission for the Indians to work in their fields, though they would be paid cash for their work. The missionaries have put a stop to all communication between the Spaniards and the Indians (error 12); they also prevent the Indians from cultivating the fields of the Spaniards (error 13). All this is clear from testimonials I duly present. One of them is by Captain Don Joseph de Urrutia, and the other is by the pastor and ecclesiastical judge of this villa (error 14). In them can be seen the other discomforts which my parties suffer. Would Your Excellency therefore, order Captain Don Joseph de Urrutia to take the Indians who are needed for work and see to it that they are not hindered from working for the Islanders, and are paid the daily wage in the presence of the captain?

Since my parties also suffer continuous damage in their fields from the cattle of the missions, though the fields are fenced in (15), would Your Excellency give orders so that these cattle do not enter the fields of the Islanders; also, because their cattle and horses are harmed, would Your Excellency command Captain Don Joseph de Urrutia to see to it with all care that the citizens suffer no harm in themselves, in their fields, nor among their cattle and animals? For all that has been here requested, may a penalty be imposed to insure observance, and the needed dispatch be issued and sent to Captain Urrutia with a penalty attached to enforce it; and may the writings I have presented (error 16) be returned to me, as they are needed by my parties? Therefore, I ask Your Excellency that after the presentation of these writings or provisions, would you give orders as I have requested, and give your decision to the general auditor?

DOCUMENT [NO. 2][5]

The Mirror of Truth which Shows the Errors I Checked in the Preceding Petition [1741].
Fr. Benito Fernandez de St Ana Presidente

I confess that some of the errors I noted (they are errors because they fail to tell the truth), I did so, not to make a defense of the Religious, the Indians, and the missions, but because it seems to me to be entirely fitting to make known errors to you and to His Excellency, so that it be evident that the allegations are made to gain the desired ends, which are prejudicial to the honor of the missionaries and the liberty of the natives. Also, may your Excellency thus get to know the needs which these attorneys mention and decide for yourself what is appropriate and what is agreeable to the royal treasury, who is being petitioned.

The attorneys for the families have not been content to say what the petition expresses but through the testimonies they have proposed to Your Excellency matters that are quite foreign to what is actually going on. There are also some improprieties, such as to make the statement that the Mission of San Antonio is only a gunshot away from the presidio, and then to proceed to mark off sites and distances from one Indian pueblo to another; also, they say that the Mission of San Antonio is not in communication with the presidio; that the Fathers live in great eagerness to lash the Spaniards, promising a reward to anyone who should deliver them into their hands. It seems to me, therefore, to be very much the place to dispel all the impostures and falsehoods and to mention where in the petition these attorneys do not speak the truth, though, it is not my concern to weaken the authority of the informants and to have them repulsed on other occasions by the highest tribunal of His Excellency.

Error 1   The statement that the families of the Canary Islanders are the first settlers of Villa San Fernando is not true, since (and it is a fact) the villa is joined to the Presidio of San Antonio and was settled fourteen years before by soldiers and citizens who lived on plots of ground in the houses they built, with crops they planted, and the irrigation ditches they dug (these the families now possess). It is clearly seen that these families are not the first settlers of Villa San Fernando, for it was already established and settled before they came. They can only have the glory that this pueblo and presidio, already founded, enjoy the name of "villa," which His Majesty gave when these families came in 1731. The case that this does not stand in the way of giving the title of the new founders is that this glory should be given also to other citizens, for only with them could the number which the law requires for founding a new villa be completed. Their labors in digging irrigations ditches and in building residences in the same region are not in vain; much land, which borders on the families' houses and belongs to the King our Lord, is left uncultivated. This land can be divided with the same rights that these families have for water, and other favors can be gained by electing a magistrate. Thus, what is today a villa by name only can become populated in a few years and be a villa in reality.

Error 2   The hardships and labor, which the families have endured since the first days of their arrival, are ordinary ones which human nature must put up with in all parts of the world; compensation is had by obtaining help from others who are in the same difficulties in this Kingdom of New Spain. The lands given by the King our Lord were opened and cleared, and they vie in richness with lands in the rest of the world. The land was fertilized already and a great supply of running water was ready to be drawn. This work had been done previously by the soldiers and settlers. During the time the Islanders were building their home, they lived with citizens and soldiers. With help from the royal treasury they were decently clothed and were supplied with implements, seed, and other needed items. To no one did they pay tax, nor do they now pay tribute to the King our Lord; a few extortions took place, but they were common in the entire province. There is a war with the Apache Indians; and problems that cause war in Europe are met with. These problems loom large but they are far less than the problems caused by hostile Indians in these regions. And so the notable discomforts and hardships which (as the Islanders say) they suffer, are, or seem to be, those of delicate women rather than those of manly men, who are called the first founders and settlers of a villa in the vast province of Texas.

Error 3   From the court in Mexico [City] to the Presidio San Antonio and the Villa San Fernando the distance is 370 [1,125 miles] leagues and not 500 [1,500 miles]. It is a vast expanse and that in a large stretch of land; this is conducive to enlist the charity of the Most Excellent Lords of the Viceroys.

Error 4   The hardships which the families suffer in matters spiritual, which the benign influence of the Most Excellent Viceroys cannot forestall, consists in this, that they have no large church. It is true, however, that they attend Mass in an adobe church, which they found already built. It has served and does serve the soldiers, the citizens, and other families as a place where they can assist at divine services (as all others in this country do). In measures temporal, the flat roof leaks. Not having other spiritual hardships, which can be characterized as serious, they cannot say truthfully that notable hardships are endured in spiritual matters.

Error 5   The room which served as a church from the beginning was constructed for a church and never was nor now is a soldier's quarters. The times when Mass was said in the guardroom has not been more than twice in a long stretch of ten years. It seems, then, that the attorneys for the families do not speak the truth in saying that Mass is said in a guardroom and that the place is unbecoming, and that it is a soldier's quarters that serves as a church today.

Error 6   If the citizens of the Villa San Fernando would work together to build a new church (whose walls are already almost finished, for they had more than two years to do this and the wood was cut [for them]), without doubt the building now would be complete and they would not have to ask the royal treasury to pay all the expenses. It is not true to say that they were ready to work together and give personal labor to build their church, for, as I have said, there is not much more to do to finish it, and the soldiers and the citizens are not refusing cooperation in doing what they can in that construction, if only the families would divide the work and would not engage in quibbling and walkouts that end up in untruths.

Error 7   The attorneys say that the only work the families have to maintain their livelihood is farming. If this is true, then the Islanders are lazy, for their fields are full of undergrowth. When the King our Lord gave them the land, it was clean and clear. Since it is not just to accuse them of the crime of laziness, for then the purpose of his Majesty in bringing to this province from the Islands would be frustrated with rising cost for the royal treasury, it must be stated that the families do not have only one kind of work, that of farming, for many of them roam about. In truth, the families of the Canary Islands could not exceed sixteen, and those who are only farmers are least in number. It is a fact that one of the attorneys is not a farmer; he is the high constable; neither are Señor Francisco Arrocha, Señor Antonio Rodriguez, Dionis [Manuel de Niz?], and other [farmers]. The three Leals are more merchants than farmers. One of the Islanders is a carpenter and four are soldiers. The breeding of cattle, raising vegetables and fruit, and making cheese do not bring exceptional profit in these regions. And so the attorneys do not speak well in saying that the only work of the families is farming their lands.

They also say that in this province one cannot engage in trade and so it is necessary to be employed in the work of farming. They ought to cite the family of the deceased Don Miguel Núñez and of Joseph Antonio Rodríguez. Citizens, as also high constable, an Islander, who maintain themselves quite comfortably by trading; there are others who maintain themselves by trade alone. And so it is not true to say that in the province there is no trade nor that one cannot be sustained by this work but that all are forced to the hard work of farming.

Error 8   Corn harvested by the Islanders is much less than what they could harvest, and by not having more, they often lack to supply the soldiers and other citizens who have no land, for land has not been given them. Never has it been the case of having no demand for corn, for they could always sell to the captain of the presidio of San Antonio without going to the pueblos of the Indians. It is not certain or true, then, that the farmer Islanders have no market to sell their corn, nor is it necessary for them to bring it to other provinces as a last resort.

Error 9   There is no decree from the Most Excellent Señor, the Marqués de Casafuerte, saying that the captains of this province are to buy, at the price of three pesos, from the Islanders, and from no one else. It is an error that destroys rectitude and frustrates the regulations of his Excellency, the Lord Marqués de Casafuerte.

The attorneys for the Islanders do not speak the truth when they say that they have such a decree in their favor. Only the captains can impose the obligation on the soldiers (according to regulations) to buy corn at three pesos. They would not be able to compensate for the cost and default by arranging to give rations to the entire company and their families. As so his Excellency never gave such a decree and thus did not obligate the captains.

Error 10 In this country there are no other crops than those planted by some of the families and by the Indians of the missions, who consume the corn and sell what is left over to procure clothing for all the Indians, and other items that are needed in civilized life, so that the Indians continue to improve their lot. One must note here that the condition is not attained whereby the produce of the crops is sufficient to meet the expenses incurred by the missionaries in behalf of the Indians. It is necessary to use the alms given by the King our Lord for their maintenance, and other alms given by devout faithful. The Fathers share in the hardships endured in order to maintain the Indians. They direct and exhort and even help the Indians personally in building, planting, drawing water, and other activities. The attorneys speak very poorly when they say that the apostolic Fathers in these regions profit by the sweat of the Indians. They should say rather that the charity and zeal of holy faith make the missionaries work like carpenters, bricklayers, teamsters, and even slaves of the Indians with no temporal reward. It must be made known how contrary the real conditions are to what is insinuated by the words which the attorneys of the families inserted in their petition: *The missionaries give them the corn at two pesos, since they have no expense in harvesting it, for they force those same Indians of the missions to cultivate and work the fields.*

What the attorneys tried to do by these words they inserted in their petition, and also by the following words: *The citizens cannot succeed in having the Indians work on their farms, not even by paying them,* is to deceive the higher tribunal in this: that the crops sown by the Indians are not for the Indians but for the missionaries and their own interests; and also because of these crops, the missionaries do not permit the Indians to go out and work for daily wages and for the Islanders on their farms. It is certain that there is no such interest for the missionaries nor is it because of this personal interest that they do not allow the Indians to work for others. And so by placing the mirror of truth in the hands of reason, one clearly sees this to be a most unfortunate error, which these lawyers made in regard to the missionaries; it also shows the little respect they have for the higher tribunal of this vast kingdom by presenting falsehoods to their face and in their presence.

The reason why the missionaries do not allow the Indians to work for outsiders is, as I have said already and noted previously, that on this river of San Antonio in 1716 [1718] the King our Lord through the service of the apostolic Fathers as missionaries, founded the Mission of San Antonio on the same site where he gave possession of lands to the Islanders. His Excellency the Lord Viceroy, who then governed this New Spain, set up in that same year of 1716 [1718], or in the following year, the Presidio of San Antonio de Bejar, next to the mission, to guard and defend it from hostile Indians in the vicinity. In the following years, about a league and a half [4.5 miles] south of the mission and presidio, the missionaries founded also Mission San Jose. About this time and during these same years, for the greater comfort of the soldiers and of the citizens and Indians, the missionaries and the captain decided to transfer Mission San Antonio to the opposite side of the river and to the east; the presidio remained where it was on the west side. In this way, the presidio and citizens could use the water from the arroyo of San Pedro, which is full of water; the Indians dug another irrigation ditch from the San Antonio River. Thus, without the Spaniards embarrassing the Indians, two pueblos were formed: one for the Indians and one for the Spaniards. In March of 1731 on the same east bank of the San Antonio River and about a league [3 miles] south of Mission San Antonio, the Mission de Nuestra Señora de la Concepción de Acuña was placed. In that same direction and two leagues [6 miles] away, the Mission San Juan Capistrano was founded. To the west of this mission and on the other side of the river, Mission de Nuestro Padre San Francisco de la Espada was established. It has a road to the north to Mission San Jose, which is about a league and a half away [4.5 miles], and from this mission in the same direction and distance is the Presidio of San Antonio. On the San Antonio River, then, six pueblos have been founded: three on the east side and three on the west side of the river. On the east side are Mission San Antonio, Mission de Nuestra Señora de la Concepción, and Mission San Juan Capistrano. On the west side are the presidio and villa, which today is called Villa of San Fernando, Mission San José and Mission de Nuestro Padre San Francisco de la Espada. In the same year of 1731 (after these five missions were founded) the families from the Canary Islands came and joined Presidio San Antonio and its inhabitants; they were given possession of land and water, together with the citizens and soldiers, and later the title of Villa San Fernando was bestowed.

The second point I ought to note is that the King our Lord and his Most Excellent Lord the Viceroy, to further the spread of our holy Faith, which is the first goal, wanted in the second place to have each mission be a pueblo of Indians; so much the more pleasing to His Majesty and to His Excellency the Lord Viceroy were they, when they became more populated and better organized pueblos, tending towards those ends which always are of importance to the royal Crown.

I mention in the third place that there is a notable difference between these new pueblos of Indians and the Villa San Fernando (made up of families presumed to be the founders). These people are Christians, brought up on the Canary Islands and educated, trained in work, and knowing how to sustain and clothe themselves, and all this is achieved by the sweat of their brow. Then, the land they possess, the water they use, and the sites on which they built their houses were already cleared and open and cultivated. Lastly, as already stated, they found houses already built and a presidio to defend them. Little or nothing of all this did the first Indians have or find. First, because the founding Indians were savage Indians, brought up as wild beasts in the hills with no work to do except to hunt to keep alive and be clothed. Secondly, to convert these savages to the faith, it was necessary that these Indians with the help of the missionaries should clear the land and cultivate the fields for planting in order to have food, and also that they work hard at digging an irrigation ditch from the San Antonio River. And so one sees why the missionaries can refuse permission to let the Indians work for outsiders.

The Islanders say that at the expense of the royal treasury a church should be built for them in which they can attend divine services. Without such expense, the missionaries want each pueblo and every new foundation for the Indians to have a church, where the Indian Christians attend divine services and the gentiles are instructed in Christian Doctrine. Also, the Indians should have a house to live in and a granary to store their grain; there should be a house for the missionaries all other things needed for men to live civilly in pueblos and in the holy faith. Nothing of this can be had by diverting the Indians to that which the Islanders demand.

The missionaries do not allow the Indians to work for outsiders not because of personal interest but to safeguard the spiritual and temporal welfare of the Indians and to reach the goal set by His Majesty and the Most Excellent Lord the Viceroy. And that goal is to have the Indians, after their conversion to the holy faith, form a new settlement for the Crown, where the new children and subjects live as comfortably as they can (this is what our royal monarch desires), and thus win over the gentiles, who on seeing the good treatment and convenience those already enjoy, will be moved to join the missions. Book 4, Title 3, Law 1.

The missionaries foresee many inconveniences which the families do not know, either because they do not want to or because it is convenient for them not to know. These Indians of the missions (as said before) are born in the forest and do not do the work which civilized life brings with it; now they work in their own pueblos with great moderation and even this means great hardship for them and some Indians leave the mission for that reason. If these Indians would be obliged to do a day's work to keep alive and clothe themselves, it seems certain that they would draw back and revert to the full freedom of the forest and live only to hunt and in complete liberty. For this reason His Majesty directs by his laws (Book 6, Title 1, and Law 20o) that the Indians are not obliged to work until they have spent some years in the mission.

Every day the missionaries see to it that the Indians of all ages and conditions of life recite the Christian Doctrine and by this gentle influence gain good knowledge; at the same time the missionaries go on explaining the sacred mysteries. This could not be done if the Indians were day laborers; they could not then be maintained as they are now cared for at the mission; nor could they attend catechism instruction regularly. The missionary thinks it best for the Indians to form their pueblo leisurely and attend daily catechism and not be forced to work every day. Besides, the planting done in the missions and all the work is performed by the community. Only the Indian who is a Christian and is strong enough to take care of the old, the infirm, and the non-Christian unfamiliar with work, is capable of becoming a day laborer. [If] these Indians become day laborers, [then] they and their wives and children maintain themselves with difficulty. If those who can work daily are working for the Islanders, then the others in the mission would necessarily die, for no planting would be done in the mission. Not only would the Indians suffer hardship, as was said, but the rest of the province would be forced to go to the granaries of food at rising prices, which is the purpose of the petition presented to the higher tribunal of His Excellency by the attorneys for the families. That this would be so is very evident. In each mission there is only one corn field and only one granary for all the Indians and beyond this there is no planting done, neither by the missionaries nor by anyone else. This would be ascribed then to them, to the missionaries, and to their own interests; in the end no mission would plant and products could be sold at the price desired by the Islanders. I spoke to Señor Juan Leal, one of the lawyers, and made the same remark to him. He replied that it was not his intention to hinder the planting done by the Indians but only that they should not sell corn that is left over at the regular price. But this is what they intend in their dubious claim, which I hold to be unjust in both Spains for it is completely opposed to natural reason. These Indians are settlers and natives; the Islanders are settlers and foreigners. The two pueblos of natives were founded long before the families left the Canary Islands; the other two [three] were founded at the same time and somewhat before the families entered this province. The King our Lord wants and commands that the natives live a civilized life and go clothed and walk in our holy Faith. Means are not wanting for the Islanders to clothe themselves. It seems to be something beyond reason to expect these pueblos of Indians to give out goods they need themselves for clothing, and other items needed to live a civilized life and establish their pueblos. It is something beyond an irremediable crime to begin to think that the King our Lord brought from the Canary Islands men who thought to justify such injustice to the natives. And so the claim of the lawyers made that they found things unreasonable is contrary to what our royal monarch wants and commands.

Error 11   The captains of the Presidio of San Antonio always used up the corn that the Indians harvested. This past year of 1740 not one family had corn for itself and the deceased Captain Don Joseph de Urruita was forced to buy corn at Mission San Antonio. Though it is true that Captain Don Gabriel Costales of Bahía paid for corn obtained from the missions to supply his soldiers, it is not true what the lawyers say that the captains did not buy corn from the Islanders because the missionaries sold it for two pesos. What alone is true that a captain does not buy from the families because they have no corn to sell or because it is more convenient for him to buy corn in the missions.

Those who can issue the few authorizations for payment for corn—payments which are much needed by the missions—are the captains of the presidios of San Antonio and of Bahía. These two the Islanders intend to compel by higher orders to buy from them and no others. Then the five pueblos of Indians could neither sell or find a buyer. It would be necessary then to have recourse to His Excellency so that the royal treasury start a store where the Indians in establishing their pueblos and a civilized life can find plows, hoes, hatchets, and other implements; metates, kettles, pots, and other domestic utensils; cloth, flannel and wool, and other items for clothing; and also some medicine and treatment for the infirmed.

Error 12 Neither is it true that the missionaries hinder all communication between the Indians and the Spaniards, as the lawyers say, for one can see at every step the Indians of the missions among the neighbors, and the soldiers, and the Islanders. Although the Fathers see them in the mission and outside of it, they say nothing or do anything to have them withdraw from such contact and communication. All the Spaniards, who want to and without any distinction, enter the missions. What the Fathers are concerned about is that some Spaniard of less note, and others who have only the name of a Spaniard, should not enter the cabins of the Indians, and that the intruders should not buy the domestic utensils given by the Fathers to the Indians, who are to live and maintain themselves at the mission. These items are metates, kettles, pots, hoes, and other needed articles. It is certain that some Spaniards do this, and if it becomes necessary, I shall present a juridical statement. Some persons enter the cabins of the Indians and take advantage of them. For this reason and because of other disadvantages, which I omit, the Fathers do not want the Spaniards to go from cabin to cabin, except those who, because of their office or character or customs, are persons from whom trouble is not expected. The Father also prevent Indian women from going to the presidio, but they allow all to go about with great care because of troubles experienced in the past from this sort of communication. Also, the Fathers want the Spaniards to trade with the Indians in the presence of the Fathers, since quarrels arise when this condition is not observed, even though it be trading only for hides. No one is hindered from trading with the Indians if the conditions are observed. Although the testimonies (which the lawyers do not present) say just the opposite, what I say is true and reflects actual events, as can be seen by all in the province.

To say that all communication between the Indians and the Spaniards is completely hindered is a falsehood, uttered by these lawyers. I have said already that the planting done in the missions is the work of the Indians community for the Indians, and all the implements and other needed items belong to the community. The Spaniards, who trade with an Indian, ought to understand that those items, which are sold or used, belong to the community and if obtained are gotten deceitfully; the best items cannot be supplied and the most valuable are wasted. Every Indian receives an abundant ration of corn for himself and his family, so that they live happily and contently in the mission. This ration of corn is often traded by the Indians for things of no value; this robs the community of corn that could be purchase clothing and other needed items. When this cannot be done, the Indians suffer hunger or must flee to the hills for food; nothing is remedied by this. So much is bought for the Indians as is obtained from the amount of corn that is sold. Therefore, the Fathers justly try to avoid such deals because of bad consequences, and because the Fathers later on must ask for alms to maintain the Indians and obtain what is needed for civilized life.

Indians riding down the streets of early Béxar were a common sight, especially on trade days. Daughters of the Republic of Texas Collection at Texas A&M University-San Antonio.

Error 13   I do not see how the Fathers hinder the Indians from being trained and I am ignorant of the ways of training the Islanders have. But the Fathers used effective means to teach the Indians how to use the axe and clear the lands, and also how to plow and plant an irrigate the fields, how to build houses, become carpenters and tailors; and this the Fathers also achieved with greater effort: they have taught the Indians the mysteries of our holy Faith. Fathers speak a purer Spanish than the Islanders do, and I find no special trade in which the Islanders may train the Indians, and much less can they educate the Indians in the way of holding meetings, or in the exercise of some diversion. They can train the Indians in what the Indians desire and in other matters also. But the Islanders are not to curse, swear, or blaspheme in the presence of the Indians, and much less let them see in the presidio and the villa actions which will teach them to offend God; thus they can show (which is very difficult) the practice of sweet charity.

Error 14   Among the points brought up in the testimonials (which the lawyers do not present and which the attestors should not give) it is said that the Fathers (mainly those in Mission San Antonio) live in great eagerness to lash the Spaniards. It is certain that those same lawyers, and most of those who live in the presidio, often entered the mission (when the Father, whom they accuse, was the minister) and the inference is that some shameful consequences rest on all. But this is not the case, for neither the lawyers nor those who testify speak the truth. Such an individual (and there are not three of them) because of the sins of relapse has been threatened with the penance of being whipped in order that he may amend, but this threat does not have the desired effect. This remedy was applied with great moderation to a servant of a citizen, and from this one case the testifier says without any distinction that the Father wanted the Spaniards to impose a penance. This was saying what he wanted to say and to testify to something he should not have testified. What the Father always wanted to find out was: who was entering the homes of the Indians, was he a sheep or a wolf, who was entering his fold? All the missionaries who live in Mission San Antonio should be vigilant, because not far from the presidio and the Villa San Fernando is a place where not infrequently bandits entered, who, if they are not hostile to the royal treasury, are opposed to royal service. It is the great pleasure of the King our Lord to have the new subjects of His Majesty receive the holy faith, be trained in pure customs and suffer no harm in their goods and furnishings.

Error 15   They say in their petition that their fields are fenced in and that nevertheless damage is done to them by the cattle from the missions; in the testimonies (which they did not present) is added the note that the damage is caused mainly by the cattle of Mission Concepción. Father President ignores it all. One of the lawyers, Señor Juan Goraz, agreed that in years past the first alcalde gave orders to the second alcalde, Señor Vicente Travieso (who is the other lawyer) and to the secretary, Señor Francisco Arrocha. The main reason for this (so great as to be prejudicial) was the fact they did not want to submit to the statement he was drawing up, and which had been made known to the families, namely, that the fields should be fenced in and the entrance remain open. In that year all the fields were not separated but some fields were fenced in, as the governor of the kingdom, Don Joseph Francisco Juaregui y Urrutia had ordered. Other fields neither now nor previously were fenced in, as had been ordered. Last year at the request of the missionary of Mission San Antonio, because of the havoc wrought among the cattle of the missions by the Islanders, a lieutenant as interim captain and high magistrate of the villa and missions, went to examine the fields to see if the Islanders had them fenced in. He found (as said already) that some sections were enclosed and others were wide open. At the same time with little distinction, the lawyers told the higher tribunal that their corn fields were fenced in, whereas the magistrate of the country saw with his own eyes that they were open, and so the falsehood of the attorneys could not be indeliberate. The attorney ought to say that the mission cattle caused some damage in the fields because some of the families of the Islanders disobeyed their alcaldes and superiors by not wanting to enclose their fields, as was evident to him when he was alcalde. For this reason the President did not make a case of it. It is not true to say that Father President made no mention of it at all.

From Señor Carvajal, a citizen of the Villa San Fernando, an ox was bought for Mission Concepción. Since the ox was used to eating the corn of the Islanders, it returned to its old pasture away from the mission. Señor Carvajal saw this, as Father President indicated, and ordered it to be killed, and the Islanders knew this. This was one instance of many that could happen because of the open fields. So the President put the case. It does not seem certain that no case was made of the information given by the families. What actually happened was that with the fields open the cattle of those same people came in and ate the corn, as did also the cattle from Mission

Concepción. For this reason, though they continued to kill and mistreat the cattle of Mission Concepción, the Islanders would often kill also the cattle of other Islanders and citizens. In this past year of 1740 in the presence of the magistrate the villa, Father President demanded in the name of the Indians the cows that had been killed, and defended the cause of the Indians to their satisfaction, and as all desired. During all this time the magistrate told me nothing nor did he say if he was asking justly or unjustly, and much less, did he say where such decrees stop. And so the one who attests to the damage done to the corn fields of the Islanders, ought to testify also to the fact that the fields were not enclosed, and also that they suffered loss and even greater damage done by their own cattle, because of the stand they took in not wanting to fence in their fields, as they had been ordered to do.

Error 16 This last error reminds us of what the lawyers retain in their writing and inserted in their petition, according to the information I received from a zealous man of our faith. I am certain that the Señor Fiscal advised that all the writings be returned. The Señor Auditor agrees with this. As so his Most Illustrious and Excellent Lord Viceroy commands it and the reason why the lawyers do not show the writings I ask for is because they want to keep them secret and not let them out to those who would make known the truth. Zeal for our holy faith placed in my hands this petition I presented and it is a faithful copy. Besides the testimonies, there is given only the name of the authors and some points they testify to. And so I cannot reply to all that has been said but I ought in justice tell the Most Excellent Viceroy that none of the testimonies has value because what is said comes from the deceased captain, or is a supposition, or is given by one who is so advanced in age and so broken in health that he would not know how much has been affirmed in this testimony. As to the testimony of the pastor, I have no doubt that it is his, since this is not the first time that he has testified, mainly against Father President. This was not given by a wise person and I propose that his testimonies tend to harm others and our holy faith, which I must defend. Knowing how the pastor acts unreasonably and how much evil can come to the Religious, as can be seen in the decrees drawn up by the governor of the New Kingdom of León, Don Joseph Francisco Jauregui y Urritia, I must say that what the pastor testifies has no value or credibility, whether his testimony be against the Religious or against the Indians and their pueblos.

Having mentioned some of the errors contained in this petition, I must make known in all truth what the missionaries are doing in the province for the Indians, both Christian and infidel, from a motive of charity. There were some missions in nearby provinces, and after increasing expenses incurred by the King our Lord in establishing warehouses to supply the missions, the results were not too satisfactory, for as the goods were easily obtained and were given by the King our Lord, so easily were they squandered. When the time came for planting some fields, before or after conversion, the Indians began to trade, and not having food or clothing, they returned to the free and pagan way of living and ambushed the Spaniards on the road to kill and rob them. To meet these problems the first apostolic missionaries, who came from the province of Quaguila [Coahuila], decided to take over the domestic management of the mission; they saw to it that the Indians and everything that the missions had, belonging to the community, giving to each Indian what was needed for substance; what was left over was to be sold for clothing and the needs of the mission. This method was followed and the good results were clearly seen in the mission and also in the stability of many souls, and all this without warehouses and their expenses. What those missionaries did in the missions of the Río del Norte, which belonged to the Province of Quaguila, the missionaries of the Province of Texas also did, without being criticized by any governor of this province, not even by Brigadier Don Pedro Rivera, the inspector. These were persons who did not judge things according to outward appearances but according to essentials. If one looks at the exterior accomplishments of the apostolic missionaries, one will see what the ignorant say: the missionaries have profits, for they order the Indians to plant the fields, to look after the cattle, to build homes and establish pueblos. But how many see the purpose of the missionaries in tackling such problems, which suggests in no way avarice on the part of the missionaries. Their motive is zeal for the holy faith, which is being planted in the souls of the Indians and takes hold of them by the methods employed. The old Fathers of the Province of the Holy Gospel in Mexico decided on this method in the enlightened and exalted spirit of Venerable María de Jesús de Ágreda. This can be seen in a copy of a letter which Father Alonso de Benavides, custodian of New Mexico, sent to the Religious of he Holy Custody of the Mission of San Pablo of the Kingdom, from Madrid in 1631. It was printed in Mexico by Joseph Bernardo de Hogal in 1730.

Since that method achieved the ends desired by those Fathers and was followed also by the Fathers in this province, it will not result, as the lawyers for the Islanders say, in any cleavage in the religious institute but will result in planting the holy Faith in these vast dominions, which to King our Lord possess in these regions. All this and what I have verified through individuals of the highest character in this country is a sufficient answer to what the families claim through their lawyers. The planting and sale of corn directed by the missionaries are not for themselves or by themselves. Not to allow the Indians to work for others is not for gain on the part of the missionaries but for the spiritual and temporal welfare of the Indians, so that they convert to our holy faith the non-Christians, who see and observe the advantages the converted Indians have by living in the missions.

I ask you then, and in justice plead, that what is contained in the dispatch, that they have won, be not put into practice, because of what I have said. What the lawyers claim is unjust. Only lawsuits will result between the families and the pueblos of the Indians, since both sides have equal rights to sell their products. If it pleases the Most Excellent Viceroy, he will say and with good reason that the missionaries in this province have very little intelligence, for they ask of him solutions that cannot be reached by reason alone without laws. By protesting against the obstinacy of the lawyers in the first place, advice can be given His Excellency that they live quietly and leave us in peace, and we shall do all that the King our Lord desires.

I ask also that you decide, if it please you, to give me the testimony of it all, or the same decrees that touch the welfare of the Indians and their pueblos.

This is what I ask of you in justice and swear that nothing is of malice.

Fr. Benito fernabndez de St Ana Presidente

[Rubric]

San Antonio as Seen by Governor Winthuysen, ca. 1744

INTRODUCTION TO DOCUMENT

Early governors of Spanish Texas initially resided at Los Adaes, a settlement composed of Mission San Miguel and Presidio Nuestra Señora del Pilar. The fact that Los Adaes was located in modern Louisiana demonstrates just how closely Spain and France contested this international boundary during the eighteenth century.

In 1741, Tomás Felipe de Winthuysen, arrived at Los Adaes to take up his post as the newly appointed governor of Texas. The rampant smuggling occurring along the border occupied much of his time in office. This was also during the period when hostilities between the Spanish and the Apache Indians worsened. While in office, Winthuysen made a tour of Texas, including a visit to San Antonio where he noted the various communities found there. He submitted his report on Texas in 1744, a year after his term ended.

Although still a frontier settlement, Winthuysen saw the potential for the community to grow.

DOCUMENT[6]

In the first place, the vast province of Texas and the New Philippines starts at the Medina River, and at a distance from it of approximately six leagues (18 miles) are the presidio of San Antonio de Béxar and the villa of San Fernando, bound on the north [east] by the San Antonio River and on the south [west] by the San Pedro River. The latter does not have as much water as the former, which has its source two leagues [6 miles] from the said presidio. It has so much water not only does it supply irrigation for the fields of the presidio, villa, and five missions, but it could also supply a much larger population. Furthermore, its waters are very soft and healthful and the soil is exceedingly fertile since experience has shown that all kinds of grains, plants, and fruits can be grown.

The construction of the presidio amounts to nothing, since only the crudely shaped houses form a square plaza without any additional rampart. Consequently there have been, and still are incidents of the Apache entering at night and stealing horses, which were tied in the plaza. This is not due to a scarcity of quality stone because nearby there are excellent quarries. However, timber is scare, because it is too far away, and the felling of trees and their transport would require a guard for protection because enemies are raiding this county and the settlements.

There are five missions protected by this presidio: four belong to the College of Santa Cruz de Querétero and one to the College of Guadalupe de Zacatecas. They are located as follows: The Mission of San Antonio [de Valero] is one league [3 miles] from the presidio, south [east] of the river. It has two priests and approximately four hundred families of diverse Indians tribes, most of whom are now Catholic. Because of the conscientious efforts of the priests [the Indians are] expert in many crafts, such as masonry, carpentry, black-smith's trade; making wool and cotton goods, straw beds, and coarse woolen cloth worn by the men, women, and children. The tribes represented at this mission are among the most warlike and skillful in shooting arrows. It is to be noted, however, that these people as well as the Indians of the other tribes and missions, because of their great fear of the Apaches, do not dare attack them by themselves but only with the help of the Spaniards. Experience has shown, should the latter not be there, the Indians would return to the woods.

The mission of [Nuestra Señora de la Purísima] Concepcíon de Acuña is about two leagues [6 miles] from the presidio south of the river. It has two priests and about three hundred families from different Indian tribes. Although not warlike, they are still experts in the mechanical trades, as seen by the structures they and other [Indians] have constructed.

Mission San Francisco de [la] Espada is located about four leagues [12 miles] from the presidio, northwest of the river. It has two priests and approximately two hundred families from diverse Indians tribes, and they are industrious like the former Indians. Every day more gentiles are added to the mission by the encouragement of their relatives who are there and have become Catholics.

Mission San Juan Capistrano is situated more than four leagues [12 miles] from the presidio, south of the river. It is [in] a somewhat unhealthy area. It has two priests and approximately one hundred and fifty families of Indians of good dispositions, but very cowardly.

The mission of St. Joseph de los Guadalupanos is at a distance about three leagues [9 miles] from the said presidio and northwest of the river. It has one priest and about one hundred and fifty Indians, who are industrious like the others.

The villa of San Fernando is contiguous to the said presidio. It is not at all progressive, since its settlers [the Canary Islanders] are more given to prejudice than to progress.

1772 Presidial Regulations Resulting from Rubí's 1766–68 Inspection Tour

INTRODUCTION TO DOCUMENT

The presence of so many historic mission compounds in the American Southwest hides the fact that the northern frontier of New Spain was an active war zone during much of the eighteenth century. These missions, by producing horses, cattle, corn, and other goods, attracted raiding parties on a fairly regular basis. Life for their inhabitants meant constant danger due to nomadic Indians who came looking to carry off horses and even men, women, and children. As noted by Governor Tomás Felipe de Winthuysen in his 1744 report on San Antonio, the Indian converts at Mission Valero were well trained in the use of the bow and arrow. In fact, in 1745, the residents of Valero reportedly helped to drive off an Apache raiding party that attacked Presidio de Béxar.

The Marquez de Rubí conducted a two-year-long inspection tour of New Spain's northern frontier military outposts that resulted in a final report recommending changes to make borderland defense less costly and more effective. Rubí noted in his report that San Antonio's location outside the presidial line meant that it was "the place most exposed in actuality to the invasions and raids of various tribes of warlike Indians of the north." Thus, he recommended Presidio de Béxar and its outpost, Arroyo del Cíbolo, receive additional troops at the expense of presidios along the Louisiana border. France's recent cession of Louisiana to Spain as a result of its defeat in the Seven Years' War (French and Indian War, 1754-1762) had eliminated the need for troops the Louisiana border.

The presidio was not a strictly military village inhabited only by soldiers. Troopers often brough their families with them when they transferred from one post to another. Moreover, soldiers often married into local families, creating strong links to the community. The presidio served as a market for local products and a customer for artisans practicing blacksmithing and other trades. Hence, the regulation intended to strengthen military-civil relations, realizing that drawing more civilians to the areas was key to it growth and defense.

DOCUMENT[7]

… San Antonio de Béjar, with its detachment at Arroyo del Cíbolo, obtain their advances at the royal treasury in San Luis Postosí.

The Presidio of San Antonio de Béjar, not included in the line [of forts], will consist of a captain, who will also be the governor of the province, two lieutenants, and ensign, a chaplain, and seventy-six soldiers, including two sergeants and 6 corporals.

The annual appropriations for the presidio of San Antonio do Béjar shall be 29,580 pesos, distributed this way: [19]

- Annual salary of the governor of the province of Texas, in that capacity and as captain of this company . . . . 4,000.
- To each one of the two lieutenants 700 pesos . . . . 1,400.
- To the ensign. . . . . 500.
- To the chaplain . . . . 480.
- To each one of the two sergeants 350 pesos . . . . 700.
- To each one of the six corporals 300 pesos. . . . . 1,800.
- To each one of the sixty-nine soldiers 290 pesos . . . . 20,010.
- For the gratuity from the common fund at 10 pesos annually per private . . . . 690.
- Total . . . . 29,580.

1. With the justified aim that protection by well-regulated presidios will foment settlement and commerce in the frontier area, that the strength of presidios likewise will be augmented by a great number of inhabitants, I order the commandant-inspector, captains, and officers, and other persons on no pretext to impede or dissuade people of good reputations and habits from entering and settling in their districts; and when the presidio is no longer large enough to contain the incoming families, they are to expand it on one side, the work being in common since it redounds to the benefit of all. At the same time I order the captains to distribute and assign lands and town lots to those that ask them, with the obligation that they cultivate them and that they keep horses, arms, and munitions for use in expeditions against enemies when necessity demands it and they are so ordered. In the distribution of lands and town lots, preference will be given to the soldiers who have served their ten-year enlistments and to those who have retired because of old age or illness and to the families of those who have died; to all these will be delivered the balances due them, as well as the one hundred pesos that should have accumulated in the treasury of the common fund, in order that they may provision themselves for their labors.

2. I expressly prohibit the molesting of merchants selling goods, provisions, and other goods (that are not prohibited) or of artisans who wish to work at the presidio, nor are they to be impeded in their establishments, sales, or transient labors; the captain, as chief and governor of the settlement, will be responsible in these matters.

I have determined that the line of the frontier [forts] is to be formed of the presidios of Altar, Tubac, Terrenate, Fronteras, Janos, San Buenaventura, Paso del Norte, Guajoquilla, Julimes, Cerro Gordo, San Sabá, Santa Rosa, Monclova, San Juan Bautista, and that of La Bahía del Espíritu Santo, as shown on the map drawn up by the engineer-in-ordinary Don Nicolás Lafora; also besides the eleven that are to be moved, that of Janos and the outposts of Robeldo and *Arroyo del Cíbolo* are to be guarded by detachments from the presidios of Santa Fé and *San Antonio de Béjar* and their enclosures strengthened, constructing them according to the plans of the same engineer.

More than one degree of latitude outside the proposed line [of forts] is situated the town of San Antonio de Béjar, almost equal distances from the two aforesaid presidios of San Juan Bautista and Bahía del Espíritu Santo; it is the place most exposed in actuality to the invasions and raids of various tribes of warlike Indians of the north, who attack the haciendas and opulent missions in that vicinity while pursuing Lipan Apaches, who are their hated enemies. In order that the settlement be adequately protected, I order that its company be reinforced to the level expressed in the regulations and that the residence of the governor, which had previously been in the presidio of Los Adaes, be moved there; the companies from Los Adaes and Horcoquisac are to be moved to San Antonio, and from them will be recruited the troops to complete that of said villa.

From this new company a detachment of 20 men, in charge of a lieutenant of that company, will be stationed permanently on the banks of the Arroyo del Cibolo in order to guard the ranches belonging to various inhabitants of San Antonio and to make less vulnerable the intervening area of almost 50 leagues [150 miles] between that villa and the last presidio mentioned above.

Royal Decree on Wild Cattle and Horses, 1778

INTRODUCTION TO DOCUMENT

Newly appointed Commandant General of the Interior Provinces, Teodoro de Croix, reviewed the condition of the Province of Texas and was not pleased with what he found. While the crown had made a substantial effort in time and treasure to promote the development of Texas' frontier settlements, the region had failed to live up to royal officials' expectations and remained lacking in both economic and social progress. Croix reasoned that the large number of unbranded wild cattle and horses provided a steady resource for "vagabonds" and other shiftless people to live outside the bounds of the law. Recall that in his report to the Viceroy that Father Fernandez had mentioned "bandits" living near the missions. Croix intended to bring order to the frontier while at the same time protecting the herds against possible extinction.

Commandant General Croix decreed that all unbranded cattle and horses belonged to the King. He created penalties, which included fines, imprisonment, and possible banishment, for anyone found guilty of taking the King's livestock. Law-abiding subjects could obtain a license and pay a head tax to capture unbranded cattle. Funds from these fines and taxes went to the Mestaña Fund as part of royal revenue earmarked for use for the betterment of the province

Croix's decree, although apparently primarily aimed at lowering crime, was unpopular with the province's residents who were used to hunting cattle and horses for gain. Church officials attempted to explain that the threat posed by Apache Indians had prevented them and others from conducting their annual round ups, resulting the large number of cattle that Croix referenced. Nevertheless, the Viceroy in Mexico City upheld the decree.

DOCUMENT[8]

Year of 1788
Number 88

Proclamation of good government issued by the Lord Commandant General of these Interior Provinces and promulgated in the settles of this [province] of Texas, declaring that wild, unbranded cattle and horse belong to His Majesty, whose above disposition has served as the origin for the erection of the Mestaña Fund, arranged according to the provisions ordered observed in the before-mentioned proclamation.

DON TEODORO DE CROIX

Cavallero de Croix, of the Teutonic Order, Brigadier of the Royal Armies, Governor and Commandant General of the Interior Provinces of Nueva España, Superintendent General of the Royal Treasury, etc.

His Majesty has entrusted to me the administration and government in chief of these and the other Interior Provinces of Nueva España, with the same faculties and duties as those formerly held by the Viceroys of the city of Mexico. Among them, one of the most important is that of overseeing the upright administration of justice in the affairs both civil and criminal, whether public or private [de oficio o a intancia de parte]; [of seeing] that delinquent persons are processed and prosecuted until, the punishment earned by their crimes having been executed, they abstain from relapsing into other crimes, thus serving as an exemplary lesson to others; [of seeing] that scandalous public inequities shall cease, as well as enmities, factions, and disputes among citizens, or among citizens and their judges, which disputes general contribute a great deal to the ruin of the treasuries and [even] the settlements; and finally [of seeing to] the establishment of order and dispatch in all matters of royal finance, war, government and policing of the provinces, whereon depends their greater development and the happiness of their inhabitants.

It is my desire to satisfy completely the sovereign confidence with which the royal piety has seen fit to distinguish me; thus, in addition to the reports and notices I previously tried to acquire, I shall consider it necessary to make a personal review and examination of the state of this province and its settlements, [to determine] the cause of its backwardness, [and] its failure to secure the advance which might have been expected of the extended time which as mediated since its foundation and the advantages offered by its fertile terrain and abundant waters. In this way I shall be able to apply the appropriate remedies with greater intelligence and knowledge.

I am well assured that the hostilities committed by the enemy have been solely for particular cause. They have principally and primarily been brought about by laxity of conduct—the frequency and facility with which the crimes are committed with impunity, especially those of theft, incontinence, scandalous concubinage, prohibited games and drinking, and the lenience with which many vicious, slothful, idle, and vagabond persons have been allowed to establish themselves and live, with no other purpose than that of propagating and extending their perverse habits, and contaminating the children of good and honorable subjects.

[The vagabonds] live off the goods, wealth, and cattle of these [honorable men]. On the pretext that [the cattle] are wild and without brand or owner, they have run them, taken them, and destroyed them at will, thus encouraging discord among families and a lack of subordination to and respect for the Governors and other Justices who have as their duty the administration of justice.

In order to prevent the repetition of similar excesses and disorders in the future:

I order the Governor of this province, the captains of its presidios, the *alcalde ordinaries*, and judges who exercise the royal jurisdiction, each in the territory, district, and population to which his own jurisdiction extends, to proceed with the greatest care in the investigation and punishment of those crimes which are committed therein.

They will form against the offenders the appropriate criminal cases, which they will prosecute, substantiate, and determine in the first hearing, conformable to that provided for in the laws of the Kingdom, General Army Ordinances, and the Regulations for the Presidios. They will impose upon them the penalties signified for each kind of crime in the royal credulas and the repeated proclamations which have ben published, without altering or moderating them whatever pretext; least of all shall they allow the criminals to settle by *composición*.

[I further order] that they dedicate themselves with particular effort and assiduity to the banishment of the detestable vice of incontinence and scandalous concubinage, watching over these persons of both sexes who are [publicly] known for it. They shall give me account of the cases formulated against them and the penalties imposed on them, so that, if I should find it suitable because of the nature of their excesses, I might remove them from the provinces and assign them such labors, presidios, or other destinations as they shall deserve. The same [measure] shall be taken with respect to the vagabonds and slothful and idle persons, over whose conduct [the officials] shall keep incessant vigil. They shall strive to ascertain the resources by which they live, and try to find some means of making them useful subjects of the State, whether by assigning them some land which they may keep and cultivate, or by obligating them to learn and work in some industry or profession in which they can acquire enough to maintain themselves and their families.

Should it be impossible to mend their ways, and should they remain incorrigible in their idleness and sinful life, they shall proceed to institute the appropriate cases against them and impose on them the penalty of banishment to public works for the space of six years, for rations only and without salary. Of this, too, they shall give me an account, so that I might give approbation and designate where they should serve [their terms].

I charge and entreat the most Reverend Bishop of this diocese, his Provisor, Priests, and Ministers of Doctrine and Missions, to contribute such part, as I am led to expect by their zeal to improve [the people's] customs, to banish idleness, crime, and public inequities, and to encourage industry and dedication. They shall make use of the gentle means which are proper to their ministry, and when these do not suffice to remedy the excesses they have knowledge of, they shall notify me or the magistrates responsible for their punishment, in order that appropriate measures may be taken to avoid scandal, offenses against God, and [other] bad examples for republics.

Another contributing factor in these [evils], as well as the lack of application in agriculture, industry, and professions, has been the liberty with which anyone, up until now, has considered himself authorized to go out and build corrals and stockades, then round up, enclose and take possession of wild and unbranded cattle and horses. Their breed has been diminished considerably by the excesses which have been committed. Now these animals, both the cattle and the horses, belong to the Royal Chamber and Exchequer [Real Cámara y Fisco de Su Magestad], first because they are strays and have no known owner, and also because they are born and raised in his unappropriated lands, not given in grants or [otherwise] alienated.

In order to avoid their complete destruction and injuries suffered by individual growers, many of whose branded cattle have been killed and left in the field, without utilizing anything except the fat, which is employed in the manufacturing of soap, I order that provisionally and for now, until I should proscribe other rules upon greater and more extensive examination, the following [rules] should be kept and observed.

1. No person of whatever quality or condition may go out and round up, kill, or take wild unbranded cattle or horses in the entire district of this province and its frontiers. The penalty for him who should act contrary to this rule shall be the loss of the animal or animals he may have taken, the payment of a four peso fine for each head of cattle, or two [pesos] for horses, and the suffering of eight days imprisonment in the public jail on the first offense; double the fine and term of imprisonment for the second; and for the third [offenses], the same doubled fine and exile for four years at hard labor, and rations only without salary, in whatever royal or public works he might be assigned to. For the imposition of these penalties, no other proofs shall be necessary than that of apprehending the animals in his possession.

2. No citizens or cattle-grower of whatever class may take from the province any herd of cattle or horses, even if they are domestic, branded, and of their own breeding stock, without first obtaining for that purpose a license from the magistrate. [The license] shall be issued in writing free of charge, without carrying any other duties than those of sealed paper, or, in its absence, those [duties] which should be extended to [especially] qualified [paper]. [The license shall contain] an individual listing of the number of head to be taken out, their kind, and their respective territories. The magistrate should keep a verbatim copy of the [license] in a book to be formed for this purpose, so that there will always be evidence of the cattle which have been removed, by which persons, and from what lands and which owners. The penalty for any transgressor shall be, for the first offense, the lost of the branded animals he

removes; for the second offense, the loss of the [animals] and payment of a four peso fine for each head of cattle and two [pesos] for each horse; and the third time, he shall suffer besides these penalties exile for two years at hard labor for rations only and without salary, in those royal or public works to which he may be assigned.

3. In order that these cattle raisers may not suffer damages, nor lose their branded cattle's breed, nor be able to appropriate to themselves a greater number than is truly and legitimately theirs on the pretext that it is their stock, they shall be allowed to brand only at those times designated as suitable by the magistrate, and with their attendance or the attendance of some person commissioned for that purpose. Each year, after the branding is done, an individual list will be made up of the number of each kind [of cattle] marked with [his brand] by each cattle raiser. After being signed by the grower and by the magistrate, it shall be kept in the book mentioned in the antecedent article. [This will insure] that there will be evidence, in these lists and in the export licenses which are also to be kept, of the breeding cattle he has branded and those he has removed, so that there may be full of those he has left and the breed they may have produced. The following year he will be allowed to brand only those which belong to him, under threat to the transgressor of the same penalties as expressed in the antecedent article.

4. Because I wish to facilitate all possible mitigations and encourage industry and application in good, honorable citizens, by just and moderate means, I invest the Governor of this province with the faculty of granting licenses to go out and take wild and unbranded cattle or horses in the times, seasons, and sites to be designated. Six r[eal]es shall be paid for each head of horses and four for each head of cattle taken, which shall be presented before the Governor or before someone commissioned for that purpose. Thus, with cognizance of the number [of animals] taken, he may charge the corresponding amount and deposit it for now in some locale to be appointed for this purpose under triple lock and key, one to the first ranking *alcalde* [alcalde de primer vote], and the other to the eldest *regidor*. Therein shall be kept the wealth produced by this tax, the fines that are imposed, and the register [libro de assiento], in which, under the signature of the three, shall be evidenced clearly and distinctly the amounts of each entry. It shall be forbidden to spend or remove any amount of [the ingress], since it is to be applied to the Royal Treasury and invested for those purposes to which it shall be destined.

5. Finally, various royal credulas, laws, and ordinances have repeatedly prohibited the sale of firearms or side arms, powder, munitions, or implements of war to the pagan Indians, whether those we are at war with or those with whom we are at peace, or indifferent towards, because of the consequent injuries to those subjects who provide themselves with them and learn to handle them. Deceit and negligence [of these laws] have brought about the many damages and unfortunate deaths which have occurred. Therefore, I order the Governor and magistrates to exercise the utmost zeal and care in overseeing the observance of the afore-mentioned prohibition and punish with full rigor those who should contravene it, imposing on them the penalties designated for these crimes without moderating them on any pretext whatsoever. In order to insure that these measures come to the attention of everyone and no one may allege ignorance, they will be published as a proclamation and affixed at the usual places in the customary form. The original shall remain in the Secretariat of Government of this province; the appropriate copy shall be passed on to the Governor at the *Ayuntamiento* of this *villa* to be placed in the Cabildo's Archive, so that the said measures may appear therein.

Royal Presidio of San Antonio de Vejar,
January eleventh, seventeen hundred seventy eight.

    El Cav[alle]ro De Croix
    [rubric]

    Antonio Bonilla
    [rubric]

Change Comes to the Missions, ca. 1792

INTRODUCTION TO DOCUMENT

Missions as instruments of conversion overseen by a missionary were always intended to be temporary institutions. The plan all along was for the mission to became a self-sufficient and self-governing Indian pueblo once the neophytes gathered there had adopted Spanish culture to the point where they were essentially "white" (i.e, Spaniards). Church officials initially believed the process could be completed in ten years but practice showed that converting a local indigenous population usually took several generations.

Although the missions received some funds from the royal war chest, they were expected to contribute to their own operations. Although some revenue came from the sales of surplus crops, the largest source of wealth came from raising livestock. By 1770, Apache raids on the missions had abated so the cattle drives to markets in Louisiana became common. In 1778, though, the Commandant General of the Internal Provinces, Teodoro de Croix, decreed that all unbranded cattle found on land yet granted by the monarch belonged to the King. Hampered by this ruling, the missions began to suffer serious financial woes because they could only increase the size of their herds through natural increase or by paying what amounted to new taxes.

While the financial situation affected decision to secularize the missions, the reality was that the lack of new religious recruits no longer could justify their continued existence. As noted by Fr. Jh. Francisco López, a religious official sent to inspect their status, the missions—especially Mission Valero—had become Spanish towns and no longer functioned as missions. Hence, it was determined to withdraw their missionary personnel and replace them with regular clergy. Mission property, which had been held in common, was distributed among its former residents. Former converts still living in houses along the west wall of the mission gained title to those properties as well.

DOCUMENT[9]

In view of this high purpose and to satisfy the obligations of my conscience, I bring to the consideration of your Reverences several facts. This Mission of San Antonio de Valero, which I administer, offers no proximate and founded hopes that in the future new gentiles will congregate, so that missionary activity could be exercised; nor can it be said truthfully that the faith will be spread among the few individuals in the mission, for they are so instructed in the Christian dogmas and gospel teaching, in the obedience due our Mother Church and the commandments of the Supreme Shepherd, in the respect due to priests and missionaries, and in just submission to our Sovereign and his royal courts and officials, that they are not now, nor can they be called neophytes, or even Indians, since most of them, being children of marriages between Indians and white women, are mulattoes or half breeds, as can be seen in the census list, sent to the viceroy by the Lord Conde de la Sierra Gorda, interim governor of this province, and by me to the Guardian Father of the Apostolic College. It can therefore be inferred that this mission cannot be called a mission of Indians but a gathering of white people. The few pure Indians who remain are, in trading and communication, as intelligent as the others. Consequently, the College ought to disassociate itself and give the mission over to the bishop so that he takes care of their souls.

The first point I make is obvious from the fact that in the sixty and more leagues [180 miles+] surrounding these missions of Béjar there is no nation of Indians which can be converted. Those who are at a greater distance to the east, north, and south, cannot be taken out of their land without violence to their nature, without offending the laws of humanity, the pontifical regulations, and repeated decrees of his Majesty.

nor has it been possible for the missionaries to win them over by favors and kindness, so that they freely leave their lands and congregate in one of the missions. At different times from 1703 till the present year of 1792 various and costly experiments have been made in vain toward this end. Secondly, it is evidently true, shown not only by the long time of eighty-nine years since the mission of San Antonio was founded, but felt also in the trade and communication with those Indians, that although they have not given up entirely the traits that are proper to and inseparable from their natural low way of living and their fickleness, they nevertheless are seen to be more civilized and cultured than many other Indians and pueblos in lands beyond.

Finally, the experience of so many years has taught us that the best fruit we can promise ourselves for the future of these Indians will be only to preserve in them the faith and Christianity they have received, just as it is preserved in the other Christian pueblos by the help and preaching of their pastors. But no apostolic increase in spreading the faith can be made among them, and yet this is the proper and special office of the missionaries, to which alone our efforts ought to be directed.

In carrying out this resolution, which Your Reverences will judge always to be fitting and in conformity with the decisions of higher government, it does not appear that any difficulty will arise, either from the Indians (they have tried again to free themselves from the economic management of the missionary, and because of this, or because of other motives, the General Commandant had drawn up in 1780 a plan, which had no results, by which the care of these souls would come under the Ordinary), or from the Ordinary, since the Mission of San Antonio is so close to the Presidio and Villa of San Fernando, divided only by the river, that the pastor of the Spaniards can take charge also of the spiritual care of the Indians.

. . .

In regard to the other missions of this Province I consider it highly important that without making any changes in the Missions of Espiritu Santo and Nuestra Señora del Rosario de la Bahia, the other four missions on the River of San Antonio be reduced to two by joining Mission Espada to Mission San José, and Mission San Juan Capistrano to Mission Purisima Concepción, both because of the advantage of having the first two on one side of the river and the last two on the other side, and also because the lands and goods are joined in their respective boundaries, and those of Mission Concepción are also adjacent to those of San Juan Capistrano. Thus only two missionaries will be in charge, and they should reside in Mission San José and Concepción, since their churches and the houses for the missionary are larger and better. The other two missions will be pueblos or settlements of visitation. In this way and by giving over the Mission of San Antonio and the administration of Nacogdoches to the bishop, the holy College can make greater progress in converting the infidels, which is the main objective of its apostolic zeal and the only purpose I have in writing this report. In this way the King Our Lord will be spared new expenses, and our College, without increasing the number of missionaries, will be able to use these five superfluous missionaries for new conversions which, it seems, can be made on the coast of San Bernardo, in Refugio, Brazos de Dios, and Orcoquiza. Thus the faith will be spread in that direction and the aforesaid missions will not be abandoned. At the beginning of their foundations it was judged necessary to have more missionaries, but at the present time they can be adequately maintained by only two missionaries, if the union which I have suggested is accepted.

But one must remember that this is possible only by leaving the administration of temporal affairs to the Indians, by keeping them in their respective pueblos without merging their lands and goods, and by freeing the missionaries from the administration and care of temporalities, so that they will look after only the spiritual welfare of the Indians, who will work for themselves and seek their own well-being. . . .

It is certain that as soon as the Indians receive the goods, they will misuse them, sell them, and give them to the Spaniards, and by using up their small patrimony in games, drunkenness, and other vices, they will want more when they return to the house of their Father missionary, asking for help to alleviate their hunger and to clothe them; and when the poor missionary will have to dismiss them from his door in sorrow, not being able to help them sufficiently, even by sharing with them the bread of his own sustenance, he will have to practice patience, charity, and compassion, and will see many of his poor Indians go hungry, naked, and dejected, and exposed to serve the Spaniards to get food. But since these are consequences that will follow transferring the goods to their awkward management and misconduct, they are also unavoidable conditions which keep the Indians in the natural sphere with all the rest of them. This is neither surprising to the Indians, nor is it proper for the apostolic institute to strive to suspend the course of divine Providence, which in its hidden design maintains all the natives of this America in the condition of the most lowly, humble, poor, and abject men.

The most zealous, prudent, and holy missionaries, who have been in these Indies from the beginning of the conquest up to this day, as we know from history and as can be seen in the abundant fruit obtained by their evangelical preaching in all the converted pueblos, thought undoubtedly that they fulfilled their task of preaching and exercised their apostolic zeal by instructing the Indians in the catholic religion, by teaching them to live as Christians, as obedient sons of the holy Church and true subjects of our Sovereign. The true charity, which impelled them to win so many souls, did not influence them to draw the Indians from their natural place of abode, to help them in their bodily miseries, to lift them up from their humble dejection, and to throw on their shoulders the duty of protecting and defending these helpless men, except in so far as these duties were conducive to the teaching and instruction by which they tried to educate them. And when, through the goodness of God our Lord, we can say that in these four missions of which we speak our missionaries have now done all the duties imposed by the apostolic institute, having all the Indians in their care (except a few who have come recently) well instructed and nourished in Christianity, and in all that is required by necessity and precept to reach salvation if they want to be saved. We sympathize surely on seeing the miserable state in which they would be left by the surrender of their goods, and we shall be content in having, after all, imitated our venerable predecessors. We shall make known to all who till now have been deceived, and who have entrusted to us the management of temporalities, that we have used them only in so far as they have been conducive to keeping the Indians together and as a help in in structing and teaching them. This, for the most part, has been achieved.

Finally, some could object to this report, claiming that the Indians, should they lack the shelter and protection from the missionary, would abandon themselves and become lazy by not cultivating their land, by leaving the missions, and some perhaps would join pagan nations to make war against us, tired of the heavy yoke of Christianity and apostatizing in great numbers from the faith and thus lose their souls. But just as the pastor, the preacher, the confessor are not responsible for these and greater willful evils committed by bad Christians because of temporal discomfort and not because of lack of instruction and teaching, neither can the apostolic missionary be held responsible for the fatal results that come to the bad Indians of his mission because of the lack of material things. In truth, if the Indians have not apostatized up to this day and have remained in the mission, submitting to the yoke of Jesus Christ after so many years of instruction, if this has been due to the temporal comfort which they have had under the protection of the missionary, little or nothing has our apostolic institute achieved. This is not easy to believe when we see that the more unskilled Indians of these missions, with the exception of one or the other, have received more instructions than many other pueblos in lands beyond. Thus if perchance they are lost tell them what God told Israel: *perditio tua ex te* [destruction is thy own.] These Indians will perish because of the evil inclination which prompts all evil Christians to permit law, of the good and the bad, or because of the lack of gospel teaching, but because of the evil inclination which prompts all evil Christians to permit themselves to be carried to perdition. Although the missionaries must deplore their perdition, it is not their task to try to remedy the situation by means of material help. Otherwise, charity would compel them to care for the widows, orphans, helpless men and women, who perhaps would not be given to so many vices, if the help of clothing and food would be given to them as it is given to the Indians.

On the other hand, the King our Lord (may God protect him) is the father and protector of the Indians and has taken measures to favor and protect them in all his courts and provided a remedy against robbers and other bad Christians, who rebel and go to gentile nations to make war against the provinces. For this reason secular leaders have pillories, chains, prisons, gallows, and other fitting punishment for such evildoers. And even if we suppose that many of these will perish, the apostolic institute always will come out ahead by assigning those five missionaries to other new conversions, for then, if one or two perish by their own free will and with full knowledge of God and his law, ten or twelve will be gained in the new conversions of those poor gentiles, who till now are in the shadow and darkness of paganism and on whom the light of the gospel has not shone.

Some will be lost because they wanted to be, though we did not give them material help, but this is not the proper duty of an apostolic missionary; others will be lost because of lack of spiritual help, of evangelical preaching, which is the only thing that pertains to the missionary. Hence, *ceteris paribus* [other things being equal] our first duty should be to help the gentiles in need and not to prevent the bad conduct and voluntary perdition of bad Christians.

Because of all these reasons I feel a grave responsibility to tell your Reverences the repeated voices of my conscience, which I am heeding by this report: namely, that the missionaries should not be increased here only for managing temporalities and with no other hope of further apostolic progress than to conserve what till now has been achieved; nor should other souls be lost where zeal could be exercised with greater results in the ministry. Because this is the dictate of my conscience, I signed in this Mission of San Antonio on September 7, 1792.

. . .

Kissing the feet of your Reverences, Fr. Jh. Francisco López
President – Rubric

Description of Texas in 1803

INTRODUCTION TO DOCUMENT

The year 1803 marked an important change for Texas. The province, located on the farthest northeastern frontier had always presented the Spanish with the problem of defense. In 1763, however, France transferred Louisiana to Spain, thus effectively relocating the Spanish border eastward to the Mississippi River. The move relieved pressure on Texas, leading to orders to abandon Los Adaes and the other settlements along the Texas-Louisiana border. As a result of this decision, San Antonio became the new capital of the Province of Texas in 1773. That respite during which the need to defend the old border was relaxed came to an end after a resurgent France reclaimed Louisiana and then sold it to the United States in the act known as the Louisiana Purchase.

The Spanish were forced to take stock of settlements in the province shared the boarder with an aggressive neighbor. The Spanish mission period had essentially produced three communities: Nacogdoches, La Bahía (Goliad), and San Antonio de Béxar. The latter had just received a new addition to its residents: the troopers of the Second Flying Company of San Carlos de Alamo de Parras and their families, who took up quarters on the old ground of Mission Valero. It is this military company that gave its name to the old mission.

DOCUMENT[10]

The province of Texas, whose extent until now has ignored a fixed point, is confined to three small centers of population, to wit: San Antonio de Béxar, Bahía de Espíritu Santo, and the settlement of Nacogdoches—the first the capital, the second a presidio situated a distance of fifteen leagues (45 miles) to the southwest on the coast, and the third located near the boundary of Louisiana. [Note: Faulk says La Bahía is forty leagues (120 miles) from Béxar, the actual distance is approximately 90 miles.]

The villa of San Fernando de Béxar, also called Presidio de San Antonio, is composed of 2,500 souls, including the troops. It is located on the very fertile banks of a river, and is susceptible to singular blessings which are not realized because of the general poverty of the inhabitants. They have restricted their work to the raising of corn, not as much as they are capable of—as experience has demonstrated—for years of abundant harvests they waste part for the lack of hard work: as to beans, chile, and some sugar cane, all they are accustomed to producing is enough for their annual maintenance, except the last which benefits two or three individuals who make small portions of sugar. The rest they sell or eat.

They have never learned to manufacture textiles or rope, nor is there any raising of cotton. There is so little wool that its owners send it to Saltillo to sell it because there are not yet ten thousand head of sheep living in this province. No one recognizes that raising them would be to his benefit. There is no wheat nor flour mills; other branches of agriculture are entirely foreign here. The same is true of the arts of every class. They suffer a damaging shortage of good cattle for which reason the scarcity of meat is almost continual; and it is true that if the hunters (*carneadas*) did not find buffalo annually between the months of May and October to supply the need in part, the greater portion of the families would perish in misery. The capturing of wild horses (a species which greatly abounds in this province) is the second object which particularly calls the inclination of all the inhabitants.

On the opposite bank of the river is the mission of San Antonio de Valero, secularized some years ago; its actual population encompasses the Company of San Carlos de Parras and amounts to 362 souls. The civilian inhabitants (*vecinos*) raise corn, beans, chile, and only Don Antonio Baca, who is from Béxar, posses land and water there beneficial to sugar cane. The harvests are small for the same reason already explained as applying to the Villa de San Fernando.

Following the course of the river, one encounters at a distance of one league [3 miles] four missions near one another, in ruins for the most part, although in ancient times they were very opulent. Their population consists of three hundred souls, among whom are a few Indians, some Spaniards, and people of other castes who are occupied as the rest in raising corn, beans, chile, catching horses and butchering at the accustomed time.

Zebulon Pike Visits San Antonio de Béxar in 1807

INTRODUCTION TO DOCUMENT

President Thomas Jefferson sought to obtain information about the region called Louisiana that the United States had just bought from France. Most famous of his efforts was the expedition of Lewis and Clarke, who journeyed to the Pacific Ocean and back by travelling along the Missouri River and crossing the Rocky Mountains. Other Jefferson-sponsored expeditions did not fare as well.

Army officer Zebulon Pike travelled across the Great Plains to the front range of the Rocky Mountains, where Pike's Peak still bears his name. Not wishing to enter the mountains during winter, he turned his expedition southward and venturing into New Mexico. Moreover, this route gave him an excuse to explore Spanish territory. Found and taken into custody by the Spanish, Pike and his men were escorted out of Spanish territory on by a circuitous route that took them through San Antonio.

Pike, who was treated more as a visiting dignitary than a dangerous interloper, met several important Spanish officials who would play prominent roles in the approaching period of unrest which would soon engulf Mexico.

DOCUMENT[11]

June 7th. Came on 15 miles to the [Medina] river Mariano—the line between Texas and Cogquilla—a pretty little stream [on which was a] Ranch. Thence in the afternoon to Saint Antonio. We halted at the mission Saint Joseph; received in a friendly fashion by the priest of the mission and others.

We were met out of San Antonio about three miles by Governors Cordero and Herrera, in a coach. We repaired to their quarters, where we were received like their children. Cordero informed me that he had discretionary orders as to the mode of my going out of the country; that he therefore wished me to choose my time, mode, etc.; that any sum of money I might want was at my service; that in the meantime Robinson and myself would make his quarters our home; and that he had caused to be vacated and prepared a house immediately opposite for the reception of my men. In the evening his levee was attended by a crowd of officers and priests, among whom were Father M'Guire and Dr. Zerbin [in charge of the military hospital at the Alamo]. After supper we went to the public square, where we might be seen the two governors joined in a dance with people who in the daytime would approach them with reverence and awe.

We were here introduced to the sister of Lieutenant Malgare's wife, who was one of the finest women we saw. She was married to a Captain Ugarte, to whom we had letters of introduction.

June 8th. Remained in San Antonio.

June 9th. A large party dined at Governor Cordero's, who gave us a toast, "The President of the United States—Vive la." I returned the compliment by toasting "His Catholic Majesty." These toasts were followed by "General Wilkinson." One of the company then gave "Those gentlemen; their safe and happy arrival in their own country; their honorable reception, and the continuation of the good understanding which exists between the two countries."

June 10th. A large party at the governor's to dinner. He gave as a toast, "My companion, Herrera."

June 11th. Preparing to march to-morrow. We this evening had a conversation with the two governors, wherein they exhibited an astonishing knowledge of the political character of our Executive, and the local interest of the different parts of the Union.

June 12th.   One of the captains from the kingdom of [Nuevo] Leon having died, we were invited to attend the burial, and accompanied the two governors in their coach, where we had an opportunity of viewing the solemnity of the internment, agreeably to the ritual of the Spanish church, attended by the military honors which were conferred on the deceased by his late brethren in arms.

June 13th.   This morning there were marched 200 dragoons for the sea-coast, to look out for the English, and this evening Colonel Cordero was to have marched to join them. We marched at seven o'clock, Governor Cordero taking us in his coach about two leagues [six miles], accompanied by Father M'Guire, Dr. Zerbin, etc. We took a friendly adieu of Governor Herrera and our other friends at Saint Antonio.

June 14th.   When we left Saint Anthony, everything appeared to be in a flourishing and improving state, owning to the examples and encouragement given to industry, politeness, and civilization by the excellent Governor Cordero and his colleague Herrera; also to the large body of troops maintained at that place in consequence of the difference existing between the United States and Spain.

. . .

Population and Chief Towns.   St. Antonio, the capital of the province, lies in lat. 29° 50′ N. and along 101° W., and is situated on the headwaters of the river of that name; it contains perhaps 2,000 souls, most of whom reside in miserable mud-wall houses covered with thatched grass roofs. The town is laid out on a very grand plan. To the east of it, on the other side of the river, is the station of the troops.

About, two, three, and four miles from St. Antonio are three missions, formerly flourishing and prosperous. Those buildings, for solidity, accommodation and even majesty, were surpassed by few that I saw in New Spain. The resident priest treated us with the greatest hospitality, and was respected and beloved by all who knew him. He made a singular observation relative to the aborigines who had formerly formed the population of those establishments under charge of the monks. I asked him what had become of the natives. He replied that it appeared to him that they could not exist under the shadow of the whites, as the nations who formed those missions had been

nurtured, taken all the care of that was possible, and put on the same footing as the Spaniards; yet, notwithstanding, they had dwindled away until the other two missions had become entirely depopulated, and the one where he resided had not then more than sufficient to perform his household labor; from this he had formed an idea that God never intended them to form one people, but that they should always remain distinct and separate.

. . .

The population of Texas may be estimated at 7,000. These are principally Spanish, Creoles, some French, some Americans, and a few civilized Indians and half-breeds.

Rebels & Royalists Bring Devastation to San Antonio de Béxar, 1813

INTRODUCTION TO DOCUMENT

The years of 1811–1821 proved to be the bloodiest and most contentious decade that San Antonio had ever witnessed. The "Grito de Dolores" issued by Father Miguel Hidalgo on September 16, 1821, set off a chain of events that led to the Battle of Medina. Just twenty miles southwest from San Antonio de Béxar, the battle was the largest land battle ever fought on Texas soil. On August 18, 1813, more than 1,300 Mexican revolutionists and American volunteers were killed or executed by victorious Royalist forces under the command of General Joaquín de Arredondo when the action turned against them. Arredondo's troops then entered and occupied the town, executing hundreds of rebels and their suspected supporters, many facing a firing squad in the city's two plazas.

The wrath of the Spanish wrought on San Antonio was intensified by the earlier execution of Governor Teodoe Manual María Salcedo, General Simón de Herrera, and more than ten other Royalists following the rebels' defeat of the Spanish Army at Rosillo Creek on March 29, 1813. Many Béxareñoes, including José Francisco Ruiz, José Antonio Navarro, and Martín de Veramendi, fled to Louisiana to escape the vengeful retribution. The devastation during this period was so great that Texas' population in 1821 was estimated at only half of what it had been ten years earlier.

The following account was recorded by an American living in San Antonio during ca. 1809–1813, who went by the name Carlos Beltran. Beltran, who later moved to Chihuahua, gave his diary to W. W. Mills, another American living there. Mills then passed on the diary to John Warren Hunter, who then passed had it published.

Beltran's account is followed by the priest of San Fernando asking for permission to remove and bury the corpse of slain prisoners still on Main Plaza eight months after they had been executed.

DOCUMENT[12]

... The Indians—Apaches, Lipans and Comanche—came in quite often, and usually took what they wanted, and on various occasions committed the most inhuman outrages. They had no fear of the Spanish soldiers and held in contempt the efforts of the native Mexicans to punish them for their misdeeds. During the first ten years of the century, that is, from 1800 to 1810, inclusive the Comanches alone were credited with having carried into captivity over 200 women and children from San Antonio and its environs. Among the poorer class there was scarcely a family that did not mourn the loss of one or more of its members, carried into captivity by these Ishmaelites of the plains.

I took part in repelling these savages on several occasions, and in the course of time these simple Mexicans began to look to me for leadership. By permission of the Spanish commandant, in January, 1809, I organized a small company for public defense. We were to furnish our own mounts, serve without pay, and in the capacity of minutemen, were to be in readiness at all times to repel an enemy and to pursue the marauders. The authorities would furnish nothing save guns and ammunition, and the old broken muskets they gave us had the appearance of having seen service in the war against the Moors. These I took to my shop and put in a state of repair, but at best, the could not compare with the American hunting rifle. Many of these later found their way into the country, and I made it a rule to buy, when possible all that were brought to me for repairs, and by this means I secured about a dozen or more, which I put in good shape and taught my men how to use them with good effect.

. . .

From the morning of Senor Aldama and Salazar's arrest [March 2, 1811], I was under continual espionage and the home of Señora Rodriguez came to be regarded by the Spaniards as the harbor of spies and malcontents, and more than once was the senora threatened with arrest and summary punishment. Finally, my shop was closed and I was put on ticket of leave, that is, I was required to report to headquarters every morning. Following this, my company of Mexicans was ordered disbanded.

I was ordered to turn in all of the guns belonging to this company. Some eighteen or twenty of these guns were American hunting rifles and were my own personal property, and I refused to turn them in, but hastened to conceal them. For my refusal I was arrested and placed in the Alamo carcel, where to my astonishment I found twelve other Americans, a number of whom had been imprisoned there for two and three years. It was in this dungeon that I first met Josiah Taylor, who, a few days later brained one of the guards with a benchleg and made his escape. Along this time, five more Americans were brought in and from them were learned that an army of determined Americans had taken La Bahia and were forcing the Spanish back on Béxar. This was good news to us as it gave us hope for speedy release from the cruelties of the hated Gachupin [European Spaniard]. Further than the report of these new prisoners, we had no means of learning the affairs on the outside, since we were held almost entirely "incommunicado."

On the 28th of March [1813], we heard heavy cannonading, which we regarded as an unmistakable announcement that our countrymen were coming. We had no means of knowing the strength of the forces on either side, but we knew we were Americans, and we knew from experience that one American soldier was a match for ten of the hirelings and ex-convicts of Spain. The cannonading seemed to grow louder, fiercer, and finally ceased, and we sat in silent suspense, until aroused by the sound of horses' feet, as if a cavalcade was hastening past the Alamo. This sound increased into a roar, and we could only surmise that the Gachupins were pouring into the town from the field of utter defeat. All that evening and through the long weary hours of the night we waited and listened to the sounds through our prison bars—a night which was fraught with the most aggravating suspense. Our guards had failed to bring our rations the evening before, and this fact looked suspicious, but we bore our hunger in patience, strengthened by the hope of speedy release.

Along about 3 o'clock we heard a great shout and tumultuous cheering, and we could no longer doubt the issue of the battle. There was no mistaking those cheers: no soldiers in all the world can surpass the American in the battle yell, or his exultant cheers over a victory. Then came a great commotion just outside our prison walls; the doors were thrown open, and seventeen of us—Americans—were led forth to freedom by our own brave countrymen!

General Herrera, Governor Salcedo and Cordera, in fact, all the Spanish officers were prisoners, and were assembled under a strong guard at the Quartel de Gobiernacion on the Main Plaza. Don Bernardo Gutierrez was nominally in command of the American forces, which consisted of about 800 Americans, the remainder being made up of Mexicans and Indians, some 1,300 in all. The Mexican contingent was commanded by a brave, patriotic Mexican by the name of [Miguel] Manchaca, a native of San Antonio, as were most of his men.

In this command was a company commanded by Captain Antonio Delgado, a son of the Colonel Delgado who was executed by Salcedo, and whose head was still exposed on a pole at the Alamo crossing. When Captain Delgado saw this gruesome relic of the doting father, he burst into a fit of weeping, which soon changed in to a paroxysm of uncontrollable fury. He hastened to the quarters, he found Salcedo with other Mexican officials, and with drawn sword forced his way past the guards and rushed upon Salcedo with the rage of a demon and would have slain him but for the interference of the Americans, who seized him and after a struggle bore him away.

Gutierrez and other leading Mexicans were present, but it was noticed that they remain quiet and offered no restraining hand. Doubtless they were moved to non-interference when they reflected that their fate would have been that of their friend and comrade, Colonel Delgado, had they fallen into the hands of the merciless Salcedo. A few hours after this attempt of Captain Delgado, the Spanish officers were removed to the Alamo prison, and right here, Colonel Kemper, the American commander, made a mistake which resulted in one of the greatest tragedies of the age, and ultimately thwarted all designs of the expedition. He allowed Manchaca's Mexican to guard the prisoners in the Alamo!

As before stated, Gutierrez was in nominal command. The Americans, as a matter of policy, conceded to him the authority of commander in chief, while mentally reserving unto themselves the privilege of doing that which suited them best. No sooner had Gutierrez found himself in possession of the then greatest stronghold in Texas, at the head of a victorious army, and his most hated enemies, Herrera, Salcedo, and others, cooped up in the Alamo dungeon, than he began to magnify his office on a great scale and to the degree quite startling to the American officers. These had agreed to release the Spanish officers on their parole of honor; Gutierrez sent them to prison heavily guarded by Manchaca's men.

. . .

José Sanchez, a near friend of mine, and nephew of Señora Rodriguez, was a member of Manchacha's company, and at the battle of Rosillo received a severe wound. He was conveyed to the home of his mother, who lived at one of the missions below town, and the evening following the address of Gutierrez to the army, I, in company with Pablo Rodriguez, who had but recently returned from a long captivity among the Comanche, went to the Sanchez home and spent the night, nursing and administering to José, the wounded man. Some time before day we started back to town, and while passing the Alamo at dawn, we met a large body of horsemen, coming from the direction of the river crossing. They drew up in front of the Alamo, and merely through curiosity, we drew near to learn the mean of this unusual movement. When we approached, we saw the Spanish prisoners were being brought out and mounted on horses for their accommodation, and to our surprise, we noticed that each prisoner was being securely bound with ropes to his horse.

I knew Captain Delgado quite well—we had always been on the most friendly terms—and, observing me closely watching his movements, he briskly asked what I was doing there, and who sent me to spy on his actions. I answered by saying that I was there on my own volition and that considering the high station held by these prisoners I thought it a shameful humiliation to their dignity and manhood to tie them on their horses when there was absolutely no reason for such brutal treatment, and that I would immediately report the matter to Colonel Kemper. This seemed to nettle the captain, and he ordered us away. We hastened to town and reported the procedures to Colonels Kemper and Ross, who went straightway to the quarters of

Gutierrez and demanded the return of the prisoners without delay. They told Gutierrez that they had pledged their honor, as American soldiers, for the safety of those men and that without proper assurances that their lives would not be placed in jeopardy while in the hands of Delgado, they would be returned to the Alamo.

Gutierrez gave them every assurance that his orders for their safe delivery on board a vessel at Matagorda would be carried out to the letter; that Captain Delgado was a true soldier, in every respect worth, reliable and circumspect, and furthermore, if he should allow any evil to befall the prisoners in his custody he would have him shot immediately upon his return.

The Spaniards and five Mexicans rode away from the Alamo that morning to an ignoble death. General Simon de Herrera, Ex-Governor Cordero, Governor Manuel de Salcedo, Lieutenant Colonel Herrera, Captain José Mateos, Juan Ignacio Arbido, Francisco Pereira and Gregorio Amado—these were the Spaniards. The following were Mexicans: Captain Miguel Arcos and his two sons, Luis and Pancho, Antonio Lopez and Lieutenant Juan Caso. Lopez was not connected with the army in any way, and his offending was in connection with betrayal and arrest of Colonel Delgado.

A few miles below the city the escort halted on a small creek that flowed into the San Antonio River. Here the prisoners were untied and dismounted one at a time, and each man was tied to a tree, hand and feet. Realizing that their end was near, these unhappy men begged to be spared until a priest might be brought from town to administer the last rites of the church, but this was refused. "You sent my father into eternity, denying him the consolation of religion in his last extremity," said Delgado, addressing Salcedo.

Ex-Governor Cordero was the third man to be led to the fatal tree. Before his arms were pinioned about the tree he called one Lieutenant Santos to him and handing him his watch and ring, asked him to convey these articles to Dr. Orramel Johnson, with the request that he forward them, if every opportunity presented, to someone in the City of Mexico—wife, mother, or relatives—I have forgotten which. [Note: The editor is mistaken. Manuel Antonio Cordero was serving as the governor of the Province of Coahuila at the time.]

When the fifteenth prisoner was securely bound to a tree, deliberate preparations were made for the shocking tragedy. Herrera exhorted his companions in misfortune to face the ordeal like men and die like true soldiers, loyal even in death, to their master, the King. Seeing their long keen knives in preparation for the carnival, Lieutenant Herrera, a mere youth, warned Delgado of the day of signal retribution and defied him to do his worst.

Manuel Salcedo begged to be permitted to die like a soldier. He asked to be shot, and for reasons that probably will never be known, his request was granted. He was the first to be executed and then, at a signal given by Delgado, the men chosen for the [line obscured] gleaming knives, cut the throats of the remaining fourteen.

. . .

In less than an hour the moment of our leaving the outskirts of Bexar the streets and plazas of that unfortunate city were swarming with the mounted minions of Spain. When the route of the [Republican] army was complete at the Medina, Elisondo, with 200 picked cavalrymen, began the pursuit, and as a result of his inhumanity the trail from the banks of the Medina to Béxar became dotted with the corpses of men whom his infuriated soldiers had overtaken and slaughtered. The wounded who had fallen by the wayside, overcome by fatigue and the extreme heat, those on foot or mounted on horses, which from wounds or other causes were unable to carry their riders beyond the zone of danger—all alike were devoted to the merciless slaughter.

The city was at the mercy of the avenger, and making a pretext of retaliation for the blood of Herrera and Salcedo, the Spanish soldiers, unrestrained, spread over the town on their hellish mission of pillage, rapine, and murder. Homes were invaded, and where resistance was offered, the defenders were butchered on their own threshold in the presence of their horrified families, the women and even tender girls, mere children were outraged, and in numerous instances, cruelly murdered and their nude bodies dragged into the street. Upon entering these homes the first demand was for mescal, or aguardiente; the next was for dinero. Granted or denied, the procedure was always the same: everything of value was seized, and that which could not be borne away was ruthlessly destroyed, and throughout the long hours of the night the air was rent with the exultant yells of a drunken soldiery, the wails of little children and the screams of outraged mothers and daughters, and for many years afterwards the people of San Antonio spoke of that awful night as "La Noche Triste"—the night of sorrow.

With his main army, Arredondo reached Béxar early in the afternoon of August 20th. The patio, or parade ground of the Alamo barracks, had been converted into a sort of carcel, more properly a prison pen, and here, upon the Royalist general's arrival, he found that his industrious subordinate, Elisondo, had cooped up in this pen nearly 800 prisoners, including citizens of all stations—all awaiting the verdict of the commander in chief, who lost no time in establishing his tribunal and from whose decision there was no appeal. Those who were taken with arms in their hands were first led into his presence, only to be ordered to immediate execution, and until sunset that evening intermittent volleys of musketry, on Military Plaza, proclaimed to the terrified inhabitants the revengeful policy of the triumphant Gachupin.

In former years a merchant who dealt largely in grain erected a large granary in the rear of his store on Main Plaza. On account of an insect known as the gorgojo (weevil) which in that climate was very destructive, and rendered it difficult to preserve corn from its ravages any great length of time, this granary was built as a protection against that pest. It was approximately 20 x 40 feet in dimension. The walls were about twelve feet in height, with flat roof and contained only two small opening besides the doorway. These opening were in the south wall, merely for ventilation, and could be closed at will. The entire building was of adobe and when the door was closed the interior was almost wholly without ventilation.

At sunset, on the 20th, further executions were deferred until the following morning. A list of patriots whose sympathies for the Revolutionists were well known was furnished Arredondo, and from this list of names—men already under arrest—he selected 300 of these patriots and ordered them transferred at once, from the Alamo carcel to this granary on Main Plaza. The order was immediately carried into execution. It was a still sultry August night, and the temperature, even at best in the open air was intensely oppressive, and without a drop of water and without any means for ventilation, these 300 citizens were thrust into that small space, the door was closed, guards were stationed outside, and later, one of these was severely punished for having repeated to a citizen how those unfortunate prisoners fought and struggled for a position neat the little openings where they might obtain a breath of fresh air. The next morning when the door was thrown open eighteen had died of suffocation, four expired shortly after being removed, while more than half of the survivors had to be lifted and carried from the building. These, when partially restored, were taken before Arredondo, and before the noon hour most of them were stood up against the bloody wall on Military Plaza.

Unsatisfied with the blood of the patriots and to give a broader scope to his consummate malignity, the inhuman Gachupin turned the vials of his fiendish rage against the innocent women and young girls of the devoted city, and more than 600 of these wives, mothers, and daughters were arrested and driven into an enclosure near the banks of the river, known as the "Quinta." These were furnished with metates, seized and taken from their own homes, and with these stone implements they were forced to grind the corn and bake the tortillas for the entire Spanish army. Over these unhappy women was placed a guard and taskmaster, a Spanish Sergeant, brutal, cruel, beastly, obscure, and immoral, and he, with the troops under his command, no less cowardly and depraved, found their chief delight in the inflection of every indignity, injury, and mortification upon these helpless women and girls. I know whereof I write. Señora Rodriguez and her daughters, the eldest who became my wife, were among the victims of Spanish persecution, and I have the truth from their own lips, fully corroborated by the testimony of scores of others of their fellow-sufferers.

Until the first of September public executions were daily occurrences on Military Plaza; the adjacent country, even at the greatest distances, was scoured in quest of refugees, who, when found, were brought in, the women sent to the "Quinta," the children turned upon the street to starve and the men delivered into the hands of the executioner. Property owned by patriots and all suspects was confiscated and passed into the ownership of Royalist, chiefly Arredondo's officers and favorites. Elisondo, with 500 dragoons, had been dispatched in pursuit of Toledo and slaughter marked his path from Bexar to the Sabine.

The Province of Texas is once more prostrate under the iron heel of the tyrant; her once beautiful capital, San Antonio, is now a city of desolation, strewn with the wrecks of her former glory, and clad in the habiliments of irretrievable woe. Her homes are tenantless, her fathers and sons are either seeking in the fastness of the mountains, in the solitudes of the wilderness or have been consigned to bloody graves, while her gentle matrons and fair daughters have become the enforced slaves of inhuman masters. Truly Texas is fallen, and the Spaniard has stamped in burning characters of hell his eternal shame on the walls of Béxar.

DOCUMENT[13]

Most Excellent Sir:

For quite a while I have been wanting to point out to His Excellency my strong desire to give Christian burial to the corpses in the plaza. To begin with it is hard for me to understand how Christian burial has been denied a group of men who were put to death for their crimes, while at the same time others are running around, guilty of the same crimes, but have been pardoned. Why deny that mercy to the dead. Secondly, it is hard for me to watch the disdain with which the corpses are treated by children, who throw rocks at them. Thirdly, [three words illegible] of His Excellency. I hope His Excellency will grant me that favor. God should grant such a merciful act. May God grant His Excellency a long life.

San Fernando de Bexar
9 March 1814.

Br. José Darío Sambrano

PART 2: MEXICAN TEXAS

Stephen F. Austin Arrives in San Antonio in 1821

INTRODUCTION TO DOCUMENT

The decade of 1810–1820 left Texas devastated. Not only had property been destroyed, the population of the province had been cut in half by death and exile. Spanish officials, who had issued a limited number of empresario grants in Louisiana, decided to award Missourian Moses Austin a grant to bring American colonists to Texas. In 1821 Mexico declared its independence from Spain but decided to follow through with revamping the nation's immigration policy.

Moses Austin died before he could fulfill his contract. Nevertheless, his son, Stephen F. Austin, took up his father's plan. In preparation for bringing American immigrants to Texas, the young Austin embarked on a tour of the region. It is important to note that he was met at the Louisiana border by a party led by Erasmo Seguín, then serving as alcalde of San Antonio. The relationship formed by the two men lasted well into the future.

DOCUMENT[14]

[August 12. 1821] This morning at daylight three men who had been dispatched from the Gal. [Guadalupe] by Erasmo[Seguin] to St Ao. returned with others & brought the glorious news of the Independence of Mexico—the Spaniards hailed this news with acclamations of "viva Independencia" and every other demonstration of joy—Erasmo invited us to breakfast with him on various Spanish dishes sent out by their wives and started in high spirits and arrived at St. Antonio about 11 ock.

Remd at Bexar untill the 21st purchased mustangs—mustang hunting etc. Indians killed 1. wounded 1 Sp.

[Austin stayed in San Antonio until August 21st but left no description of the town.]

Mexican Border Commission Views San Antonio, 1828

INTRODUCTION TO DOCUMENT

The exact location of the border between Louisiana and Texas remained unsettled throughout Mexico's wars for independence and into its early republican period. In 1827, Mexico sent a commission to Texas to visit the disputed border in order to provide the government with information need to help settle the issue. General Manuel de Mier y Terán headed the scientific expedition which included several specialist who were to assist in gathering and recording data. Naturalist Jean Louis Berlandier served Mier as zoologist and botanist while a junior officer, José María Sánchez y Tapía, acted as cartographer and draftsman for the expedition.

All three men kept journals and recorded their impressions of San Antonio. As visitors coming from the interior of Mexico, they viewed the town as disheveled and its inhabitants lacking in energy. They were not impressed by what they saw.

The expedition proved important because Mier y Terán quickly determined that Mexico was on the verge of losing Texas because of the number of Americans entering the region. He noted that the new arrivals retained their attachment to their former homeland and would never assimilate due to the fact that they were becoming the dominant population. Mier y Terán's warnings prompted the Mexican Congress to pass the Law of April 6, 1830, which restricted immigration from the United States. Despondent over the impending loss of Texas, the general committed suicide in 1832 while on duty in Tamaulipas.

Description of San Antonio & Environs in 1828 by Jean-Louis Berlandier

DOCUMENT[15]

An enormous battlement and some barracks are found there, as well as the ruins of a church that could pass for one of the loveliest monuments of the area, even if its architecture is overloaded with ornamentation like all the ecclesiastical buildings of the Spanish countries. In the barracks of that mission lives a presidial company, long since come from Nueva Vizcaya [Coahuila] from a presidio called Alamo de Parras, which retained its name in Texas. It is to be regretted that those who founded San Fernando de Béxar did not join it to the presidio of the Alamo, located at a much more favorable site. Convinced of the dangers which another flood could produce, recent authorities have several times proposed establishing the town there. Composed of some one hundred houses, the quarters of the Alamo is considered part of San Fernando de Béxar. It is subject to the same authorities, and is separated by the river.

    The streets of Béxar are not very straight, not because of the winding river, which flows to the east of the houses, but also because that admirable regularity characteristic of every town founded by the Castillians in the New World was discarded there. Two large squares, separated from each other by the church and some houses, do not draw the traveler's attention at all. The houses are for the greater part *jacales* [huts] roofed with thatch. The better ones are of a heavy and course construction, and the larger number have fireplaces—in a word, there are already hints of a region lying outside the tropics. The inhabitants are gay and not very hardworking, and the dance is the chief amusement of the lower classes. Most of the families are linked to the military of the presidial companies, and it is to the great defect in the organization of these troops that the lack of agricultural progress observable in the region should be attributed. These soldiers, continually in the wilderness, or going to and from one presidio to another, cannot devote themselves to laboring in the fields. They content themselves with their pay, albeit this reaches their hands only after a thousand detours. The most comfortable off of the private citizens at the Mexican presidios are not lovers of farming; I have often seen them go elsewhere, sometimes even to the Anglo-American colonies, to seek the grain necessary for their subsistence. They much prefer to carry on a wretched trade, in which they have an infamous monopoly, to the detriment of the poor people—particularly since a law of the state excludes from retail trade all aliens who have not been naturalized. When they are reproached for their indolence, they allege that the Indians do not allow them to go out to cultivate the fields, which is partly true. But what I have never understood is why, although there are well-watered lands about the houses and the missions—even inside the presidio—one sees no planting there, whereas, moved by a principle of laziness, they go to sow *de temporal* [dry farming] fields of corn six or seven leagues [18 to 21 miles] from the dwellings (in localities truly exposed to attack by the indigenes), solely in order not to have to take the trouble of watering the fields.

From the brief idea which we have given of Béxar it can easily be seen that, if it did not have troops stationed there, that the greatest misery would prevail. Indeed, as the presidial companies are not paid in silver, money is extremely rare in the area. It is to the bad financial administration of Mexico that one should attribute the audacity of the indigenes: because the soldiers are badly paid and frequently without horses, or else very badly mounted, the indigenes are sure that after they have committed a theft or crime the soldiers will find themselves unable to go in pursuit. The military have been without pay or clothing not only for months but even years, and they have been on campaigns against warring tribes in the meantime. They feed themselves by hunting game in the wilderness. When the commissioners of the ports send some few thousand piastres to theses wretches, there is always some speculator—guilty of the crime of embezzlement—who uses that money to buy merchandise to sell to the soldiers at an immense profit. These petty tyrants abound in almost all of the republic. They are especially common far from the central government, which cannot keep under surveillance the conduct of employees situated at such a great distance. During my sojourns in the Interior Provinces [states] I have witnessed actions which, under a well-regulated government, ought to lead their perpetrators to the gallows, at least.

Cuidad de Béxar resembles a large village more than the municipal seat of a department. There is no paved street and no public building. Trade with the Anglo-Americans, and the blending in to some degree of their customs, make the inhabitants of Texas a little different from the Mexicans of the interior, whom those in Texas call foreigners and whom they scarcely like because of the superiority they recognize in them. In their gatherings, the women prefer to dress in the fashion of Louisiana, and by doing so they participate both in the customs of the neighboring nation and of their own. . . . Unfortunately for the creoles of Texas, the agricultural industry which they have shown in our time is so wretched that a monopoly over them by the American colonies founded in this department is to be feared. Several times have Béxar and Goliad gone to seek grain and cattle in those colonies. They cannot vie in any respect with those industrious colonists, much more hardworking than they, who are supplied with implements useful to their labors. If the creoles have some well-built wagons, they are very few; in general, on seeing them one would believe oneself to have gone ten centuries backwards in the elementary and necessary arts. Their wagons [carts], which one would believe to have been built without any tools, ride on wheels made of one or two joined pieces which have a lenticular shape and which are drawn transversely by some large tree trunk. The rest of the wagon [cart] is nothing but on assemblage held together by ropes or rawhide; sometimes there is not even a wooded peg. Oxen, as badly harnessed as the wagons are defective, are the only animals used for draft of plowing.

In regions where man struggles with the land, it is only when cultivation is extended and perfected that the herds multiply. In Texas the inhabitants find themselves in completely opposite circumstances, for the raising of domestic animals on the immense plains covered with pasture is completely independent of the progress of agriculture. I agree that the great obstacle to the prosperity of the herds is the presence of the indigenes who steal or kill them. Nevertheless, those errant and nomadic tribes—enemies of the sedentary arts of and peace and [who are] continually at war with one another—raise horses. Lastly, the foreign colonists have had to overcome the same obstacles and today are full of such animals as oxen, cows, horses, pigs, etc.

When the indigenes are at peace with the presidio, ranchos are found on all of the banks of the river streams. Independently of the missions they sow the most necessary grain, and the need for foodstuffs is less urgent. But these proprietors—more active than their fellow citizens—often lack field hands at harvest time, even if paying good wages. At the time for cutting sugar cane, I have seen a piastre paid to each worker, and even so there was difficulty in finding a sufficient number. At Béxar as at Laredo, at Goliad as at [San Juan Bautista del] Rio Grande, and in most of the

presidios everything is military, for this is the most pleasant life of the indolent....
I shall content myself with pointing out that the inhabitants [of Béxar] are not at all
farmers. More than a century after it was colonized the region remains static, and it
will never be covered with fields except in more active and harder-working hands.
What surer wealth than the products of a flourishing agriculture? By coastal trade,
they would send their cotton to the United States and their grain to Campeche, as all
the [Anglo-American] colonists have learned to do. But, ever distaining what lies under
their noses, the inhabitants of Béxar (and even some Anglo-Americans), struck by the
immense riches which have come out of Mexico, are forever searching for mines. At
Béxar, one rarely talks about a well-cultivated field or a splendid harvest, but rather
hears it that here or there—in a fluvial terrain covered with fossils—there is a gold
or silver mine. So avid are they for metal, the cause of human frailty, that one sees
people buying from the Indians granite from the cordilleras of the interior, because
they believe that the flecks of mica are small scales of silver. It is perhaps due to false
rumors about the existence of mines of precious metal that many adventurers from
the north have several times tried to incite small revolutions, because the ignorant
have imagined that gold and silver flow there in large waves.

Description of San Antonio in 1828 by José Mara Lino Sánchez y Tapia

DOCUMENT[16]

By a conservative estimate it may be said that the Mission of San Antonio de Bejar, on
the banks of the beautiful river that bears the same name and whose headwaters are
about two leagues [6 miles] to the northwest, was founded between 1690 and 1693.
Both the temple and the fortifications built as a defense against wild Indians are still
preserved. The small settlement within the enclosure is composed of one company of
frontier troops known as the Alamo Company, the name given to the place. In 1730, the
missions of Concepción, San José, and San Fernando were moved from the frontier
of Texas and rebuilt in the vicinity of Mission San Antonio. In the same year the *Villa
de San Fernando* was founded on the opposite bank of the river and was joined to
the settlement of the *presidio* or Mission of the Alamo by a bridge of trees was built,

the two making one place, as one might say, through the middle of which runs the aforementioned river.* The streets are not exactly straight, for they curve at various points, and the buildings, though some are made of stone, show no beauty, nor do they have conveniences. There are two squares, almost joined together, being merely divided by the space occupied by the parochial church, but neither one is worthy of notice. The commerce, which is carried on by foreigners and two or three Mexicans, is very insignificant, but the monopoly of its is very evident. I could cite many incidences to prove by assertion [that foreigners illegally dominate commerce?], but I do not wish to be accused of ulterior motives. Although the soil is very rich, the inhabitants do not cultivate it because of the danger incurred from Indian attacks as soon as the get any distance from the houses, as the Indians often lurk in the surrounding country, coming in the silence of the night without fear from the troops, for by the time the latter notice the damage done it is already too late. No measures can be taken for the maintenance of a continuous watch on account of the sad condition of the troops, especially since they lack all resources. For months, and even years at a time, these troops have gone without salary or supplies, constantly on active service against the Indians, dependent for their subsistence on buffalo meat, deer, and other game they may be able to secure with great difficulty. The government, nevertheless, has not helped their condition in spite of repeated and frequent remonstrations. If any money arrives, it disappears instantly, for infamous hands are not lacking to take it and give the poor soldiers goods at double their normal value in exchange for what they have earned, suffering the inclemencies of the weather while these inhuman tyrants slept peacefully in their beds. I am not exaggerating; on the contrary, I keep silent about many worse things I could say. The character of the people is care-free, they are enthusiastic dancers, very fond of luxury, and the worst punishment that can be inflicted upon them is work. Doubtless, there are some individuals, out of the 1,425 that make up the total population, who are free from these failings, but they are very few.

[*The opening of the paragraph taken from Carlos E Castañeda's translation of Sachez' journal.]

This pen and ink drawing by Gary Zaboly depicts a trooper of the presidial garrison of San Antonio during the 1830s. Courtesy of The Alamo.

General Mier y Teran Assesses Condition of Texas Towns in 1828

DOCUMENT[17]

I have spoken of the savages and foreigners and now I must consider the situation of the Mexicans. Those who live in Texas, whose number surely totals less than four thousand souls, constitute the three towns of Béjar, La Bahía, and Nacogdoches. The grand resource of the subsistence of these populations is the soldiers pay. One of the errors that we commit in Mexico is the belief that presidial soldiers are men who engage in agriculture. This is so untrue that we must consider that these troops are so alien to agrarian tasks as are those who are in the garrisons of [San Juan de] Ulúa and Veracruz. When we speak of frontier communities, it is necessary to discuss the military companies because they are the most numerous among the inhabitants. When we say they are not farmers, we realize that the greatest calamity that can occur is to have no means of providing for the troops, and, that these places can easily go to ruin. In the entire Mexican federation there is scarcely a more miserable little town than Laredo [then in the state of Tamaulipas, not Texas] and others located. Like it on the banks of the Rio Bravo. . . .

Focusing on Tejas, the three towns are isolated from one another and from the rest of the Mexican population. They cannot resist the feared uprising of the colonists and of foreigners who have entered clandestinely. Rather, however much we might think to help the Mexicans, they must be considered already under the power of the agitators, and therefore, the Mexicans must be considered already expelled entirely from Tejas. . . . We cannot rely on aid from Béjar, because the town has none, even in peaceful times. What we can expect in the case of a revolution, whose first consequence would be to cut [Béjar] off from the coast, because the town is under the control of foreigners, who are the sole owners of the wagons [*carros*] that can be used to travel in this county. . . . But in Béjar, which is the most important town among all those that have been embraced by these disasters [misrule and revolution], where there is greater number of farmers and industrious people, new worries have arisen with the admission of foreigners. At any moment they expect a revolution to break out, for which, all necessary elements exist and for which many indications can be seen: parties of foreigners cross the county in different directions without [the authorities] knowing the purpose of such extraordinary travels; they enter and depart from the Mexican towns; they travel to the encampments of the savage nations; and they travel all over the colonies and the entire frontier. . . . The foreigners also know that they are feared and distrusted, and are afraid of being seized unawares and thrown off their land. In short, here you see everything in agitation that precedes a great upheaval.

San Antonio de Béxar in 1828 by J. C. Clopper

INTRODUCTION TO DOCUMENT

A resident of Austin's Colony, Nicholas Clopper settled in Clopper's Point near the mouth of the San Jacinto River. This location, later sold to James Morgan, became known as Morgan's Point. Clopper was accompanied by his son, Joseph C. Clopper, Harmon Gregg, and a few others, traveled to San Antonio. The younger Clopper chronicled their time there in his journal.

Nicholas Clopper, who had connections to Cincinnati, Ohio, later organized the purchase of the Twin Sister cannon during the Texas Revolution. Harmon Gregg's son, Josiah Gregg, later visited San Antonio on his journeys through the southwest.

DOCUMENT[18]

We cross the Salou a small stream within five miles of San Antonio—Musquite prairie continues the earth here is covered with small smooth grey flint stones from an ounce to two or three pounds in size—the land is ascending for a couple of miles when we are on an exceeding high country—two miles further and we come to a Spanish fort and magazine commenced some years since and left unfinished—this stands on the summit of the circular ridge within one mile of San Antonio commanding a view of the town and the vast plain on which it stands—from this spot San Antonio has a very striking resemblance to one of Uncle Sam's handsomest and largest country villages—the curious traveller feels stimulated to urge on his jaded steed satisfied from this *first blush* that he shall be transported with a nearer view of its proportions its lofty domes—its elegant simplicity and natural beauties—he hurriedly descends the eminence in a fever of body and mind—comes to a little canal which he beholds with rapture extending itself abroad o'er the thirsty land and watering beautifully verdant and flourishing fields of corn—enters a regular avenue of huge cotton wood trees—thinks of the grand Avenue leading to U. Sam's house—asks who it was who so slandered this people by saying that they are but little superior to the lowest grade of the human family—surely the labour and utility of these canals—the beauty and taste displayed in the planting of this avenue is a flat contradiction to it all—he passes on—thro' the midst of this friendly shade—on the right stands a massy pile of ruins—for what purpose were these stones piled one upon another and why were they thrown down—this he discovers was one of the strong holds of Popish delusion, in which the Royalists in 1810–11 sought refuge from the avenging fury of the Patriots who battered down the mighty walls with their cannon—it is now a garrison—A few yds before him he sees the exceedingly serpentine San Antonio, coming winding around the town and gliding by as if hurried with important despatches to the Gulph of Mexico—he looks with mortification and disgust at the order of architecture which suddenly presents itself on his left he crosses the little river and beholds the same wigwam style of building which constitutes the principal part of the town—he proceeds on finds that the streets intersect each other very irregularly presently enters the public Square this is laid off at right angles being about 150 by 300 yards in the centre of which stands the Church—a large clumsy stone building—that seems to have been standing for Centuries. It has a steeple of the same materials, very well modelled of octagonal form—in this is hung 2 bells kettle-toned and of different sizes—these have their tongues tied with ropes and are made to bellow most horribly by two barbarous boys who stand close by and jirk these engines of torture to the utter dismay and confusion of the astounded stranger perhaps 40 times per diem—this Church has also a skylight dome at the opposite end.

In the midst of this Square the traveller stands and contemplates the buildings around him—he had before entering been disgusted with their dwellings that [he] first met—being formed of branches of the Musquite tree set up end ways in all the zigzag varieties of their growth having the interstices daubed with mud—these *hollow squares* are thatched over with the swamp flag and stand ready to receive their inhabitants who carry in a few chests a palate or two and some dried skins and the mansion is furnished. But the public square presents to the strangers eye a more solemn picture each side is formed of one unbroken solid wall except where the streets pass thro'—these walls have doors at neighbourly or family distances opening into what may more properly be termed cells than rooms—as few of them have windows—none indeed have sashes nor is there a pane of glass in the town—they seem more like port holes than windows—having bars like a prison grate; or dark shutters—these walls show no roof above them but seem to stand as we may suppose do the ruins of an earth-shaken or sacked and burnt City after the buildings had been battered down to the last story by a destroying and victorious enemy—these walls are about 18 or 20 ft in height the roof is invisible from the outside—is formed of huge cedar logs as rafters on which are laid small boards—these beams have a descending inclination from the back walls outwardly so as to rest upon the front walls about 2½ ft below their height. the roof is then covered with a cement from 8 inches to a foot in thickness from off which the rain is conducted by wooden troughs passing thro' the walls and projecting 3 or 4 ft into the Square. Thro' this square and the heart of the town runs a canal for the purpose of watering the garden lots, as the water by small outlets may be conducted from this to all parts of the place—the traveller hears around him a confusion of unknown tongues, the red natives of the forests in their different guttural dialects—the swarthy Spaniard of a scarce brighter hue—the voluble Frenchman—a small number of the sons of Green Erin—and a goodly few of Uncle Sam's Nephews or half expatriated sons—he feels himself now for the first time in his life a stranger truly in a foreign land and enters a door for a short residence that he may discover something more of this people—but what he has seen we will let him make known in his own proper person. I find that Father has obtained a house and opened his goods.

Mr. Gregg is convalescent, tho' like Lyndsay and Patrick continues in a very debilitated state—business tolerably brisk profits moderate—some difficulty in dealing with the Mexicans, not understanding their language—form an acquaintance with two or three families—become some what a favourite with our landlady who has two pretty daughters—accompany them several times to the fandangos—waltzes and reels the principal forms of dance among them—always performed in the streets. Men do not select their partners—this is more gallantly left to the ladies—the former placing themselves in a line on the floor and when the latter arise and face the object of their choice—it sometimes happens that two or more make the same selection and then there is a good deal of elbowing among the fair ones—there are always managers to regulate matters—often solicited but never participate in the intricacies and mazes of their figures—delicacy forms but a small part of female character in San Antonio—their very language seems almost to forbid the cultivation of this most beautiful of the Graces—unmarried girls are very vigilantly kept from all intercourse whatever with the other sex unless one of the parents be present—soon as married they are scarcely the same creatures—giving the freest indulgence to their naturally gay and enthusiastic dispositions, as if liberated from all moral restraint—The complexion of the native mexican is a shade brighter than that of the aborigines of the country—the men are not generally well formed in feature or person—are extremely ignorant in all the advanced arts of civilization—the majority not being able to read—they are astonishingly expert in the management of horses—not surpassed perhaps by any other people on the Globe. They are completely the slaves of Popish Superstition and despotism—distinguished for their knavery and breach of faith. The softer sex are generally handsome in person and regular in feature and of rather a brighter hue than the men eyes black, sparkling, holding most intelligent converse when disposed in the still language of the affections—were long black hair handsomely adjusted into curls and puffs on public occasions—they are remarkably addicted to dress and Jewelry and on festal occasions appear as richly arrayed as any females I have ever seen—exhibiting no small degree of taste and are certainly among the vainest of their sex. But all this show lasts no longer than till they reach their homes, where they instantly appear as if they might soon be numbered on the Charity list.

The Gochapines or European Spaniards that dwell among them are exceptions to these remarks. These are mostly intelligent and wealthy—became acquainted with a daughter of one of them. And often have I regretted my ignorance of their bewitching language. She was of the middle size her person of the finest symmetry—moving through the mazes of the fandango with all the graces that distinguish superiority of person of mind and of soul—her face was perhaps not sufficiently oval to be of that form most admired as the model of beauty—her features were beautiful forming in their combination an expression that fixed the eye of the observer as with a spell—her complexion was of the loveliest—the snowy brightness of her well turned forehead beautifully contrasting with the carnation tints of her cheeks—a succession of smiles were continually sporting around her mouth her pouting cherry lips were irresistible and even when closed seemed to have atterance—her eye—but I have no such language as seemed to be spoken by it else might I tell how dangerous was it to meet its lustre and feel its quick thrilling scrutiny of the heart as tho' the very fire of its expression was conveyed with its beamings. I felt lonely and sad as a stranger in that place and a vision so lovely coming so unexpectedly before me could not fail to awaken tender recollections and altogether make an impression not soon to be forgotten.

The 16th of Sept. the anniversary of the Declaration of Mexican Independence was celebrated with a great deal of order and unanimity and considerable enthusiasm of feeling. A stage was erected in the public Square very much resembling a huge bedstead with a tester and curtains reaching down like drapery to the platform and made fast to the four posts at the tops of which were flying their own National flag that of The United States, of Great Britain and of France—while that of Old Spain formed a carpeting for the stair case ascending to the stage. The Soldiery and citizens both ladies and gentlemen paraded the streets in the afternoon in the evening an oration was delivered from the stage by a Priest—was told it was an excellent and patriotic composition—but I thought badly delivered and apparently with but very little effect on the multitude—a large table was set covered with wines and other liquors, sweetmeats etc "*pro bono publico.*" The Square was then lighted up with lamps and candles and every thing cleared off for the enjoyment of the "dearly loved fandango" five or six setts at it at once.—never before did I witness so large a collection of such happy beings. Thus passed off their day of Independence.

Continue to be myself "chief cook and bottle washer" for our company of Invalids in San Antonio—have some amusements in teaching the girls A. B. C.—and learning their language with them—old lady no longer afraid to trust them to my discretion—have opportunities of witnessing their manner of living. Every family has in the yard an oven built in form of a cone solely for the purpose of roasting the heads legs and tails of animals—on such occasions all the connexion round, are invited, skins are spread on the earth—when these delicacies are thrown down in the centre of the waiting circles, and every one that is fortunate enough to have a knife makes a lively use of it till the whole head is fairly demolished and as many of the legs as can be possibly crowded after it. When they have to pay for their meat in market a very little is made to suffice a family it is generally cut into a kind of hash with nearly as many peppers as there are pieces of meat—this is all stewed together. The way in which they obtain their bread is worthy of notice. They raise only Indian corn—this is soaked in lime or ley till the rind of the grain is taken off it is then ground on a concave stone about 12 inches wide and 20 in length with legs cut to it 6 or 8 inches long—the hinder being somewhat longest so as to give the stone an inclination from the body of the grinder—a handful of corn is laid on this and masticated with another stone resembling a roller but cut so as to fit the concavity this operation is always performed by the women, and in a kneeling posture—they generally go over it a third time—if they wish to treat their friends with very white bread the whole family gather round the pot of corn and grain by grain bite off the little black speck at the end of the germ—when the dough is already a small portion at a time is taken and patted in the hands till thin as a flannel cake—this cake making operation is always accompanied with tunes and words that seem peculiarly to chime in with the patting ceremony it reminded me very much of our tuneful ladies in a *finery starching* scene. These cakes are baked on sheet iron and when eaten hot with butter or gravy are very palatable—but soon get tough—they answer the natives for spoons with which they all dip into the same dish of meat and peppers prepared as above—one spoon not lasting longer than to supply with two mouthfuls when a new one is made use of. Very few families are supplied with the common necessary kitchen and household utensils—not even with chairs—sitting on skins spread upon the earthen floors of their dwelling thus live the commonality throughout the northern provinces of Mexico.

  The population of San Antonio is differently estimated from three to five thousand—they must rapidly improve with their increasing intercourse with the Americans. There is kept up here a garrison of three or four hundred soldiers for the defence of the place against the Indians but more particularly that very powerful tribe the Cumanches who are supposed to be 6 or 7,000 warriors strong and are continually at war with the Mexicans in some one part of the Province of Texas Saw about 20 or 30 of this tribe, who came in to trade—they are fine looking men—and the largest in frame considered collectively, I ever saw—are remarkably proud and overbearing toward the Mexicans

Mounted Béxarenos exhibiting skill on horseback. Daughters of the Republic of Texas Collection at Texas A&M University-San Antonio.

whom they heartily despise Allways on horseback in their travels and warfare—are expert horsemen—use the bow the lance and the shield not having many firearms among them—their mode of attack is generally by arranging the lances in front, the guns in the center and bows in the rear—their horses at full speed accompanied with the fury and yellings of demons—they are among the bravest and most warlike of the Mexican tribes—friendly in their disposition toward Americans and dreading the deadly rifle. The Lapans are a branch of the Cumanches and the next most formidable tribe in Texas. These two tribes range from the Brazos River to the Rio Grande and the mountainous country south of Santa Fee but are rarely known to molest American traders in those countries. Have abundance of figs peaches and melons here—very little attention paid to the cultivation of fruits tho' it is a climate very congenial to most of tropical productions—fall from a grape tree very seriously hurt—sell off our goods at auction—make arrangements for journeying to the east.

Take a ride with Captn. Lindsay toward the head of the San Antonio river which rises 6 or 7 miles above the town or rather gushes a full sized river of the lesser magnitude from under one of the immense hills north of the town. We become bewildered among the hills woods and and are disappointed in seeing the romantic spectacle but feel in a measure compensated by witnessing a few miles farther N the most picturesque and pleasing scenes of country that ever gratified our views—immense hills—extensive vales—barren rocks—luxuriance of verdure—deer starting up from before us and bounding over the adjacent landscape—blue mountains towering in the distance, as it were to shut out the view of infinitude—the whole lovely in its original wildness, and most impressively imposing in sublimity. Such is the scenery around San Antonio— forming an immense and complete ampitheatre 6 or 7 miles in diameter, within which nearly the whole plain is a rich and productive soile and may be watered at any time of the year by canals of little expense from the San Antonio river—and certainly there never was a stream better calculated for the purpose of manufacturing machinery— but all is in the possession of a people too ignorant and indolent for enterprise and too poor and *dependent* were they otherwise capacitated. Begin to understand the "common parlance" of the place tolerably well. Landlady and girls most willing to assist me—am asked all about *my country*—how far to it—how many relations I have—what religion they profess—tell them some were Roman Catholics—greatly delighted. By the by this family are pretty strict in the observance of their forms—repetitions of "Our fathers"—"Ave Marias"—"Credos" etc for indeed the religion of this place is understood by very few if any as a gracious affection of the heart and soul but a mere requisition of personal mortification in form of penances etc. Old lady very anxious to know when I would visit her country again—tell her perhaps in two or three years—informs me by that time her prettiest daughter will be marriageable and wished I would bring her some Jewelry with me—gives me a brass ring with a blue glass sett as a remembrance from her daughter whose delicate fingers at the same time were ornamented with more than one of gold—put it carefully in my pocket however, seemingly much flattered by the *distinguished* compliment.

City Ordinances for San Antonio de Béxar, 1829

INTRODUCTION TO DOCUMENT

After achieving independence from Spain and finally jettisoning the monarchy with the ouster of Emperor Agustín de Itrubide, Mexicans opted for a federal republic signaled by the adoption of the Constitution of 1824. Former provinces which had been virtually autonomous under the Spanish were charged with organizing themselves into states that would coexist and share power with the newly established national government. In 1827, the Legislature of Coahuila and Texas, while producing its own state constitution, requested municipalities within its borders to submit their own ordinances.

Civil government in San Antonio de Béxar had existed since 1731 with the establishment of a town council or *cabildo* by the Canary Islanders. Hence, rules and regulations for the town had already existed for a hundred years. The current town council, by now called the *ayuntamiento*, drew on these existing regulations and customs when preparing its ordinances for the legislature.

The 1829 Ordinances covered governance, public heath, public facilities, beautification projects, and revenues raised through taxes and fines. Unlike the descriptions from visitors from both the Mexican interior and the United States that deemed San Antonio as a rustic and somewhat lawless place, these regulations show that, even though on the frontier, life in San Antonio was well regulated.

DOCUMENT[19]

The Duties of the Alcalde [Mayor/Judge]

Article 17. The laws of the State [of Coahuila y Tejas] have already made known the qualifications necessary for this office and do hereby declare his following duties:

FIRST: He shall direct himself on all working days to the legal business demanded by his office and shall dedicate himself to the best administration at all times.

SECOND: He shall take special care that these city ordnances [governing law and order, public health, trade and taxes, etc.] are carried out faithfully in each and all its parts.

THIRD: He shall make an inspection of the archives of the municipal government every six months, and shall see that the secretary write out the proper index on each record book.

FOURTH: He shall take care also that a census of the general population be kept in a corresponding record book. This census is to include the names of parents or the heads of families that make up the community with their full names, ages, place of birth, their employment or type of office, their marital status, and the number, age, and sex of their children. This census shall contain the names, ages, type of employment, place of birth of all male and female servants even if they are not related to the family.

FIFTH: In this same book, a notation will be made of all births and deaths that occur in each and every family as indicated in the particular census taken at the end of each year by the city attorney (*procurrador síndico*) and the secretary.

SIXTH: He shall recognize the arrival of the political chief of the department to a meeting in session with all the formality prescribed in Article 14 [e.g., offered a courteous greeting upon being presented to the council].

Regarding Public Health

Article 19. The maintenance of public health shall be one of the principal duties of each and every member of the municipal government.

Death on the early San Antonio frontier was a fact of life. This painting captures the funeral procession for an infant. A fiddle leads the way, while mourners discharge firearms as they go. Daughters of the Republic of Texas Collection at Texas A&M University-San Antonio.

Article 20. There will be a committee on heath made up of an alcalde, an alderman (*rejidor*), the city attorney (*procurrador síndico*), the curate, and two residents that the municipal government will elect.

Article 21. It shall be the duty of the municipal government that the two preceding articles be carried out and that the following provisions be observed.

FIRST: That the individuals responsible for the actual cleanliness of the acequias that passes through the city preform their duties and that these individuals do a perfect job by the last of February, not allowing new water currents through the acequia until it be examined by the chief of police, the president of the municipal government, and city attorney. If, upon examination, the acequia is not properly cleaned, those responsible shall immediately comply with their duties, being made aware that they shall be fined in a manner equal to their delinquency.

SECOND: It shall be the duty of the citizens whose property borders the acequia, and especially the city attorney, to guard that no dead animals, pelts, or any other corruptible refuse be cast into the acequia. Those found at fault shall be fined in a manner equal to their offence.

THIRD: It shall be the duty of the city attorney that the streets, plazas, and all other public parks be kept clean of all trash, rocks, small carts, lumber, and anything else that might impede traffic or soil their appearance. It shall be his duty to see that the owners of homes next to these streets and plazas wash and sweep the front area of their homes at least on Saturday of each week.

FOURTH: It shall be the daily duty of each employee (an individual in the business of selling edible goods) that the public be sold only the best quality of meats, bread, fruits, and other edible goods. He shall not defraud the public of its money nor shall he combine foods that may be dangerous to public health.

FIFTH: It shall be the duty of the chief of police, or in his absence, that of the alcalde, to see that any citizens of the country or foreigner who wishes to practice medicine in the community immediately come before proper authority and present those documents that indicate his training in the medical profession. Furthermore, it shall be the duty of those in authority to inspect, each year at least, the medicines that are sold to the public. They shall also inspect doctors, pharmacists, and all those involved in the medical profession and whose responsibility it is to administer these medicines and introduce new ones.

SIXTH: The slaughter of bovine livestock, lambs and sheep, or bristle-producing animals for consumption by the public shall be cared for outside the city limits.

SEVENTH: It is prohibited to maintain any kind of livestock, regardless of their number, within the city limits. All livestock should be cared for away from the city.

EIGHTH: All those in the business of selling (vendors) meats and white bread are obliged to make public the cost of their products in terms of ounces. It shall be the duty of the city attorney to watch carefully that all business transacted in these matters be kept honest. Those not complying (with the law) shall forfeit the right to do business upon being found guilty and may possibly serve a jail sentence.

NINTH: A professional mason builder authorized and paid by the alcalde when under contract shall be obliged to plan and keep in good order all streets and houses to be constructed. All citizens interested in these matters shall seek his services through the office of the alcalde.

TENTH: It is prohibited to construct homes from bulrushes (tulle) or grass. Those unable to obtain less combustible building material will need to bring their case before local authority.

Regarding Public Welfare

Article 22. It shall be the duty of each and every member of the municipal government to make known the number of *aucsilios* in his possession that are available to the individuals of this community—both native citizens and foreign—for the safety of their lives and interests.

Article 23. Each individual foreigner who is a subject of this country or any other country shall come before the alcalde within 24 hours of his arrival to the city. He shall present his passport and make known the intent of his visit and observe the general laws of the nation and the particular laws of the state.

Article 24. The city attorney and the other members of the municipal government has the responsibility to oblige all city homeowners to maintain good fences, along those parts of their properties bordering public streets. These citizens are not permitted to burn refuse in the patios of their homes. Furthermore, they are obliged to keep all their animals well fenced.

Article 25. It shall be the duty of the first alderman and the city attorney to make an annual inspection of all shops and retail stores wherein weights and measures are utilized, for the purpose of inspecting, correcting, and doing away with all faulty measuring devises. They shall also take care that all inspected measuring devices are kept in order through the rest of the year.

Article 26. It is entirely prohibited to engage in all type of card games, and the owner of an establishment permitting these games will be punished with (full) rigor of the laws.

Article 27. Retail stores, pool halls, and other establishments of public business and amusement shall be visited and guarded by the ordinary civil and military patrolmen. They shall see to it that these business establishments are closed by 10 PM and that dance socials end at the hour designated ahead of time. Dance socials (fandangos) are to take place on evenings before official feast days.

Article 28. There will be two weekly patrols charged with the safety and maintenance of public order. The chief of police shall assign eight armed men to each patrol. Each patrol shall be on duty from 9:00 PM until 3:00 AM and perform those duties required of them by the police department and those assigned to them by the municipal government.

Article 29. The designated patrol shall be supervised by the alcalde or one of the aldermen serving in rotation who has been appointed by the alcalde.

Article 30. When in the judgement of the chief of police or that of the municipal government it is deemed necessary to increase the number of patrols or the number of patrolmen beyond that designated by Article 20, it can be brought into effect.

Article 31. In order to preserve newly planted trees, and other wooded areas within the city around which livestock is afforded pastureland, two rural judges (*jueces de campo*) shall be selected each year from among neighbors, ranch owners, and those in open farm areas (*labores de rumbos espuestos*). It shall be their exclusive duty to provide suitable wood-storage locations from which to take firewood; to determine the amount of necessary firewood; to preserve pecan and other fruit trees; and finally guard against forest fires that occur each year.

Article 32. It also shall be the duty of the two forest experts mentioned in Article 31 to construct, to maintain, and to repair the fences around the newly planted trees. They shall take care that the roads are maintained and that necessary ones be opened. They shall repair bridges. Also they shall be put on guard for thieves who might cause damage to the maize land, orchards, and other croplands assigned to their care. They shall turn in all delinquents and information on the nature of their offense to the alcalde, who in turn shall uphold and faithfully carry out those laws that both the forest rangers and the alcalde knowingly and weekly pledge to support.

Article 33. It shall be the duty of the municipal government to appoint a commissioner with legal power to enforce justice among the citizens who have residence in one of the three wards or blocks (*cuarteles o' mansanas*) in which this community is divided. The first commissioner shall administer justice to the citizens living on the left bank of the [San Antonio] river in the area known as the Alamo and La Villita. The second and third commissioner shall serve the rest of the citizens of the community. Their districts shall be divided by the main streets originating from the

Alamo bridge and running in a straight line to the opposite bank of the creek in the next populated sector. One commissioner shall be responsible for the district north of the line, the other for the district south of the line.

Article 34. It shall be the duty of the commissioners to care for their appointed tasks faithfully; first, clean and adequate maintenance of the streets; secondly, to inform the alcalde within 24 hours regarding any stranger or new neighbors moving into their respective districts with the intention of taking residence; and thirdly, to take action against unruly drunks, gamblers (*taures*), individuals given to public scandal, and any other reportedly suspicious character. All such persons shall be apprehended and immediately brought before the alcalde. Fourthly, [a commissioner] shall take immediate cognizance of differences arising between neighbors in his respective district and especially those where mutual damage has occurred in such places as planted orchards or in fenced areas. He shall also be aware of damages caused by domestic and other animals engaged in providing transportation, providing that the damages do not exceed 10 pesos. Fifthly, he shall take care that the water resources in his district are fairly distributed by causing the water currents to flow through an irrigation ditch serving the majority of the citizens, and that the *acequia* and its tributaries designated for use by the city are kept clean. Sixthly, in keeping with his obligations, he shall keep close watch over all those things in the district related to public safety, health, welfare, and beautification, inasmuch as his resources permit, giving a weekly account of all his business to the alcalde and even more often when the nature of his business warrants it.

Article 35. It shall be the duty of the commissioners of the four missions (Valero, San José, Concepcíon, and Espada) to assist the rural judges (*jueces de campo*) with their authority, advice, and goodwill, so that they may carry out the duties charged to their care.

Article 36. The chief of police, upon notifying the alcalde, may request help from the military authorities to protect individuals whose business interests oblige them to leave the city.

Regarding Beautification of Public Places

Article 43. It shall be the duty of the municipal government:

FIRST: To preserve the growth of the *alameda* planted northwest of the city and to watch that it contributes to the beautification of the city in keeping with available means.

SECOND: It shall encourage those having residence along the banks of the river, aqueducts, and creeks, as well as those living next to the city plaza, to plant all types of shade trees, provided they do not cause damage and in keeping with recommendations of the municipal government.

THIRD: A statue depicting "Liberty" along with the national coat of arms shall be located in the front part of the hall where the municipal government meets. The hall shall be decorated further as time goes on with pictorial representation of the first national heroes and all those who efficaciously and directly contributed to its independence from the year 1810 to 1821. There shall be other patriotic symbols and engravings (*geroglíficos*) that promote national pride and interest.

Regarding the Creation of City Treasury Funds

Article 44. In order to obtain funds, the municipal government shall adopt previously practical measures of taxation, both public (*proprios*) and arbitrary (*arbitrios*), to which this city is accustomed.

Article 47. In order to increase the above mentioned fund, the following surtax is decreed.

FIRST: One *real* annually on every 200 varas cuadrados on lots mentioned in Article 45 and which are in use for residential purposes.

SECOND: One peso annually on all lots outside city limits (city owned lands) under contract to accept *el 5° del fondo de proprios*, as has been customarily done until now.

THIRD: These lands shall be posted since it was not previously done, as community lands (*egidos*) of the city, two *leguas* long and one *legua* wide, east and west respectively. Furthermore, the products from these lands shall also pertain to the public fund.

Article 48. The funds from the excise taxes shall come from the duties presently imposed and which will be imposed in the futures on all fruit produce, commodities, national products, foreign goods imported to the city, and also from duties on transportation vehicles and all beasts of burden. In this fund shall be included fines collected in this regard.

Article 49. The following taxes are hereby in effect:

FIRST: Three *reales* on each head of livestock that is slaughtered.

SECOND: One-half *real* on each sheep or goat [slaughtered].

THIRD: Two *reales* on each slaughtered hog.

FOURTH: Six pesos annually, payable in advance, on every clothing and retail store that is stocked with merchandise brought into the city.

FIFTH: Three pesos, payable in the same manner as those in Item 4 on retail stores that are stocked with merchandise within the city.

SIXTH: Twelve pesos upon the grand opening of all new stores stocked with merchandise brought into the city. This shall include those stores which, even not closing for one day, change owners and are operated from different officers.

SEVENTH: One peso on each lottery not valued at more than fifty pesos; two pesos when its value is between 50 and 150 pesos; and in large *rifas* [raffle] the tax ratio is 2% of its total value. The prize or winnings can be confiscated in the event that the tax is not paid, and the city treasury shall allocate the money or price with the exception of one-third of its value, which shall be given to the informer of the delinquent act, if there should be one.

EIGHTH: Four *reales* on one or more musicians when they exercise their profession at dances that take place in all homes, streets, plazas, or even while playing at an event popularly called *gallo* or *serenata*.

NINTH: One peso on each individual who stays one or more nights in the city jail, provided that he is not exonerated. This peso shall be placed in the city treasury.

TENTH: One peso on each cart or wagon at each time each time it is brought into the city carrying national or foreign products.

ELEVENTH: Beside the one peso tax mentioned in No. 10, each citizens owning a cart shall pay a one-peso license annually.

TWELFTH: All mules loaded with goods of some sort and that pass through the city shall be taxed one peso per mule.

THIRTEENTH: A one peso tax shall be paid annually by property owners each day water is supplied by different canals as presently distributed in the city.

FOURTEENTH: Each [cart or wagon] load of sweet cakes [*peloncillo*] produced in the factories and mills located in the city shall be taxed two and one-half *reales* when the product in finished.

FIFTEENTH: A crop of cane that is harvested but not processed shall be taxed two *reales*.

Article 50. Besides the duty imposed in the sixth paragraph of the previous article on stores at the time of grand opening, an annual tax of six pesos shall be placed on all stores currently opened to be paid within a reasonable amount of time. All stores currently opened shall also comply with all other regulations pertinent to stores as found in paragraphs four and five above.

Article 51. All carts and mules who carry into this city fruit produce grown within two leagues [6 miles] of the city are exempt from paying the taxes mentioned in paragraphs eleven and twelve. However, all carts and wagons carrying wood will pay the following: four *reales*, those with beams [*unigas*] constructed of said woods, and one peso for those of wood shavings [*tabetas*] or bark [*corteza*] from the same.

Regarding Monetary Fines That Contribute to the City Treasury

Article 52. A fine of two *reales* shall be imposed on each individual every time he is charged with not fencing the front, rear, and the sides of his property bordering public thoroughfares. A fine of four *reales* shall be imposed on each individual who is proven responsible for spoiling, obstructing, or polluting the water in the acequia, even when it is caused by his domestic animals. A fine of one peso shall be imposed on every citizens responsible for the sanitation and repairs of the acequias and is found delinquent. A fine of four *reales* shall be imposed on an owner of a home in the patio of which trash is burned. A fine of two pesos shall be imposed on every individual who, without good reason and authorization, shoots firearms within the limits of this community or within one-half league [1.5 miles] of its environs. The owners of hogs, cows, dogs, or any domestic animal is responsible for damages that his animals might cause to other private property and, besides being liable for just compensation, he shall incur a fine of four *reales*. Furthermore, the following provisions shall be observed.

> **FIRST:** Anyone who finds one or more of the neighbors' hogs within the confines of his property or home can tie them and immediately notify the judge.
>
> **SECOND:** A fine of four *reales* per animal shall be imposed on all animal owners approaching the *juez* with the purpose of reclaiming their animals after they have been turned into the authorities, two additional *reales* for the handling charges, and all other costs incurred in their overnight care.
>
> **THIRD:** After three days, if the owners do not reclaim their impounded animals, proper authorities may take steps to sell them at public auction and shall cover the cost of damages caused by the animals and those incurred in their handling and care. Said auction shall take place only after the owner has been informed, if he is in the locality. The balance from the sales after expenses shall go to the owner if he should claim it. In the event that the owner does not, the money from said auction shall be placed in the city treasury.
>
> **FOURTH:** The constables are authorized to impound all stray hogs found in the streets. The same regulation found in the second part of No. 3 shall be carried out in the case of stray hogs.

Article 53. Drunks [*ebrios*] habitually causing scandal shall be fined, when able to pay, twenty-five pesos for the first offense, fifty for the second, and those who continually relapse shall incur the full force of the penalties for this type of delinquent in Article 123 of State Law No. 37. [Law No. 37 is referenced but not printed in Kimball's *Laws and Decrees of the State of Coahuila and Texas*.]

Article 54. Any individual sent to jail because of drunkenness, either by those on night patrol or by other proper authorities, shall be arrested for 15 days and sentenced to labor at public works or other tasks determined by the alcalde and under appropriate security measures.

Article 55. The fines mentioned in Articles 53, 54, and 54 shall not go into effect in cases where the law applies some kind of corporal punishment. Those inflicted with corporal punishment are not obliged to satisfy the others.

Article 56. All meat or bread merchants who deceive the public through false advertisement and unfair sales practice shall be deprived of their business licenses and shall be liable to a jail sentence.

It shall be the duty of the governor of the state to see that these ordinances are carried out, by having them published, officially proclaimed, and promulgated.

Given in Ciudad de León Vicaris [Saltillo] on May 30, 1829.

José Manuel Cárdenas, President
Ramon Garcia, Secretary
J. Maria Aragon, Secretary

I herby order that these ordinances be published, officially proclaimed, and promulgated, and that they be carried out.

José Maria Viesca (Governor)
Leona Vicario [Saltillo], June 6, 1829
Santiago de Valle, Secretary

Benjamin Lundy Visits San Antonio, 1833

INTRODUCTION TO DOCUMENT

Benjamin Lundy gained notice in the early abolitionist movement as one of its most ardent leaders. In 1821 he gave up a successful saddle making business in Ohio to start a newspaper called the *Genius of Universal Emancipation* whose goal was to end slavery in the United States. A Quaker, Lundy travelled throughout the United States and North America, giving lectures and promoting abolition.

One of Lundy's projects caused him to twice travel to Texas. He wanted to obtain a colony in Texas, Tamaulipas, or some other part of Medico where former slaves could settle. Although powerful political figures and intellectuals supported plan, nothing came of it. Lundy was later instrumental in promoting the view of the Texas Revolution as a Southern slaveholders' plot to strip the region from Mexico, a notion adopted by both the abolitionists and the Mexican political class.

Lundy chronicled his stay in San Antonio, which served as a stopover on his journey through Mexico to promote his plan.

DOCUMENT [20]

[August 23, 1833]   I arrived at Bexar, otherwise called San Antonio, before noon, and stopped at the public house of John W. Smith. In the afternoon I took a walk around the town, and in the evening called on my friend Juan Antonio Padilla, with whom I had become acquainted the summer before, at Nacogdoches. He continues as favourable as ever to my project.

The town of Bexar contains about two thousand inhabitants. Many of the buildings are of stone, and very lofty, with flat roofs. The larger portion however, are mere huts, constructed principally of poles, with one end set in the ground, in the form of picket-fence. These huts are thatched with a kind of coarse grass, and are entirely destitute of floors.

24th.   I rose early and walked about the town. Many of the people were stirring by daylight, while others were lying on their pallets in front of their houses, it being customary with numbers of the labouring class to sleep in the open air. I called again upon Padilla and showed him my credentials, with which he was quite pleased. He accompanied me on a visit to the authorities of the place. We went first to the political chief, and showed him my passport. He is rather a pleasant man, and speaks pretty good English. We next visited the Alcalde, who took a copy of the passport.—Then I spent the rest of the day in looking about town. There lives here, in Bexar, a free black man, who speaks English. He came as a slave, first from North Carolina to Georgia, and then from Georgia to Nacogdoches, in Texas. There his master died, and the heirs sold him to another person. This new master, being apprehended for debt, offered the slave his freedom if he would take him out of prison. The slave complied, but the master dying soon after, an attempt was made by his heirs to re-enslave the man, which however proved unsuccessful. He now works as a blacksmith in this place. I have been to converse with him, he having seen me at Nacogdoches last summer, and knowing me again when he met me here. He is highly pleased with my plans. Though he is jet-black, he says the Mexicans pay him the same respect as to other laboring people, there being no difference made here on account of colour. Padilla says it is the policy of the Mexican Government to unite all colours and treat all with respect. The

Mexicans, in this region, make as good an appearance as any people; but there are very few among them that we should call white. The inhabitants of Bexar appear far better in general than those of Brazoria, San Felipe or Gonzales. They have graceful manners and honest countenances, and exhibit tokens of wealth and independence. Both men and women are fine looking people;—less vivacious than the Haytiens, but more mild and easy in their manners.

In the afternoon I went out to the fields north of the town, where I was struck with the wonderful growth of the vegetables of almost every kind known to us further north. The Indian corn is very luxuriant. The peaches are large, and of fine flavour, as well as in great abundance. Every where, in the gardens, there are fig-trees loaded with fruit. The figs keep ripening all the year. They are sold at the rate of twelve to fifteen for a six cent piece.

Aug. 25th. Sabbath morning. I walked out and found all very still in the streets, but the stores and shops were open as usual. Some of the people were at church and some at work.

26th. I have commenced providing my own board in a small but convenient room which I have rented in Bexar, and which is to serve me as a work shop. It is reported to-day that a Mexican was killed yesterday within four miles of town by a party of Indians, probably Camanches. This tribe is very hostile to the Mexicans, but friendly to the northern Americans.

27th. I was informed early this morning, that a fellow named Morgan, who has been in Bexar for some days, had decamped. He professed to be a son of the proprietor of Morgantown, Virginia. He begged of me the loan of several articles of clothing, and two other North Americans lent him money. He was then drunk for two or three days, at the end of which he left for La Bahia (or Goliad,) without repaying loans of any kind. Another of my countrymen got intoxicated yesterday, and behaved as in "the land of the free." Being complained of by the keeper of the North American tavern, he was lodged in prison. To-day he was tried and fined ten dollars. A great part of what we hear of the bad treatment of our countrymen among the Mexicans, is caused by the misconduct of such persons.

28th. At work in my shop.

29th. Being unable to get work at my trade to-day, I walked out. Saw much stone in quarries, though the surface of the ground is generally clear. Limestone is abundant in the vicinity. Lime is used in covering the roofs of most of the stone houses in Bexar. The roof is commenced by laying cedar poles horizontally across the building from wall to wall, then across these poles smaller pieces of timber are laid compactly; and over them are put stones and earth rounded up in the middle; then over the whole a coating of parget [plaster] or rough-cast is laid. Around the roof, there is a sort of parapet, from which wooden spouts extend outwards, two or three feet, for carrying off the water. On some of these roofs, grass and the prickly-pear are seen growing. The roofs of the inferior houses are covered, some with shingles, some with bark laid after the manner of clap-boards, and some are thatched with a coarse grass which grows on the margins of the streams.–Going into the market to-day, I found good beef selling at two cents per pound.

There is news this morning of an attack by Indians, supposed to be Tiwaukanes, upon a horse-pen five miles from town. One man was wounded by them.—Information of recent date from Mexico says that all is going on well, that centralism is defunct, &c.

31st. I purchased some provisions this morning, expecting to set out to-day for Monclova, the capital of Coahuila, and the seat of government for Coahuila and Texas. I learned that the Ayuntamiento determined yesterday to send out forty men of the "civic guard" against the Indians. The people in town are in some alarm. Not a man ventures into his field, or to a distance of a quarter of a mile to procure wood, without taking his gun along with him. It looks strange to see a man or a boy with a musket on his shoulder, driving an ox-cart. having been disappointed in my plan of leaving town to-day, and my finances being reduced to the lowest ebb, I was obliged to sell some of my clothing. As there was no work at Bexar to be done in the saddling line, I determined to try to make and repair suspenders, in which business I had made some experiments during my apprenticeship. A company of merchants is now organizing to start for Rio Grande, Monclova, &c., in about a week. I must wait and go with them.

September 1st, 1833. The autumn has commenced, and I am still here at Bexar. It is the part of philosophy to bear up against difficulty, disappointment and affliction, and I will do so as long as possible. I have still some resources. I have not been obliged to beg or steal, nor am I likely to be: my case, therefore, is not yet desperate. There was not much talk in town to-day about Indians: the alarm concerning them was probably in part without foundation. In the evening I walked out of town; found the peach trees looking better here than in the United States: the hackberry, persimmon and mulberry are abundant.

2d. Busy in my shop with making and repairing suspenders.

3d. I was called up this morning to visit a sick man. Having told the people something about the cholera, they all think me a doctor.

5th. I saw this evening a large and beautiful skin which was taken from a Mexican leopard. It is fully equal to that of the African leopard, which it much resembles. There are at this time in Bexar many people from Austin's lower settlements, who have come here, on account of the salubrity of the place, to spend the sickly season.

6th. I had arranged to leave Bexar to-day with a company going to Monclova. It is now said, however, that they will not start in less than two weeks. What shall I do? My consolation is that there is yet hope for the virtuous and support for the industrious.

Sept. 8th. Another Sabbath. This is the day set apart in the Christian calendar as the anniversary of the birth of the blessed Virgin Mary. The bells of the old church are pealing merrily, and rockets are flying briskly. As high mass is to be performed; more *eclat* than usual is perhaps necessary, to draw the attention of the careless and merely formal professor to the high importance of the occasion.

11th. We had a fine shower to-day, a thing somewhat rare now a-days, as it is generally dry here during the summer months, though wet enough at other seasons. In the afternoon I walked out to recreate myself from the fatigue of sitting constantly in my shop for several days. News came by last night's mail that the cholera is raging in many parts of Mexico. Gen. Duran, chief of the Centralists, lately died of it. Letters received by the Ayuntimiento here from Stephen F. Austin at Mexico, state that the Mexican Congress will not accept the "Constitution of Texas" prepared by the self-delegated convention, until they proceed constitutionally in the business.

12th. In addition to making suspenders I have now started a new branch of business, viz., the making of shot bags from panther and deer skins. Any thing for an honest livelihood, and to keep my spirits from sinking while I am pent up here.

14th. I learned to-day that Vann, the Cherokee chief, having obtained leave from the government to arrest and take away two of his slaves who had escaped to this vicinity, delegated his authority to one Williams, who went with an assistant to a ranche thirty miles south of this place, and having made demand of the slaves proceeded to take them. One of them resisting was shot dead by Williams; the other escaped. This event has created some excitement here. I have sold to-day a shot bag and a pair of suspenders at $1 each. Thus I am quite in funds again!

16th. A splendid ball was to have taken place here this evening, but it has been prevented by the sad news of the death, from cholera, of the Vice-Governor and Chief Justice of the State [Juan Martín de Veramendi].

17th. I sold yesterday, two shot bags, and to-day I sold one to the slave-hunter Williams, before I was aware that he was the person who had shot the black man. Was it providential that this wretch should thus contribute to my support while I was engaged in the cause of freedom? Hercules will assist your wagon out of the mire, if you but put your own shoulder to the wheel. The authorities have instituted an inquiry into the slave's death; and I learn, in the evening, that the villain, Williams, who shot him, has absconded, under the apprehension that some evidence was to be produced, which would be likely to make the trial go hard with him. It is said that he went in pursuit of the slaves, on condition of receiving one-half their value, in case he should return them to Vann.

18th. I was called on to-day to visit another sick man; also a sick woman. They persist here in considering me a doctor. I still work away, however, at suspenders and shot bags.

19th. Early this morning some Camanche Indians arrived in town, with skins, &c., to trade.—A great religious parade is held here to-day. It is a sort of a religious invocation to God for preservation from the cholera. There are great apprehensions, among the people, of that terrible disease; and those who can afford it, carry little bags of camphor in their bosoms, to guard against an attack. The state of health, at present, however, is as good as I ever witnessed at any time or place. My own health has become very good.

23d. A row took place yesterday between two of our Northern Americans, or United States people. The victor was taken before the Alcalde, and upon hearing, to-day, was fined ten dollars.—A person who resides on Kimball's Creek, Texas, informs me that there is an abundance of mineral coal in that quarter, similar to that of Pennsylvania, though somewhat more sulphurous.

26th. The merchants with whom I am to go to Monclova, have engaged a team and expect to start in a few days.

28th. A man from Pittsburg, named George Pagan, stole to-day, from my room, a pair of suspenders worth $2. These Mexicans are novices in the arts of thieving, drunkenness and vagabondism, in comparison with these fellows from the North.

29th. I walked out this forenoon with Matthew Thomas, to see the cane patch, grounds, &c., of his father-in-law, Felipe Elua, a black Louisiana creole, who was formerly a slave, but who has purchased the freedom of himself and family. He has resided here twenty-six years, and he now owns five or six houses and lots, besides a fine piece of land near town. He has educated his children so that they can read and write, and speak Spanish as well as French. They are all fine looking, smart black people. He has a sister also residing in Bexar, who is married to a Frenchman. The sugar cane, of which there is a patch of about an acre on Elua's land, looks as well as that which grows in Hayti, and the land is evidently well adapted to it. The frost does not kill the roots of the plant here as it does further north, but the sprouts make their appearance in the spring, so that it is unnecessary to replant it. Besides the cane, we saw some fine looking cotton, a large patch of sweet potatoes, together with beans and other garden vegetables, the property of the same black man, and all in beautiful order.

30th. A merchant named Rubideau, who arrived here two days since from St. Louis, where I knew some thing of him in 1820, and whose character and standing is considered good, proposes to buy me a horse and to pay some bills for me, and desires me to accompany him immediately to Monclova. He is a Louisiana French creole, and is now acting as agent for the Missouri fur trading company. He says he knows all about my public career. I have introduced him to my friend Padilla. There is also another person who is going from Monclova to Mexico, that offers to furnish me with money to accompany him. These offers seem certainly to be fair and friendly.

October 1st, 1833. Another month has passed, and I am still here at Bexar.—Another religious procession took place this afternoon. Its object was "to keep away the cholera," as our North Americans here say. I went out with several others to see it. At a particular part of the ceremony all in the procession knelt for a few moments. The same thing is done by the Catholic bystanders, but it is not required of strangers. The latter, however, generally stand and uncover their heads, as a mark of respect.

5th.   Our company for Monclova being frightened, by reports of the cholera, have concluded to defer starting for a week or two. Rubideau is willing to go on, but he has an attack of the ague, of which I have undertaken to cure him. To-day some Shawnee and Delaware Indians arrived in town on their way to attack the Camanches.

6th.   There is a very cool north wind today. The Mexicans are all blanketed up as they walk abroad.

Col. Juan N. Almonte's Report: Department of Bexar in 1834

INTRODUCTION TO DOCUMENT

Juan N. Almonte, the illegitimate son of rebel priest José Morelos, held several prominent government posts after Mexico gained its independence from Spain. Educated in New Orleans, Almonte learned English and later became part of the Mexican diplomatic mission to Great Britain.

In 1834, the Mexican government asked Colonel Almonte to lead an expedition to Texas to gather facts. The colonists, however, suspected his actual purpose was to spy on them. His report documents the situation he found regarding San Antonio de Béxar and the general population of the department. Almonte later served as an aid to General Antonio López de Santa Anna during the Texas campaign.

Almonte made two observations about the Department of Béxar which set it apart from the American colonies to the east: (1) he saw no slaves and (2) the population was in decline.

DOCUMENT[21]

The population of Texas extends from Bexar to the Sabine River, and in that direction there are not more than 25 leagues [75 miles] of unoccupied territory to occasion some inconvenience to the traveler. The most difficult part of the journey to Texas is the space between the Rio Grande and Bexar, which extends a little more than 50 leagues [150 miles], by what is called the Upper Road, and above 65 leagues [195 miles] by the way of Laredo. These difficulties do not arise from the badness of the road itself, but from the absence of population, rendering it necessary to carry provisions, and even water during summer, when it is scarce in this district. This tract is so flat and rich in pasturage that it may be traveled with sufficient relays, and at a suitable speed, without the fear of wanting forage.

Department of Bexar

In 1806 the Department of Bexar contained two municipalities; San Antonio de Bexar, with a population of 5,000 souls, and Goliad, with 1,400; total 6,400. In 1834 there were four municipalities, with the following population respectively: San Antonio de Bexar, 2,400; Goliad, 700; Victoria, 300; San Patricio, 600; total 4,000. Deducting 600 for the municipality of San Patricio (an Irish settlement), the Mexican population had declined from 6,400 to 3,400 between 1806 and 1834. This is the only district of Texas in which there are no Negro laborers. Of the various colonies introduced into it, only two have prospered: one of Mexicans, on the river Guadalupe, by the road which leads from Goliad to San Felipe; the other of Irish, on the river Nueces, on the road from Matamoros to Goliad. With the exception of San Patricio, the entire district of Bexar is peopled by Mexicans. The greater part of, the lands of Bexar can easily be irrigated, and there is no doubt that so soon as the Government, compassionating the lot (*suerte*) of Texas, shall send a respectable force to chastise the savages, the Mexicans will gladly hasten to colonize those valuable lands which court their labor. Extensive undertakings cannot be entered on in Bexar, as there is no individual capital exceeding 10,000 dollars. All the provisions raised by the inhabitants are consumed in the district. The wild horse is common, so as rarely to be valued at more than 20 reales (about 10 shillings British) when caught. Cattle are cheap; a cow and a calf not being worth more than 10 dollars, and a young bull, or heifer from 4 to 5 dollars. Sheep are scarce, not exceeding 5,000 head. The whole export trade is confined to from 8,000 to 10,000 skins of various, kinds, and the imports to a few articles from New Orleans, which are exchanged in San Antonio for peltry or currency (*peleteria y mettilico*).

Lack of schools. There is one school in the capital of the Department supported by the municipality, but apparently the funds are so reduced as to render the maintenance of even this useful establishment impossible. What is to be the fate of those unhappy Mexicans who dwell in the midst of savages without hope of civilization? Goliad, Victoria, and even San Patricio, are similarly situated, and it is not difficult to foresee the consequences of such a state of things. In the whole department there is but one curate (*cura*), the vicar died of cholera morbus in September last.

Samuel A. Maverick's Account of the Siege of Béxar, 1835

INTRODUCTION TO DOCUMENT

Samuel Augustus Maverick came to Texas from South Carolina to take advantage of the business opportunity that abounded. Unlike the most Americans, he established himself in the center of Tejano culture, residing in San Antonio de Béxar. He found himself inside Béxar at the start of the Texas Revolution. After the Battle of Gonzales in early October 1835, Maverick and other Americans living there were placed under house arrest by General Martín Perfecto de Cos.

Though Maverick's journal we get a glimpse of life inside the town during the Siege of Béxar. Although under arrest, he was still able to exchange messages with the colonists conducting the siege. Accompanied by John W. Smith, another American living in Béxar, Maverick was finally released after promising to leave Texas. Instead, he joined the Texan forces and helped guide them when they attacked the town in the Battle of Béxar in early December 1835.

DOCUMENT[22]

SEPT. 5th. Leave Gonzales for Bexar, 6 miles to judge Williams. *[blank]* m. to *[blank]*, 49 m. to Cibolo, 22 m. to Salado Cr.; 5 (m) to Bejar (76 miles from Gonzales to Bejar). Arrived on 8th Sept.

SEPT. 16th. Grand Independence Celebration. (Paid Smith to 23rd, owe from 24th). Mr. Anderson's account of the Comanches.

OCT. 8th. Messrs Smith & Anderson return from Gonzales with the final resolution of the people & Ayuntamiento that they will not give up the cannon. Col. Ugartechea had first sent 4 or 5 soldiers and wagons; 2nd, 100 men under Lieut. Castinada; and 3d, set out himself at head of all his effectives, at the moment of Anderson's going, but returned. People collecting in at Gonzales. This day (8th) arrived Genl Perfecto de Cos and also Ugartechea's family from Monterey. [Genl Coml. Bexar –Perfecto de Cos. Domingo de Ugartechea, Col. Com. Cav'y]

OCT. 11th. Sunday. Attend grand mass with the soldiers with military music, &c, and hear that La Bahia was surprised and taken yesterday (10th) at break of day by about 60 Americans. One killed and one or two wounded of the Mexicans.

OCT. 12th. Great flurry and excitement by arrival of Mex. spies reporting that great crowds of Americans were on the road coming. This moment commence to mount cannon, pressing into the service Smith and other citizens (3 cannons already mounted; 2 now being mounted.)

OCT. 15th. Appointed for the meeting of the Convention. Americans on the march from Gonzales.

OCT. 17th. Arrival of courier with dispatches from *[blank]*.

(12th. Timbers &c. taken to El Alamo to fortify the quartel, & begin, on 13th, to blockade the streets, which is finished by the 17th.)

16th. Smith's doors guarded, and Col. Ugartechea's.

OCT. 17th. Arrival of Pedro Flores, as courier, with news that S. F. Austin is General of American forces. Dispatches from Gen'l Austin to Gen'l de Cos. Reports that 800 Americans are stationed at Cibolo and 500 more expected instanter. Reports that Sandoval, Comd't at La Bahia and company carried prisoners to San Felipe. (Ugartechea had this day gone out with 100 men to the Cibolo, and confronted the advance body, who having alighted & cooked, U. turned back.)

13th was the day on which the military broke the figure of San Antonio, and on the 14th the [Halley's] comet was seen in the west 45 [degrees] above the horizon, its train reaching 1/4 over the visable firmament.

OCT. 18th. Courier with communications from Cos to Austin, and my note to Austin. On 17th, finished mounting one cannon (had before only 3). All the powder &c. taken to the Church 3 or 4 days ago. Forces are divided here; part in the quartel (of the infantry) in Presidio on W. side of the rio, and the whole troop on E. side in their quartel in Alamo 300 cavalry and 2 *[200]* Infantry. (The actual number, officers, soldiers, guards etc. of Effectives is 647.)

OCT. 19th. Cos had written to Austin that if he would send his men all home & then send or come with 2 or 3, be would be disposed to hear him. This day Austin sent a mere verbal message by Pedro that he had not come to treat but to fight; and if he (Cos) would not meet him outside he would attack him inside of the town. De Cos's observation to the servant was "I want no more communications. Let the damn rascals come." His letter to Austin had on 18th been read aloud at the beat of the drum at the four corners of the public square.

OCT. 20th. Great flurry this morning on account of a report that the Americans are at the Salado (5 miles). House tops covered with sentinels &c., but soon over. Suppose the report is a false one. The Mexican spies report that some 20 of them attacked 3 on Salado; got a rifle and blanket but did not kill the Americans.

[OCT.] 21st. Bowie sent his compliments to the town.

OCT. 22nd. Reports that Rodriguez and 50 soldiers are absent and suppose [they are] gone over. Padillo is with Austin. This afternoon is the first rencontre. 12 or 15 shots discharged. 3 come in shot - one through the head, one wounded and one his gun broken. This night arrival from Rio Grande of a cavallardo and about 48 soldiers.

[OCT. 23rd] RD. Eleven soldiers came in from Rio Grande. Soldiers all in motion, and go out but nothing done. At night there was some shooting.

OCT. 24th. 41 more soldiers arrived. There appears to have been a small engagement today at about 9 o'clock on the Salado. At 10 Infantry come in with one man wounded (shot through the head). We heard at least 100 reports. Another report has it that there were some soldiers wounded in an engagement at the 2nd Mission (San Jose), which took place this morning. 24th. Saturday. No fighting, word sent.

[OCT.] 25th. Letter rec'd from [Austin] saying that the reason Bejar was not at once taken is because the colonists would disperse before all now on the march to this Place would be able to reach it. 4 or 5 hundred are coming besides those already

come. Genl Houston had arrived with part of the Nacog[doches] troops. Mexer [Mexia] & Zavalla are on the move in Texas. The great object is, when all the fighting men are brought together, to concert measures for giving general, united & effective support to the Constitution of 1824, and to put down Centralism.

It is expected that a resolution will be taken by all or most to march on to Matamoras, and from thence to any quarter thought to be best. It is expected (says Gen'l A.) that Mexir [Mexia] will raise troops to march into the interior. [He adds that] Cos might put an end to all this by pronouncing, or leaving the people of Bejar free to do so (in favor of the Constitution). Word also comes to confirm the report of Friday's skirmishing, and it appears that some 3 or 4 were left dead for the Americans to inter.

[OCT.] 26th.   Nothing. An 18 pounder just mounted was carried by [word omitted] to the Alamo, and raised to the top of the church; besides this, they have 10 (smaller) cannons mounted - 5 in Presidio, of which 4 are in the Plaza and 1 in front of the church, and 7 [in] the Alamo, of which one, the 18 pounder, is on the top of the old church of San Antonio [de Valero]. It appears that Bowie and the American party lately at the Mission of San Juan (3rd one) have gone back to the Headquarters at the Salado.

[OCT.] 27th.   Tuesday. Mexican infantry go out this morning. At 7 1/2 o'clock firing commenced, which continued nearly 2 hours (at the first Mission - Concepcion). 2 or 3 messengers then came in on a strain & they carry out 2 mules loaded with ammunition. Soon after 9 rounds of artillery are heard and brisk firing for 20 or 30 minutes.

[OCT.] 28th.   It appears from what is come out that the Mexicans had every one of their artillery men shot down & most of them killed, and both of the cannons they carried out taken from them. They left 23 dead on the ground. Out of 12 officers only one came off without a wound. They brought 42 wounded men off. 4 died on the way coming; on this morning (28th) it appears certain that 15 of these have died.

[OCT.] 28th.   Fifteen Mexican infantry out of the 42 wounded brought in are, this morning, dead; besides this havoc of the infantry, artillery-men etc. there were some of the cavalry killed. It is probable that more than 42 were brought off wounded for they [Mexicans] reported 8 (only) left dead [on the field], whereas the Padre, (who went with 10 men at the request of Austin to Gen'l Cos) reports 23 dead [on the field] and some dying in the American Camp. There must be at least 80 put past duty. The old Padre reports but one man as being touched, and he only wounded in a tender part

In the afternoon of yesterday some cavalry went towards the Mission and being hemmed in where the river was not fordable they quit their horses and swam the stream and thus saved their lives. The party of Americans were at first only 50 men, who were looking out a good camping place. As the action went on, they were increased until they were about 200 strong. The main body still remained with Austin on the Salado. They considered this as a mere scouting frolic, whereas it was an almost breaking up business for the Central party. The Mexican force was much more numerous than the American, and their infantry the best soldiers in the Republic (of the Mexican breed).

[OCT.] 29th. Several deaths. In the afternoon a large reinforcement; 2 or 3 hundred, coming to the American army came almost into the town (suppose by mistake) and then turned off.

OCT. 30th. A party of 3 or 4 hundred, with Bowie, came up on this side of the river near to town. The banter not being accepted, after staying till evening, they went down again.

[OCT.] 31st. No mass. Two soldiers missing: either killed in the course of the firing today up the river, or possibly deserted. Some more cannons mounted here and great activity to secure the place.

NOV. 1st. (Sunday) All Saints' Day: a great occasion with the Catholics. 8 o'clock this morning a division of the Fedl. force is seen 1 or 1 1/2 miles from the Alamo (north). They fired three times at Ugartechea's fort which salute is returned by two shots. Nothing more done-too far off.

NOV. 2nd. This is the people's day—for common people's souls to go to Heaven. Yesterday the Padre was sent by Gen'l Cos to say to Austin that they had better disperse and make their representations peaceably to the Government, and he would pledge himself they would be attended to. Austin returned the Padre with the word that he did not come to make representations; he would have a fight and if Cos would not come out he would go into the town. He sent word that the alternatives he [Cos] had were either to abandon the place or stay and fight.

He sent Cos word that he had extensive resources of men and money and that Mexir [Mexia] was gone to take Matamoras. When the Padre told Cos this he said it was a lie; they had not the resources spoken of &c. and that they might come on for they were not able to move him and he would stay in town.

Austin and his chief division are 1 1/2 miles above town, at the upper mill place. The rest below town on both sides of the river. Nothing done today—2nd—but a little firing at long distances (and without effect) at the picket guards of the Mexicans at the edge of La Villita about the ditch.

[NOV.] 3rd. The division of the Americans below town are said to be gone off this morning; where gone is not known. The army above are still there. The Mexicans have gone on with their work of defense briskly.—Cannons now mounted. The place could much easier have been taken with 200 men after the affair of Gonzales than it can now with 1500 men.

The quartel in the Alamo is very strongly fortified, and the streets to the plaza here well guarded; and all trees, grass, fences and other lurking places and barricades removed and being removed in order to see the Americans when they come up. This night (of 3d November) some hundred or more guns fired in the Alamo, among which is heard a number of rifles. This turns out to be a party of Americans examining the premises and meeting the picket guard. A firing is carried on from behind a couple of houses. One Mexican is killed. While this is going on 1/2 doz. rounds are given and received by the Col. & the Americans N. of the fort.

[NOV.] 4th. Redoubled exertions today in fortifying and clearing away hereabouts and mounting cannons. Ugartechea fires two guns off this morning, without getting an answer. A note had come yesterday from S. Jr. (thought to refer to Juan Seguin), saying that tonight (of 4th) a general attack is contemplated. A report is abroad among the citizens that the Americans are quarreling, and particularly Austin and Bowie. This evening at 7 o'clock the Mex. guards, whilst passing in the vicinity of the grave yard received a couple of shots and came in. No mass.

[NOV.] 5th. From the effect of a number of little reports, stories and conjectures, our house is in great dejection this morning; have been drooping some days. I still have confidence. Ugartechea fires some cannon.

[NOV.] 6th. Ugartechea fires his cannon, and there is another taken by Candalia (Ar't'y Col.), a little out of town on this side above and fired several times, but not very near the Amens., though towards them. Very cheering accounts come this afternoon of an addition of 4 or 5 hundred more men with some cannons and plenty of provisions and other supplies. A great fog this morning, arising by evaporation from the river

(spring water). Thermometer at 7 A.M. in shade out of doors is at 49°. Yesterday at about same hour a norther blew up, bringing the thermometer down 20°, from 75° to 55°. About a week past we experienced the first norther this fall.

[NOV.] 7th. Note from Austin in general terms. All the Americans are at the upper Molina General Mexir [Mexia] has sailed from New Orleans to Matamoras or Tampico with a great force etc.

[NOV.] 8th. (Sunday) Afternoon. A spying party of Americans said to be seen west of town a mile out. Capt. Barragan and some cavalry give them chase. They forced the Americans to seek safety in a gully. They took 6 horses, two frock coats and two hats, on which account the church bell was rung in joy. This evening the Gen'l fired off some signal rockets which threw things into a little helter skelter and turned out a false alarm.

[NOV.] 9th. Reported that a considerable number of men more have joined the American force. Also reported that 4 or 5 hundred soldiers are coming on to Cos from Laredo (having some reluctant Mexicans as prisoners). The Americans are keeping a good lookout for this reinforcement of the Federal Army.

[NOV.] 10th. The Federal Army (of Austin & Co.) have from time to time been receiving cannon. just heard they received yesterday one requiring six yoke (of oxen) to haul. Suppose an 18 pounder. Col. T. J. Rusk sent me his name by Peter.

[NOV.] 11th. Wrote a few lines to Rusk this morning and sent by P., evening. Holmes received a few lines from Wm. Austin and I a sibylline leaf. He writes that they are 900 strong. Some who were obliged have gone home. New forces immediately expected. Some from New Orleans certainly on the way; have seven cannon. Two hours after dark an alarm, and in about twenty minutes four or five hundred muskets discharged and three cannon. Two guns being fired close to Smith's, Cap't Solis with (Mendoza) four soldiers and some at the door entered the house where we were sitting. In his lingo he demanded who shot off the guns and why, and in a very menacing, hurried manner ordered his men, who at the word formed in a good position, cocking their muskets, and held them at a present (with bayonets). Smith (J.W.) and the women denied that we did it. He asserted and the women again earnestly protested. He then Pushed into the yard, still furious and in calling out it so happened that he was heard by Vedall [Alejandro Vidal] who owned that he had shot his guns, saying he shot at

some of the Americans on the point, on the opposite side of the river. This was a lie, but being a faithful damned dog no more was said. The Capt. tried to excuse himself and the affair ended. (He had said he was shot at as he heard the balls whiz by him; this a lie.) Vedall answered at the second call. If he had declined answering at all, they would have been fully convinced it was we, and certainly if a soldier would have said this or these men fire[d] (or with arms) they would have shot us instantly. It was certainly a fine specimen of Centralism. I did not at the time think they would fire. It occurred to me that he demanded to know if any from the American Camp had got into our premises. I knew none had and felt that his was an idle bravado and that we were safe. On a full explanation, however, I saw we were very near being shot through a mistake. Dm such a government.

[NOV.] 12th. Col. Ugartechea, who is a well-meaning gentleman, being told what occurred last night, was much concerned. We demanded again leave to go out of town. He went to the General [Cos] and two hours [after] returned. He reports that the General can't suffer us to go out of his custody; but they promise ample protection and Ugartechea closed by requesting us to shoot such fellows if they should do such a thing again. This is kind assurance of & Gen'l and Colonel, but is impracticable and useless. It seems that Ugartechea had the Captain brought up; that Candalia, the Lt. Col. of Infantry, defended his capitan. He undertook to quarrel with the Col. (Ugartechea) when the Gen'l told them to stop: "*The times don't allow brother officers to quarrel,*" and added to Ugartechea "*Assure those gentlemen at Smiths that they shall be protected. If the like insult is offered again, tell them to shoot down the rascals but they cannot be permitted to leave town.*"

[NOV.] 13th. Report of a cannon heard early this morning, and at about 10 o'clock twenty guns fired in answer to five or ten from the Mill, commenced by the Americans.

[NOV.] 14th. Quiet. Five or six shots fired by the Americans on the Alamo. Two of them hit the fort.

[NOV.] 15th. Sunday. I am engaged in making a plan. At 10 o'clock brisk and heavy firing going on by the Americans, not answered by Ugartechea, as was the fact yesterday. Shot as if by an experienced gunner. The fourth shot entering the fort took a soldier's leg off. One shot supposed to be aimed at the Church near this [house] in the middle of town, hit in a tree top on the bank of the river and fell into the water, one hundred yards from us or less. They whistled as if they were coming into Smith's. One hit the corner of Don Fernando Rodrigues' stone house. Today a flag flying for the first time, in the fort, and a man in it with his shin bone broke etc. Videll [Vidal] cut off his leg, borrowing Mr. Smith's saw. His operation was singular and savage; he (the man) died at sunset, killed by Videll.

[NOV.] 16th. Sent my project to *[Milam]* at 9 o'clock. Firing commenced a few minutes after at the fort again and after a while at the church near us (where there is a constant lookout kept and where there is a battery etc.) The balls fired at the town fell short a hundred yards or so, one falling at the picket's cannon (No. 2) in the second street, and one knocking down a woman's hen house—dreadful! The Col. did not fire in reply. Soon on the receipt of *[blank]* the firing ceased altogether and nothing more today.

[NOV.] 17th. Not a sound. The wind hardly blows. All gayety again in town. Officers riding about on their pampered and mettlesome steeds. A report circulated that a great force from Santa Anna has landed and that a considerable reinforcement will be here in three or four days.

NOV. 18th. A man from the American Camp came in last night and tells some of his friends (report perhaps general) that the Americans know that Col. Ugartechea left here four or five days ago in the night with sixty men in order to bring on those four hundred or more troops that a few days ago were on the march and returned back to Laredo; that the Americans had sent a messenger and escort to hurry on Padilla and some troops under him, who are coming from Goliad in order to *[make]* an attack, which the Americans were determined to make before Col. Ugartechea could get here with his reinforcement. This the deponent asserts positively, viz: That the Americans are going to make an attack some night. And from the very uncommon caution observed last night for the first time (and in the afternoon) in challenging citizens as they passed Musquis' corner, and (what they never did before) making them tell what business they were upon etc., it is my opinion that some news came in during yesterday afternoon about the Americans' design of making an attack. This is the first time I heard that Col. Ugartechea had gone out of the fort.

[NOV.] 19th. The Americans said to be erecting a battery one half *[mile]* this side of the mill, a little above La Garza's sugar mill. One lone gun fired (cannon); fired at the American camp at 11 or 12 o'clock at night. Nothing. No firing all day. Govr. Viesca said to have come yesterday to American Camp. He reports that Genl Mexia had taken

Matamoras. There is a report that Montezuma had gained a naval victory over the Centralists.

[NOV.] 20th.   One American cannon at 11 o'clock. This day the worst norther we have had. Thermometer 42° with rain and wind. One cannon also early this morning. After dark an American came into edge of town, enquiring for Gen'l Austin's camp. He was seized by the picket guard and carried to the jail of the Plazas. Another American was seen lying drunk below town, but before the soldiers could reach him a Mexican (friend) had sent and the American on his horse made off. It is said that the dispatches just arrived bring word that the little fort on the Nueces, on the road from Goliad to Matamoras, was just taken by Americans; six cannon and a parcel of small arms and prisoners.

[NOV.] 21st.   The soldiers who came back from hunting up the drunk men were sent again. They found an American by the road-side sleeping (or drunk). He woke up and said he was their friend (in bad Spanish). However, one of the soldiers shot a ball through him, but still speaking, another shot and killed him. They then stripped him and brought his clothes & pistol and horse to town which they are offering for sale about town. He had no gun. Señor Paplo further says that it came from Yturri's house (friend to Cos) that they speak of shooting the prisoner. This a very cold, bleak, rainy day. The Americans are raising a battery or something not far from La Garza's sugar mill, one half mile this side of the Molina where Austin is. Thermometer this morning 36 1/2°.

[NOV.] 22nd.   Sunday. Very cold. One hundred guns at least fired through the day; say seventy from the Alamo and a cannon placed on W. side of the river, and thirty by the Americans.

NOV. 23rd.   Five cannon fired this morning from the battery of the Americans at or near the sugar mill of La Garza. The weather very cold—very unusually so as S. [Smith] says. Thermometer down to 28½° after sunrise. Water in the house froze over as thick as a dinner plate. No frost out of doors by reason of the wind.

[NOV.] 24th.   Thermometer at 31°, but a little weak sunshine, now and then. The Americans were very quiet yesterday and so today. It is supposed that something is going on betwixt them and Ugartechea (at the head of the soldiers he is trying to bring in from Laredo). This whole afternoon is occupied in a far-off attack on the American dirt fort, three quarters of a mile above. Some two or three hundred discharges of

muskets, now and then the crack of a rifle is heard. The Americans have two cannons there. In the midst of the firing the Americans fired two cannon at the fort (over it) and one at the church here in town. None of the officials went out. Towards night the soldiers returned—two killed and one wounded (Mexican). The Americans in all likelihood came off untouched as the soldiers did not go within musket shot but near enough to be reached by a good rifle.

[NOV.] 25th.   Thermometer 30°. Sun shining and a fair day.

[NOV.] 26th.   Weather improving. Foraging party of Mexican soldiers etc. on the west of town (in hearing) attacked by the Americans—three killed and several wounded. Some wounded men brought in next morning report that every kindness was offered and done to them by the Americans. By their request they were left by the Americans covered up with their blankets and grass. They say that none of the Americans were hurt. The Americans took off all their pack mules (the Mexicans), say twenty or thirty.

[NOV.] 27th.   Fair day, cool. One of the soldiers of yesterday's foraging party, in running off, came by an American's horse and mounted him: he was shot through the hat. (A soldier who had taken hold of the horse a moment before had his arm broken by a rifle ball.) The same brought the horse in and to-day sold him to Smith for $46.00, horse, saddle and three pistols.

[NOV.] 28th.   Americans after the foragers this morning on the Salado, but were dodged. At 10 o'clock thermometer is at 54°—a fine day. Five or six cannon shot at the Alamo fort. Nothing done. Last night (after midnight) a great deal of musket firing from the picket guard, who reported (falsely) that they saw the Americans coming in with a great many ladders to scale the walls. Poh! No need of ladders.

[NOV.] 29th.   Mr. Cocke thinks he was shot at whilst on the ridge-pole of our (Nixon's) house [current Commerce Street, about 200 feet east of Soledad Street]. Some cannon firing.

[NOV.] 30th.   Monday. Cannonading.

DEC. 1st.   Left town, Smith having promised for us that we would go soon to the United States. After leaving town cannons fired from both parties.

[DEC.] 2nd.   We all go into the American camp from ranch of José Angel Navarro (Gefe Politico), ten miles below town. Great cannonading this day. Col. Mendoza has the calf of his leg shot off. Council of officers held instanter and Smith and myself

urge an assault. After a great many objections being urged and answered by our offering to head the divisions etc., it is finally agreed to make the attack by taking: 1st Veramendi's; 2nd La Garza's; and 3d Cardena's houses. The command to be given to Maj. Morris; 2nd Col. Somerville; and 3d Col. Jack.

[*DEC.*] *4th.* This failed, on Col. Somerville and Col. Jack saying they were not ready, so when morning (the 4th) came, there was a general breaking up. Another *faux pas* is made: the volunteers curse the officers and 250 or 300 set off for home. All day we get more and more dejected. The Gen'l (Burleson) mustered the remaining men and begged them not all to go; but some stay and retreat with the cannon to La Bahia. A retreat seems our only recourse. The spectacle becomes appalling; but it was the deep darkness that prognosticated day. Near sunset Al Feris *[Alveris?]*, Cornet of horse, deserts, coming in on a fine horse and with a white flag. His story is heard and corroborated. (Another deserter had just come in with dispatches from Cos to Ugartechea). Near dark and by the animating manner and untiring zeal of Col. Milam, these trivial matters are turned to account. An impulse is given and received; the men fall into ranks to see if we are strong enough. The mere fragment of the seven hundred, say two hundred & fifty, volunteer to make the attack next morning; (two thousand had from time to time been in camp.)

DEC. 5th. Attack made, myself *[as guide]* going with Col. Milam at the head of the right division. Johnson commanded the left.

DEC. 10th. White flag of surrender sent us.

DEC. 31st, 1835 & JAN. 1st, 1836. Men set out for La Bahia to rendezvous for an attack on Matamoras.

Importance of San Antonio de Béxar in the Texas Revolution

INTRODUCTION TO DOCUMENT

The Alamo has often been described as an abandoned mission in the middle of nowhere by both historians and filmmakers. True, the mission was closed but it was always put to some other use and never totally abandoned. It is also true that it took visitors traveling several days in either direction to reach it. However, the isolation actually added to its importance, not detracted from it.

The key to understanding much of Texas history lies in knowing the region's geography. The headwaters of the San Antonio River emerge where several geographical landforms converge, each adding to it the flora and fauna of its respective biozone. Native Americans found the region attractive because of its rich resources. The Spanish were attracted to it for the same reason. The settlements on the Rio Grande lay to the south and west while more settlements lay to the east along the Louisiana border. The San Antonio River valley marked a staging area for travelers headed in either direction. San Antonio de Béxar marked the northern outpost in the valley; La Bahía lay further downstream; and the river emptied into Copano Bay.

During the Spanish era the area east of the river represented a semi-sustainable territory whose fortunes were determined by international events. The area west of the river came to represent the frontier line that could be sustainable from the interior. This changed somewhat during the Mexican era as the area east of the river came to represent the Anglo colonies with its overwhelmingly American population. Meanwhile, the area west of the river maintained stronger connections with the interior. Hence, the San Antonio River Valley came to serve as the dividing line between Mexico and what was increasingly becoming an American version of Texas.

Both the colonists and the Mexican government understood the importance of this cultural and political border. General Mier y Terán had warned back in 1828 that in the event of a revolution that the colonists would move quickly to cut the town off from the coast. During the summer of 1835, the Mexican government planned to reinforce Béxar in order to launch a campaign to reestablish order in Texas. Even before the revolt had erupted, the colonists eyed capturing San Antonio, La Bahía, and Copano with the view of denying Santa Anna's Centralist administration their use. All three fell to the colonists and their Tejano and American allies by the end of 1835. This line became the base for the Texans from which to launch a campaign to seize Matamoros and take the war deeper into Mexico.

Additionally, defending the line against an expected counterattack by the Mexican government became an important objective. The cause for concern was well founded because Santa Anna's plan to subdue Texas called for retaking control of the towns along the San Antonio river. As he later stated, "Béxar was held by the enemy and it was necessary to open the door to our future operations by taking it."

DOCUMENT[23]

James Bowie to Governor Henry Smith [Excerpt of Letter]

February 2, 1836

"The salvation of Texas depends in great measure in keeping Bejar out of the hands of the enemy. It serves as the picquet guard and if it were in the possession of Santa Anna there is no strong hold from which to repell him in his march towards the Sabine. ... Colonel Neill and myself have come to the solemn resolution that we will rather die in these ditches than give up this post to the enemy. These citizens [at Bexar] deserve our protection and the public safety demands our lives rather than to evacuate this post to the enemy.—again we call aloud for relief; . . ."

DOCUMENT 24

William B. Travis to Governor Henry Smith [Excerpt of Letter]

February 12, 1836

This being the Frontier Post nearest the Rio Grande, will be the first to be attacked We are illy prepared for their reception, as we have no more than 150 men here and they in a very discouraged state—Yet we are determined to sustain it as long as there is a man left; because we consider death preferable to disgrace, which would be the result of giving up a Post which has been so dearly won, and thus opening the door for the invaders to enter the sacred Territory of the colonies.

DOCUMENT 25

William B. Travis to Governor Henry Smith

February 13, 1836

. . . it is more important to occupy this Post than I imagined when I last saw you—It is the key to Texas from the Interior. Without a footing here, the enemy can do nothing against the colonies, now that our coast is guarded by armed vessels—

DOCUMENT 26

Antonio López de Santa Anna
Manifesto

Béxar was held by the enemy and it was necessary to open the door to our future operations by taking it.

Eulalia Yorba: An Eye Witness Account of the Battle of the Alamo

INTRODUCTION TO DOCUMENT

The Battle of the Alamo is usually told from the viewpoint of the military combatants, ignoring that the close proximity of the old mission to the town made it possible for the townspeople the see the event as it unfolded. In fact, the battle should be seen as a community events since it not only occurred at San Antonio but also involved its residents who served on both sides. Moreover, the military occupation of the town by Texan and then Mexican forces affected the lives and fortunes of the Béxareñoes for years to come.

Eulalia Yorba's interviewer claimed that her "mind is very keen on events of sixty and seventy years ago." Even so, his article contains some factual errors such as describing the Alamo as a single building instead of a compound. The accuracy of interviews conducted decades after the battle not only depended on the subject's memory, it also depended on the interviewers ability to correctly interpret the language if the person spoke Spanish. Furthermore, writers often tended to embellish their stories even if no embellishment was required to report an interesting or historic event.

DOCUMENT 27

ANOTHER STORY OF THE ALAMO
The Battle Described by an Alleged Eye Witness
How Santa Anna's Overwhelming Force Attacked and Captured
The Enemy's Stronghold—The Death of Davy Crockett
San Antonio Express, April 12, 1896

There is now living in the United States but one person who saw the awful conflict. She is Señora Eulalia Yorba, a poor old Spanish woman, who lives in the suburbs at Fort Worth. She was born in 1801 and is therefore nearly ninety-five years of age. She was thirty-four when the Alamo was besieged. She lives with her granddaughter's family and is supplied with a little means of livelihood by the well-to-do citizens of San Antonio and Fort Worth, who take just pride in the mention of the old Spanish woman of the battle at the stone mission. Her mind is very keen on events of sixty and seventy years ago and she has been sought after by numerous writers of history of the Southwest.

The writer had a most interesting interview with Mrs. Yorba not long ago and communicated the results to the *San Francisco Examiner*. Everyone in Fort Worth knows where to find her and we were soon at her door. She said:

I well remember when Santa Anna and his two thousand soldiers on horses with shining muskets and bayonets marched into the little pueblo of San Antonio. The news ran from mouth to mouth that Colonel Travis, Davy Crockett and Colonel Bowie and the 160 or so other Texans who had held the locality against the Mexicans for several weeks had taken refuge in and barricaded themselves in that old stone mission, which had been used as a crude fort or garrison long before I came to the county. It belonged to Mexico and a few stands of muskets and three or four cannons were kept there. When Santa Anna's army came they camped on the plains about the pueblo and a guard was put about the Alamo fort. That was from the last day of February to March 4. Of course, I kept at home with my little boys and never stirred out once, for we women were all terribly frightened. Every eatable in the house, all the cows, lumber and hay about the place were taken by the troops, but we were assured if we remained in the house no personal harm would come to us.

Of course, we were hourly informed of the news. We knew that the Texans in the Alamo were surrounded by over five hundred soldiers constantly, while fifteen hundred more soldiers were in camp out on the plain. We learned that four days had been given for the Texans to surrender. We heard from the soldiers that not one of the imprisoned men had so much as returned a reply to the demand for surrender and that on the morning of March 6, 1836, Santa Anna was going to bring matters to a crisis with the beleaguered rebels. I can never tell the anxiety that we people on the outside felt for the mere handful of men in the old fort, when we saw the hostile troops as far as we could see and not a particle of help for the Texans, for whom we few residents of the town had previously formed a liking.

The morning of Sunday—the 6th of March—ah! Indeed, I could never forget that, even if I lived many more years more—was clear and balmy and every scrape of food was gone from my house and the children and I ran to the home of a good old Spanish priest so that we could have food and comfort there. There was nothing to impede the view of the Alamo from the priest's home, although I wished there was. The shooting began at six in the morning. It seemed as if there were myriads of soldiers and guns about the stone building. There was volley after volley fired into the barred and bolted windows. Then the volleys came in quick succession. Occasionally we heard muffled volleys and saw puff of smoke from within the Alamo, and when we saw, too, Mexican soldiers fall in the roadway or stagger back we knew the Texans were fighting as best they could for their lives.

It seemed as if ten thousand guns were shot off indiscriminately as firecrackers snap when whole bundles of them are set off at one time. The smoke grew thick and heavy and we could not see clearly down at the Alamo, while the din of musketry, screams of crazy, exultant Mexicans increased every moment. I have never heard human beings scream so fiercely and powerfully as the Mexican soldiers that day. I can compare such screams only to the yell of a mountain panther or lynx in desperate straits.

Next several companies of soldiers came running down the street with great heavy bridge timbers. They were quickly brought to bear as battering rams on the mission doors, but several volleys from within the Alamo, as nearly as we could see, laid low the men at the timbers and stopped the battering for a short time, Three of four brass cannon were loaded with what seemed to us a very long delay and were placed directly in front of the main doors of the mission. They did serious work. Meanwhile bullets from several thousand muskets incessantly rained like hail upon the building and through the apertures that had been made in the wood barricades at the windows and doors. The din was indescribable. It did not seem as if a mouse could live in a building so shot at and riddled as the Alamo was that morning.

Next we saw ladders brought and in a trice the low roof of the church was crowded and with a screaming, maddening throng of men armed with guns and sabers. Of course we new then that it was all up with the little band of men in the Alamo. I remember that the priest drew us away from the window and refused to let us look longer, notwithstanding the fascination of the scene. We could still hear the shouts and yells and the booming of the brass cannon shook the priest's house and rattled the window panes.

Along about nine o'clock, I should judge, the shooting and swearing and yelling had ceased, but the air was heavy with thick and heavy blue powder smoke. A Mexican colonel came running to the priest's residence and asked that we go down to the Alamo to do what we could for the dying men.

Such a dreadful sight. The roadway was thronged with Mexican soldiers with smoke and dirt begrimed faces, haggard eyes and wild, insane expressions. There were twelve or fifteen bodies of Mexicans lying dead and bleeding here and there and others were being carried to an adobe house across the way. The stones in the church walls were spotted with blood, the doors were splintered and battered in. Pools of thick blood were so frequent on the sun-baked earth about the stone building that we had to be careful to avoid stepping in them. There was a din of excited voices along the street and the officers were marshalling their men for moving to camp.

But no one could even tell you the horror of the scene that met our gaze when we were led by the sympathetic little colonel into the old Alamo to bandage up the wounds of several young men there. I used to try when I was younger to describe that awful sight, but I never could find sufficient language. There were only a few Mexicans in there when we came and they were all officers who had ordered the common soldiers away from the scene of death and—yes—slaughter, for that was what it was. The floor was literally crimson with blood. The woodwork all about us was riddled and splintered by lead balls and what was left of the old altar at the rear of the church was cut and slashed by cannon balls and bullets. The air was dark with powder smoke and was hot and heavy. The odor was oppressive and sickening and the simply horrible scene nerved us as nothing else could.

The dead Texans lay singly and in heaps of three or four, or in irregular rows here and there all about the floor of the Alamo, just as they had fallen when a ball reached a vital part or they had dropped to their death from loss of blood. Of course we went to work as soon as we got to the mission at helping the bleeding and moaning men, who had only a few hours at most of life; but the few minutes that we looked upon the corpses all about us gave a picture that has always been distinct as one before my very eyes.

So thick were the bodies of the dead that we had to step over them to get [near] a man in whom there was still life. Close to my feet was a young man who had been shot through the forehead. He had dropped dead with his eyes staring wildly open and, as he lay there, seemingly gazed up into my face.

I remember seeing poor Colonel Davy Crockett as he lay dead by the side of a dying man, whose bloody and powder-stained face I was washing. Colonel Crockett was about fifty years old at that time. His coat and rough woolen shirt were soaked with blood so that the original color was hidden, for the eccentric hero must have died of some ball in the chest or a bayonet thrust.

Juan Seguin to the Residents of Béxar, 1836

INTRODUCTION TO DOCUMENT

The Texas Revolution would forever alter the nature of San Antonio. Two fierce battles had left the town wrecked and its inhabitants facing and uncertain future.

San Antonio remained under occupation by Mexican forces throughout the spring of 1836. General Juan José Andrade had been left behind by Santa Anna with a small thousand-man garrison to care of the wounded and to refortify the Alamo. In early May, however, word of the Texan victory at San Jacinto reached the city, followed by orders for Andrade to demolish the Alamo, evacuate the town, and rejoin the rest of the Mexican Army which was withdrawing to Matamoros.

In early June, a small company of Texans under Captain Juan N. Seguin arrived to take possession of the town from the retreating Mexicans. News that the Mexican Army planned to return to Texas and resume its campaign prompted the abandonment of San Antonio. Before leaving, Seguin address the Béxareñoes, telling them that the time had come for them to side with the new government or face the consequences. By summer, the population of the town had dwindled to around forty as the residents had either left with the Mexican Army or sought the relative safety of neighboring ranches.

José Francisco Ruiz, a town leader who had been sent to the convention and had signed the Texas Declaration of Independence warned his son-in-law, Blas

Herrera, "if for any reason you should remain, then by no means should you take up arms against the Texans. Give the same advice to your friends for only God could possibly return the territory of Texas to the Mexican Government. Texas has the arms and money for her defense and shall remain forever free."

DOCUMENT[28]

TO THE INHABITANTS OF BEXAR

Fellow Citizens:

Military movements compel me to repair to Head Quarters. I have in consequence to evacuate this town, but previous to doing so, I require your aid to carry off the cattle and place them where the enemy cannot make use of them. I have no doubt that you will assist cheerfully in this measure, thereby furnishing to the supreme government of Texas a proof of your attachment to the just cause, and the beloved liberty we are contending for. If, on the contrary you fail to render the slightest service, your disaffection will be manifest; and although a matter of regret to the supreme government, yet it can then no longer treat you as Texians, but, perhaps, as enemies. Be not deceived with the idea we have no forces wherewith to repel force—time will show to the contrary and will convince you that Texas must be free.

Fellow citizens your conduct on this day is going to decide your fate before the general government of Texas. If you maintain your post as mere lookers-on; if you do not abandon the city and retire to the interior of Texas, that its army may protect you, you will, without fail, be treated as real enemies, and will suffer accordingly. My ties of birth and friendship I entertain towards you, cause me to desire your happiness, and I therefore address you in that spirit of truth while in me is characteristic.

Bexians: render every possible aid, and soon shall you enjoy your liberty and your property, which is the wish of your countryman and friend, Juan N. Seguin.

PART 3: Republic of Texas

Mary A. Maverick Moves to San Antonio, 1838

INTRODUCTION TO DOCUMENT

Samuel A. Maverick became a member of the Alamo's garrison following the Texan victory at the Battle of Béxar. He avoided death with the rest of the command on March 6, 1836, because his companions elected him a delegate to represent the garrison at the convention scheduled to begin at the town of Washington on the Brazos River. Arriving late, he added his signature to the Texas Declaration of Independence after it was already printed.

Maverick traveled to Alabama at the end of the revolution where he married Mary Ann Adams. In 1838, Maverick returned to San Antonio with his wife, Mrs. Mary Maverick. The Mavericks initially rented a house in town from José Casiano, living there for a short time. They then set up house in the Huisar property on Main Plaza located at the northeast corner of Soledad and Commerce Streets. While living there, Mary witnessed many epic events that became part of Texas' frontier history. She kept journals detailing her families experience which highlight the dangers that still faced the residents of San Antonio.

DOCUMENT[29]

SAN ANTONIO DE BEXAR.

We were now travelling up the valley of the San Antonio River, occasionally passing along the the river itself. June 13, [1838] sixteen miles to the Marcelino Creek and three miles to Aroche's rancho near Erasmo Seguin's—14th, eight miles to Jesus Cantu's rancho on the arroyo Calaveras, passing several other ranchos, eleven miles to the Salado. June 15th, 1838 nine miles to "El Presidio de San Antonio de Bexar." Senor Don José Casiano, whose rancho we passed, had offered us his city house until we had time to secure another. This polite offer we accepted and immediately occupied Mr. Casiano's house, when we entered the town. This place fronted on the Main Plaza (Plaza Major), was bounded south by Dolorosa Street and extended half way back to the Military Plaza. It is now covered by the east half of the Hord Hotel. (At present, Southern Hotel.)

The front room of the house was then occupied by my brother William Adams as a store. He was so much afflicted with the "Texas fever" that soon after my wedding he set out for San Antonio, travelling on horseback from Galveston. Before reaching San Antonio, he dreamt several times of the town and its surroundings, and when he reached the hills east of town he was struck with the faithful resemblance between the reality and his dreams. He looked upon it as something marvelous and frequently spoke of his prophetic dreams. He was twenty-two then, and he immediately determined to establish himself as a merchant in San Antonio. He bought a horse which he named Mexico or "Mex" and rode him all the way back to Tuskaloosa. William turned all his available property in Tuskaloosa into money, bought goods, brought them to San Antonio, rented the room of Casiano, and set up as a merchant. He rode back on the horse "Mex," which horse by the way, Mr. Maverick afterwards bought, and we used "Mex" in the "run-away" of '42 and when we removed from La Grange to the Peninsula in 1844, Mr. Maverick, after our arrival, put in some money with William. Dr. Launcelot Smithers was William's clerk and success seemed certain, but Smithers sold large amounts on credit to Mexicans in Coahuila; and, though the Mexicans were well to do, they never paid, and after eighteen months merchandizing William closed up without realizing the capital invested. William left February 1st,

1839, for Mother's to bring out his negros and try farming. He returned with brother Andrew October, 1839.

We lived in the Casiano house until about September 1st, when we moved into a house north of, and adjoining, the historic Veramendi place. The house we rented belonged to the Huisars. Huisar, the ancestor, carved the beautiful doors for the San José Mission—he had quite a number of workmen under him and was employed several years in the work. In the latter part of December, Mr. Maverick went to Mobile to get some money in the hands of John Aiken, his attorney. Aiken was then in Tuskaloosa, where, as Mr. Maverick's agent, he had sold to a Mr. Brown for sixteen thousand dollars Mr. Maverick's business stores in that place. Part of the money was paid down and Mr. Maverick returned to us in January.

1839.

Early in February, 1839, we had a heavy snow storm, the snow drifted in some places to a depth of two feet, and on the north side of our house it lasted five or six days. Anton Lockmar rigged up a sleigh and took some girls riding up and down Soledad Street. Early in Febuary, we moved into our own house, at the north east corner of Commerce and Soledad Streets, being also the north east corner of the Main Plaza, (Plaza Mayor.) This house remained our homestead until July '49, over ten years, although five of the ten years,—from '42 to '47, we wandered about as refugees. It was known as the Barrera place, when Mr. Maverick purchased it, and the deed dated January 19th, 1839.

The main house was of stone, and had three rooms, one fronting south on Main Street and west on Soledad Street and the other two fronting west on Soledad Street—also a shed in the yard along the east wall of the house towards the north end. This shed we closed in with an adobe wall and divided into a kitchen and servant's room. We also built an adobe servant's room on Soledad Street, leaving a gateway between it and the main house, and we built a stable near the river.

We built a strong but homely picket fence around the garden to the north and fenced the garden off from the yard. In the garden were sixteen large fig trees and many rows of old pomegranates. In the yard were several China trees, and on the river bank just below our line in the De la Zerda premises was a grand old cypress, which we could touch through our fence, and its roots made ridges in our yard. The magnificent old tree stands there today. It made a great shade and we erected our bath house and wash place under its spreading branches.

Our neighbors on the east, Main or Commerce Street, were the De la Zerdas. In 1840, their place was leased to a Greek, Roque Catahdie, who kept a shop on the street and lived in the back rooms. He married a pretty, bright-eyed Mexican girl of fourteen years, dressed her in jewelry and fine clothes and bought her a dilapidated piano—he was jealous and wished her to amuse herself at home. The piano had the desired effect, and she enjoyed it like a child with a new trinket. The fame of her piano went through the town, and, after tea, crowds would come to witness her performance. One night Mrs. Elliott and I took a peep and we found a large crowd inside laughing and applauding, and other envious ones gazing in from the street.

Our neighbor on the north, Soledad Street, was Dona Juana Varcinez, and I must not omit her son Leonicio. She had cows and sold me the strippings of the milk at twenty-five cents per gallon, and we made our butter from this. Mrs. McMullen was the only person then who made butter for sale, and her butter was not good, although she received half a dollar per pound for it. Old Juana was a kind old soul—had the earliest pumpkins, a great delicacy, at twenty-five cents and spring chickens at twelve and a half cents. She opened up the spring gardening by scratching with a dull hoe, some holes in which she planted pumpkin seed—then later she planted corn, red pepper, garlic, onions, etc. She was continually calling to Leonicio to drive the chickens out of the garden, or bring in the dogs from the street. She told me this answered two purposes—it kept Leonicio at home out of harm's way, and gave him something to do. She had lots of dogs—one fat, lazy pelon (hairless dog) slept with the old lady to keep her feet warm. When we returned from the coast in '47, Sam S. Smith had purchased the place from her and he was living there. He was a good and kind neighbor.

We moved into our home in good time, for here on Sunday morning, March 23d, 1839, was born our second child, Lewis Antonio. All my friends have always told me, and, until quite recently I was persuaded Lewis was the first child of pure American stock born in San Antonio. But now I understand a Mr. Brown with his wife came here in 1828 for two years from East Texas, and during that time a son was born to them in San Antonio. Mr. Brown, the father, died about the same time of consumption, and his wife moved away further East. The son named John Brown, is now said to be a citizen of Waco. [Lewis Antonio Maverick, however, was the first child born in San Antonio of American parents to "grow up" in San Antonio and Mary A. Maverick the first American born woman or United States woman to make San Antonio her home.]

During the summer, Sammy had difficulty teething. Dr Weideman, a Russian scholar and naturalist, and an excellent physician and surgeon, took a great liking to Sammy and prescribed for him with success. This summer, William B. Jacques brought his wife and two little girls, and settled on Commerce Street. In the latter part of August, Mr. William Elliott brought his wife and two children, Mary and Billy, to San Antonio. They bought a house on the west side of Soledad Street, opposite the north end of our garden, and we were a great many years neighbors and always friends. This year our negro men plowed and planted one labor above the Alamo and were attacked by Indians. Griffin and Wiley ran into the river and saved themselves. The Indians cut the traces and took off the work animals and we did not farm there again. Mr. Thomas Higginbotham, a carpenter, with his wife, came to San Antonio and took the house opposite us on the corner of Commerce Street and Main Plaza. His brother and sister settled in the country, on the river below San José Mission. This year the town of Seguin on the Guadalupe thirty-five miles east of San Antonio, was founded.

In November, 1839, a party of ladies and gentlemen from Houston came to visit San Antonio—they rode on horseback. The ladies were Miss Trask of Boston, Mass., and Miss Evans, daughter of Judge Evans of Texas. The gentlemen were Judge Evans, and Colonel J. W. Dancey, Secretary of War, Republic of Texas. They were, ladies and all, armed with pistols and bowie knifes. I rode with this party and some others around the head of the San Antonio river. We galloped up the west side, and paused at and above the head of the river long enough to view and admire the lovely valley of the San Antonio. The leaves had mostly fallen from the trees, and left the view open to the Missions below. The day was clear, cool and bright, and we saw three of the missions, including San Juan Capistrano seven miles below town. We galloped home, down the east side, and doubted not that Indians watched us from the heavy timber of the river bottom. The gentlemen of the party numbered six, and we were all mounted on fine animals.

Mary A. Maverick's Account of the Council House Fight, 1840

INTRODUCTION TO DOCUMENT

San Antonio during the Republic of Texas continued to be surrounded by dangers. The Mexican government refused to recognize Texas's independence and threatened another campaign to reclaim its lost territory. In addition, raids and counter raids between the Comanches and Texans led to a state of war on the frontier.

In March 1840, one group of Comanche chiefs agreed to bring in captives they held as part of a peace agreement. The meeting, which took place in the Council House located on the east side of Main Plaza, erupted into a bloody melee when the Texans informed the chiefs that they planned to take them hostage to ensure the release of all captives. What followed became known as the Council House Fight. It serves as an example of the unsettled state of the town even after Texas achieved its independence.

DOCUMENT[30]

On Tuesday, 19th of March, 1840, "dia de San Jose" sixty-five Comanches came into town to make a treaty of peace. They brought with them, and reluctantly gave up, Matilda Lockhart, whom they had captured with her younger sister in December 1838, after killing two other children of her family. The Indian chiefs and men met in

This painting depicts the arrival of a Comanche delegation into the main plaza of San Antonio on March 19, 1840. This visit would precipitate the Council House Fight which would forever change the trajectory of Texan and Comanche relations. Courtesy of McWhiney History Education Group.

council at the Court House, with our city and military authorities. The calaboose or jail then occupied the corner formed by the east line of Main Plaza and the north line of Calabosa (now Market) Street, and the Court House was north of and adjoining the jail. The Court House yard, back of the Court House, was what is now the city market on Market Street. The Court House and jail were of stone, one story, flat roofed, and floored with dirt. Captain Tom Howard's Company was at first in the Court House yard, where the Indian women and boys came and remained during the pow-wow. The young Indians amused themselves shooting arrows at pieces of money put up by some of the Americans; and Mrs. Higginbotham and myself amused ourselves looking through the picket fence at them.

This was the third time these Indians had come for a talk, pretending to seek peace, and trying to get ransom money for their American and Mexican captives. Their proposition now was that they should be paid a great price for Matilda Lockhart, and a Mexican they had just given up, and that traders be sent with paint, powder, flannel, blankets and such other articles as they should name, to ransom the other captives. This course had once before been asked and carried out, but the smallpox breaking out, the Indians killed the traders and kept the goods—believing the traders had made the smallpox to kill them. Now the Americans, mindful of the treachery of the Comanches, answered them as follows: "We will according to a former agreement keep four or five of your chiefs, whilst the others of your people go to your nation and bring all the captives, and then we will pay all you ask for them. Meanwhile, these chiefs we hold we will treat as brothers and 'not one hair of their heads shall be injured.' This we have determined, and, if you try to fight, our soldiers will shoot you down."

This being interpreted, the Comanches instantly, with one accord raised a terrific war-whoop, drew their arrows, and commenced firing with deadly effect, at the same time making efforts to break out of the council hall. The order "fire" was given by Captain Howard, and the soldiers fired into the midst of the crowd, the first volley killing several Indians and two of our own people. All soon rushed out into the public square, the civilians to procure arms, the Indians to flee, and the soldiers in pursuit. The Indians generally made for the river—they ran up Soledad, east on Commerce Street and for the bend, now known as Bowen's, southeast, below the square. Citizens and soldiers pursued and overtook them at all points, shot some swimming in the river, had desperate fights in the street—and hand to hand encounters after firearms had been exhausted. Some Indians took refuge in stone houses and fastened the doors. Not one of the sixty-five Indians escaped—thirty-three were killed and thirty-two were taken prisoners. Six Americans and one Mexican were killed and ten Americans wounded. Our killed were Julian Hood, the sheriff, Judge Thompson, advocate from South Carolina, G. W. Cayce from the Brazos, one officer and two soldiers whose names I did not learn, nor that of the Mexican. The wounded were Lieutenant Thompson, brother of the Judge, Captain Tom Howard, Captain Mat Caldwell, citizen volunteer from Gonzales, Judge Robinson, Mr. Morgan, deputy sheriff, Mr. Higginbotham and two soldiers. Others were slightly wounded.

When the deafening war-whoop sounded in the Court room, it was so loud, so shrill and so inexpressibly horrible and suddenly raised, that we women looking through the fence at the women's and boy's marksmanship for a moment could not comprehend its purport. The Indians however knew the first note and instantly shot their arrows into the bodies of Judge Thompson and the other gentlemen near by, instantly killing Judge Thompson. We fled into Mrs. Higginbotham's house and I, across the street to my Commerce Street door. Two Indians ran past me on the street and one reached my door as I got in. He turned to raise his hand to push it just as I beat down the heavy bar; then he ran on. I ran in the north room and saw my husband and brother Andrew sitting calmly at a table inspecting some plats of surreys—they had heard nothing. I soon gave them the alarm, and hurried on to look for my boys. Mr. Maverick and Andrew seized their arms, always ready—Mr. Maverick rushed into the street, and Andrew into the back yard where I was shouting at the top of my voice "Here are Indians! Here are Indians!" Three Indians had gotten in through the gate on Soledad street and were making direct for the river! One had paused near Jinny Anderson, our cook, who stood bravely in front of the children, mine and hers, with a great rock lifted in both hands above her head, and I heard her cry out to the Indian "If you don't go 'way from here I'll mash your head with this rock!" The Indian seemed regretful that he hadn't time to dispatch Jinny and her brood, but his time was short, and pausing but a moment, he dashed down the bank into the river and struck out for the opposite shore.

As the Indian hurried down the bank and into the river Andrew shot and killed him, and shot another as he gained and rose on the opposite bank,—then he ran off up Soledad street looking for more Indians.

I housed my little ones, and then looked out of the Soledad Street door. Near by was stretched an Indian, wounded and dying. A large man, journey-apprentice to Mr. Higginbotham, came up just then and aimed a pistol at the Indian's head. I called out: "Oh, don't, he is dying" and the big American laughed and said: "To please you, I won't, but it would put him out of his misery." Then I saw two others lying dead near by.

Captain Lysander Wells, about this time, passed by riding north on Soledad Street. He was elegantly dressed and mounted on a gaily caparisoned Mexican horse with silver mounted saddle and bridle-which outfit he had secured to take back to his native state, on a visit to his mother. As he reached the Verimendi House, an Indian who had escaped detection, sprang up behind him, clasped Wells' arms in his and tried to catch hold of the bridle reins. Wells was fearless and active. They struggled for sometime, bent back and forward, swayed from side to side, till at last Wells held the Indian's wrists with his left hand, drew his pistol from the holster, partly turned, and fired into the Indian's body—a moment more and the Indian rolled off and dropped dead to the ground. Wells then put spurs to his horse which had stood almost still during the struggle, dashed up the street and did good service in the pursuit. I had become so fascinated by this struggle that I had gone into the street almost breathless, and wholly unconscious of where I was, till recalled by the voice of Lieutenant Chavallier who said: "Are you crazy? Go in or you will be killed." I went in but without feeling any fear, though the street was almost deserted and my husband and brother both gone in the fight. I then looked out on Commerce street and saw four or five dead Indians. I was just twenty-two then, and was endowed with a fair share of curiosity.

Not till dark did all our men get back, and I was grateful to God, indeed, to see my husband and brother back alive and not wounded.

Christmas Time in San Antonio, 1840

INTRODUCTION TO DOCUMENT

Although a frontier town, San Antonio still exhibited a rich cultural tradition which had developed over time. As a young woman from the United States, Mary A. Maverick found the Catholic celebration of Christmas interesting. The season also was a time for the social elites for the town—Tejano and Anglo—to interact.

DOCUMENT[31]

On December 12th, the Mexicans celebrated in grand procession "Dia de Nuestra Señora de Guadalupe," the patroness saint of Mexico, and whom the priests had identified with the Virgin Mary. Twelve young girls dressed in spotless white, bore a platform on which stood a figure representing the saint very richly and gorgeously dressed. First came the priests in procession, then the twelve girls bearing the platform, and carrying each in her free hand a lighted wax candle, then came fiddlers behind them playing on their violins, and following the fiddlers the devout population, generally, firing off guns and pistols and showing their devotion in various ways. They proceeded through the squares and some of the principal streets, and every now and then they all knelt and repeated a short prayer—an "Ave Marie" or "Pater Noster." Finally the procession stopped at the Cathedral of San Fernando on the Main Plaza, where a long ceremony was had. Afterwards the more prominent families taking the Patroness along with them, adjourned to Mr. José Flores' house on west side of Military Plaza, where they danced most of the night. We were invited and went, taking with us little Sammy with his jolly golden curls and a new suit of pea green. It was all quite a novel and interesting scene to me.

The principal citizens lived in the plazas or within two blocks of them on Flores, Acequia, Soledad, Commerce and Market streets. Very few of the Mexican ladies could write but they dressed nicely and were graceful and gracious of manner. We exchanged calls with the Navarros, Sotos, Garzas, Garcias, Zambranos, Seguins, Veramendis and Yturris.

Republic of Texas Recognizes Catholic Church's Property Rights, 1841

INTRODUCTION TO DOCUMENT

Ownership of the land and buildings comprising the former Mission San Antonio pitted the city council against the Catholic Archdiocese of Texas. Located on the east bank of the river, the property had become valuable as the town began to develop. Who owned it: the city or the Catholic Church? Civic leaders viewed the mission as abandoned and therefore part of the town. Church officials, however, contended that it was still owned by the Church.

In 1841, the Congress of the Republic of Texas settled the issue by recognizing the Church's claim as valid, awarding it Valero's church, Long Barrack (the convent), and Low Barrack (the south wall guard house). The west wall had entered private hands when the mission was secularized in 1793. By the mid-1840s, developers like Samuel A. Maverick had begun to purchase land on which some convert housing still sat.

The act is important because it made possible the later rental of the church property to United States Quartermaster Department, an event that enabled San Antonio to develop from a frontier outpost to a bustling city.

DOCUMENT [32]

AN ACT CONFIRMING THE USE AND OCCUPATION AND ENJOYMENT OF THE CHURCHES, CHURCH LOTS, AND MISSION CHURCHES TO THE ROMAN CATHOLIC CONGREGATIONS, LIVING IN OR NEAR THE VICINITY OF THE SAME.

Sec. 1. Be it enacted by the Senate and House of Representatives of the Republic of Texas, in Congress assembled, That the churches at San Antonio, Goliad, Victoria, the church lot at Nacogdoches, the churches at the Mission of Conception, San Jose, San Juan, Espada, and the Mission of Refugio, with outbuildings and lots, if any belonging to them, be, and they are hereby acknowledged and declared the property of the present chief past of the Roman Catholic Church, in the Republic of Texas, and his successors in office, in trust forever, for the use and benefit of the congregations residing near the same, or who may hereafter reside near the same, for the religious purposes and purposes of education, and none other; provided, that nothing herein contained shall be so construed as to give title to any lands except the lots upon which the churches are situated, which shall not exceed fifteen acres.

David S. Kaufman
Speaker of the House of Representatives

Anson Jones
President pro tem of the Senate

Approved January, 13th, 1841
David G. Burnet

General Rafael Vázquez Captures San Antonio, March 1842

INTRODUCTION TO DOCUMENT

One of the misconceptions about Texas history is that the Texan victory over General Antonio López de Santa Anna at the Battle of San Jacinto ended the conflict the between Texas and Mexico. In reality, neither side was in condition to continue the war. Mexico, however, refused to recognize Texas' independence. By 1842, Antonio López de Santa Anna was once again president of Mexico.
In 1841, then President Mirabeau B. Lamar authorized a foray into New Mexico to establish trade and reinforce Texas' claim to the region. Responding to Texas's recent ill-fated Santa Fe Expedition, Santa Anna decided to punish the Texans and remind them that Mexico still considered the former department as part of Mexico. He ordered two forays into Texas, both which resulted in the temporary occupation of San Antonio by the Mexican Army. The first expedition, under the command of Rafael Vaquez, reached the town in March. The second and larger expedition commanded by Adrian Woll entered San Antonio in September.

DOCUMENT[33]

From the Report of Gem Mariano Arista to the Secretary of War and Navy, March 12, 1842: [The Texans] having called a meeting and after a discussion of this matter, at

2 o'clock in the afternoon evacuated the city which was immediately occupied by me; so it came to pass that I have the honor of advising Y.E., that the National Flag is once more flying over the city of Béjar, and the Mexican Eagles are again today treading the soil that they had been deprived of for the length of six years; . . .

General Adrian Woll Captures San Antonio, September 1842

DOCUMENT[34]

September 11 & 12, 1842

No. 237. Most Excellent Sir. Since dawn today, the anniversary of the glorious September 11 [1]828 [when the Spanish surrendered at Tampico to Santa Anna], this city has been occupied by the troops of the Division under my command, notwithstanding the vain resistance which about 250 of the enemy, fortified in a few of the houses in the main plaza, dared to attempt. After half an hour of firing, they were obliged to surrender at discretion, leaving in our power only 62 of them, the rest having escaped, crossing over the canals and the river, favored by the mist, the Indian corn and the woods: [an account of] which I have the honor of informing Your Excellency in order that you may condescend to pass it on to the Supreme Government. By my adjutant, Lieutenant of the 1t Regiment of Regualr Infantry, D. Antonio Villagra, who, at my side, was slightly wounded in the corner of his left eye near the nose, I am sending the flag which the enemy dared to hoist in view of your troops. By future courier I shall direct to Your Excellency the full detailed report, contenting myself now in rejoicing with Your Excellency and [in] declaring to you that the deportment of all of the chiefs, officers, and troops which compose the Division under my command has been worthy of Mexican soldiers.

God and liberty.   S. Antonio de Béxar, September 11, 1842.

No. 239. Most Excellent Sir. On the 10th at two o'clock in the afternoon, the Division under my command halted at Arroyo del Leon, about three leagues [nine miles] distant from S. Antonio de Béxar. The spies, who had been ordered out and were just returning, assured me that in the city there had been no news of our expedition, which I had to believe in as much as the march had been undertaken through the wilderness surpassing all obstacles, opening a road in the middle of the woods, passing by the head of Uvalde Cañon and following the edge of the S[an] Saba range of hills in such a manner that the Texan scouts reporting from the Leona and Nueces rivers that there had been no rumor of anyone on the known froms form [Prresidio de] Rio Grande and Laredo to the city of Béxar, the enemy had abandoned themselves to such confidence that the judges of the court appointed by the so-called government of Texas had arrived to open the sessions of the court. Upon this intellegence, convenient measures were taken and orders were released [for the army] to continue the march at seven o'clock at night and, to take possession of all of the roads and to await the day in order to examine the entrance and to seize said members of the court. In this *interim* one of the scouts returned accompanied by four citizens of Béxar who informed me they came charged by the inhabitants to implore me not to enter the city, because perhaps they would be obliged by the Texans to join them to resist us. With regret, I [thus] became aware of the fact that the arrival, of which until then there had been no notice, nor even the slightest suspicion. I knew that it was necessary not to lose time. The commissioners were made prisoners and the march was then undertaken, leavign the baggage and the loads of provisions with a force of 50 soldiers from the presidial companies under the command of Captain D. Francisco Castañeda. [The army] halted at the edge of the burial ground. Some detachments of *defensores* from Béxar, Rio Grande and the presidial soldiers were placed in the Alamo and at all points around the city. The Santa Anna battalion, commanded by Colonel D. Sebastián Moro y Moral, with one piede of artillery, formed in column supported by another under orders of Brevent Colonel D. Cayetano Montero and composed of two squadrons of the S[an] ta Anna regiment of regular cavalry with one artillery piece from the cavalry brigade. It was ordered that the signal of a cannon shot, which would be fired at daybreak, all stations should beat reveille, apprehending all individuals who should try to leave the city, while the aforesaid mentioned column would march to form in battle about the 2nd plaza called the Ayuntamiento, Juan Nepomuceno Seguin having to occupy the other plaza with the remaining *defensores* of his corps. Thus disposed, all awaited the coming of day. Whilst it dawned, one of our spies learned that a redoubt had been built and loophole openings made in the houses fronting the church and in others that formed the first block of the street leading to the Alamo. Suddenly, reveille is heard beating. Thinking that [the sound of reveille] are [from] the detachments, the order is given to fire the cannon shot and the column begins its march at the sound of the music. The reveille was the enemy's! Fortwith a few skirmishers, accompanied by my staff, on horseback [advanced]. I marched at the head of the column. A dense fog caused the skirmishers upon entering the plaza to turn to the right. The rest of us continued forward. Coming to the middle of the plaza, the enemy opened a very lively fire, which, killing a drummer, wounded the horses of three of my aides-de-camp and that of the major general. Immediately, Captain D. Marcelo Torreblanca was ordred to take possession of the belfrey of the church with 50 men of his company; Captain Ignacio Ruiz with those of his company established themselves in the hourses facing the enemy; Captain D. Ildefonso Vega, Brevet Commandant of Battalion, was prepartd to march with another [company] with orders to take possession of a house located on the right flank, while Captain D. Juan Garrido, Brevet Commander of Battalion, was possessing himself of another on the opposite flank, which they executed at once. The artillery pieces were advanced, commanded by Lieutenant D. Manuel de Frago, who placed them advantageously. Although everything was accomplished with rapidity and percision, the haughty Texans on accounbt of the halt which the column had made were making the air resound with their shouting of *hurrahs* to Texas! but their happiness was [but] for a few moments. The reproof appeared horrible, because at the same time that the fire broke upon them from all directions, the day dawned! Confined in a district of the town from which his firing was but extinguished, the encirculed enemy was about to be put to the sword in his entrenchments, which our brave infantrymen were already touching, when at the sight of a white flag I ordered the firing ceased. Several commissioners, who presented themselves to me, offered to surrender their arms provided they should be permitted to retire to their homes. I replied that if they did not surrender at discretion, they were to be exterminated without exception. They requested the time necessay to consult with the others, which having been conceded to them, they did, returning to announce that they were resigned to their fate. Moved by a spirit of humanity and in order that they might recognize Mexican generosity, I guaranteed them their lives, and the surrender of arms followed. The Texan flag which had been lowered was discovered beneath a pile of rocks where they had attempted to hide it. It is the one which I have the honor of forwarding by my aide-de-camp, D. Antonio Villagra.

Unfortuantely, a dense fog favored the flight of a large number of the enemy, who through the back of he houses, crossing the river and some large Indian corn fields, gained the forest at the time that the others hoisted the white flag; thus it was that only 62 of them became prisoners; and though various squads were ordered in pursuit of the fugitives, it was not possible to apprehend a single one.

The enemy sustained only five killed and three wounded (the latter ultimately flung themselves into the river and escaped), considering that, entrenched and behind parapets, he presented no object to the shots of our bold soldiers. Our loss has been lamentable; for besides one killed, we have twenty wounded; as to what degree, the report which I enclose to Your Excellency will acquaint you.

It remains for me to recommend to Your Excellency the chief, officers, and individual soldiers who distinguished themselves in this action, and although all at the time behaved in an admirable manner, what is most praiseworthy is that they performed all the mobvements there were orderd to make without confusion and with great percision. . . . S. Antonio de Béxar, September 12, 1842.

Frederic Benjamin Page: A "Suthron's" View of San Antonio ca. 1845

INTRODUCTION TO DOCUMENT

Travelers' tales were an important and poplar form of literature in the 19th century. With the coming of Texas statehood, visitors began to flock to the southwest, which was still considered somewhat unknown, exotic, and intriguing. The author of one such example of the genre was Frederic Benjamin Page who went by the pseudonym "A Southron." True to his nom de plume, Page's view of San Antonio is shaped by his southern upbringing. Nevertheless, he paints a colorful picture of the town as it existed as the Republic of Texas came to an end. As an American, he marveled at what a bright held for future development under the hands of his industrious countrymen.

DOCUMENT[35]

... The last twenty miles of this day's journey we found very fatiguing, being annoyed by dust, and retarded by deep and heavy sand, though our pace was somewhat quickened by discovering a large and fresh Indian trail, and seeing an unknown party on horseback, and smoke ascending from Indian camps nearby and around us. Nothing quickens the pace of a traveller like the sight of a wild Indian. It lifts one from his saddle and bears him "along and aloft," with the speed of a locomotive, which

The skyline of San Antonio in 1840 during the tumultuous days of the Republic of Texas. Daughters of the Republic of Texas Collection at Texas A&M University-San Antonio.

defies alike both time and space. It sharpens one's vision, and for a time the blood courses rapidly about the heart.

On the following morning we rode to the Cibolo and took a field breakfast, with appetites that a sultan might have envied. Here the country altogether changes its appearance and suddenly becomes more picturesque and beautiful, and plucking some of the jewelled flowers which checkered the "green pastures" whereon we sat, we remounted our horses, and towards noon of a lovely May day, crossed the beautiful river and entered the ancient and somewhat dilapidated city of San Antonio de Bexar. Here

"The violet blows beside the stream,
The blood-root in the wood,
With daisies all the meadows gleam,
Like stars on solitude!
The lilac blooms by larches thin,
The grass springs green and gay,

> And song and beauty usher in
> The laughing month of May!"

The city of San Antonio is about one hundred and twenty or thirty years old—is five hundred miles south-west from Natchitoches, and contains about three hundred houses. It lies on the San Antonio river about 180 miles from its mouth, into which there is a good port one hundred miles only below the town.

The morning after our arrival we were visited by a *norther*. We felt its effects quite severely for a while, till it moderated, and ended in a shower of rain. These northers in some parts of Texas are quite frequent and severe, but they generally terminate in twelve or twenty-four hours. Their effects are often limited to particular districts of country. Those who desire a minute description of them, together with more comprehensive details of the climate, &c. of Texas, are referred to the interesting works of Mrs. Holley and Mr. Kennedy, by far the best and most descriptive that have been written upon the country. And here we cannot refrain to allude to some excellent "Notes on Texas," which first made their appearance in the *Hesperian*, a monthly periodical published in Cincinnati, Ohio, and to wish them a more extended circulation. They contain the most intelligent, accurate, and impartial view of the early history, &c. of the country, that we have ever seen, and it is much to be desired that the author would revise them and give them to the public in such a shape as they really deserve, and which would ensure for them a more general and extensive perusal.

The approach to San Antonio from the east is over a gently rolling country of tolerable soil only. A great portion of the land we passed immediately on our route from the Colorado, was arid, sandy, and quite barren. For some twenty miles or more after passing the eastern line of the county of Bexar, the soil is of a deep heavy sand, often a coarse gravel, and the road in dry weather, heavy, dusty, and fatiguing; yet even here, in this sandy land of promise, the scenes are full of rural grace and loveliness, and abound with pictures for the artist and daguerreotype. The soil and appearance of the country generally now begin to improve, and continue so as you ride farther west. Here it is that nature always smiles. Above all countries in the world this is the paradise of flowers. The prairies in spring-time are carpeted with the nopal, or prickly-pear, with its tufts of red and yellow rose-like blossoms—redder than scarlet, yellower than gold—while the hyacinth and jonquil, prairie rose and jasmine, and yellow-flowered honeysuckle, passion-flower and sweet syringa, everywhere blossom and diffuse their delicious fragrance through the air, and give to the whole neighborhood the appearance of a flower-garden. Here it is you are favored by a softer and more fragrant breeze, and charmed by a clearer sky, more "beautifully blue" than any you have elsewhere seen.

> "Hic ver perpetuum, atque alienis mensibus sestas"
> [Here is spring forever, and strange months rest]

We crossed the Salado three miles from town, and as we gained the summit of the hills which commands a view of the city, the whole panorama of the green valley of San Antonio burst upon the sight. All its charms were revealed to us at once, like the flower which blooms in the hand. "What freshness! what beauty! what solitude!" Here it is, as Ossian has it, the green hills lift their dewy heads—the blue streams rejoice in the vale. Before us we saw the venerable but decayed city, to the right the Alamo and neighboring mountains, to the left the missions of San José and Concepcion, "rearing their gothic heads, like the old abbeys of Europe," and the beautiful San Antonio river, like a cord of silver, gliding through the valley of flowers—the valley of love! Oh! how I felt my heart swell as I gazed on the landscape, and wished those whom I loved most were with me to enjoy it. I am sure they would have been happy!

> "Hic gelidi fontes, hie mollia prata, Lycori,
> Hic nemus, hie toto tecum consumerer aevo."

> [Here who are cool springs, here soft meadows, Lycori,
> Here the forest, here all you consumerer ages."]

CHAPTER XIV.
COUNTY OF BEXAR.

San Antonio de Bexar—Its Antiquity—Mexican Cabins—Delicious Climate—Fine Bathing—Passion of Love—Earthly Paradise—The Alamo—San Antonio River—Water Power—Manufactures Anticipated— Canon de Ugalde—The Soldier's Retreat.

The San Antonio country, emphatically so called, is one of the loveliest and most fertile regions on the face of the globe, and the city of *San Antonio de Bexar*, in the hands of Anglo-Americana, will soon be made the most desirable residence on the American continent. San Antonio has quite a feudal aspect at present, and its churches, and towers, and moats, and bridges, remind one of some of the dilapidated cities of Old Spain, to which it formerly belonged. It was settled by Spaniards, and by emigrants from the Canary Islands, as early as 1730, and once contained a population of some ten or twelve thousand souls. It is built chiefly of stone, and is embosomed in one of the loveliest and most enchanting valleys that can possibly be conceived. The city is regularly built after the Spanish fashion, and its military and civic square, with a fine large church in the centre, reminded me of the Place d'Armes and cathedral in the city of New Orleans. The church is built of a kind of lime rock which abounds in this region, and forms the chief material of the walls and houses of the main part of the city. The population of the city has now dwindled to a few hundred souls, but will soon be augmented to as many thousand. Its consequence is at once indicated by the number and variety of its names,—Presidio de San Fernando—La Villa de San Fernando—City of San Antonio—City of San Antonio de Bexar. The streets extend at right angles for some distance from the main part of the city, where one might easily imagine himself either in Mexico or Havana. Farther on, the frail cabins of the frail and imbecile occupants—half Mexican, half Indian, and who are as idle and lazy as may well be—are indiscriminately made of adobes (unburnt brick), tapia, mud, and reeds, with thatched roofs, and now and then a buffalo-hide to fill up a crevice and keep out the sun—What Sancho calls the "inclemencies of the heavens," rarely occur in this delicious climate. These primitive huts, probably, are somewhat like those rudely constructed hovels to which Waverley was conducted by the Highlanders when rescued from the hands of Gilfellan, some "sixty years since,"—

> "A little cottage, built of sticks and reeds,
> In homely wise, and wall'd with sods around."

They seldom have other than dirt floors, with deer or buffalo-skins spread out for carpets, and which serve the double purpose of bed and chairs; and where the indolent occupant spends most of his time, like the Turk in dreaming away his existence over his chocolate and cigarrito, in preference to coffee and the pipe. He knows no care but rejoices like the Persian at the rising, and the Swiss at the setting sun. It is the delicious climate, no doubt, which makes the life of the Mexicans so joyous and happy. Music and dancing, hunting and the chase, cards and love, make up their whole existence. Love is here, as Dupaty describes it among the Romans, an amusement, an affair, a caprice, and rarely a necessity, for they feel it very early and instinctively, and the heart loves directly.

The air here is always balmy, and elastic as a morning zephyr. It is as fresh as a rose leaf; and the mind and body both seem buoyed up by it. Those who have breathed the nitrous oxyde gas may have some idea of its elasticity, and sweetness, and its happy effects upon the soul. Hygeia makes this her chosen residence, and health, beauty, and freshness forever bloom among her votaries. The youthful pulmonic, and the aged invalid, may here add a cycle to their frail existence, and those from the icy regions of the north, where nature is hourly wasting from the inclemency of climate, may here renew their youth, and have length of days, with contentedness of spirit and joyousness of heart. The ills that flesh is heir to rarely find their way to this ambrosial region of the south.

There is a legend that, as Aristonus was changed by the gods into myrtle after his death, so the Mexicans are turned into *muskeet trees*, and so far from fading, they possess the marvellous property of renewing themselves every few years

Here—

> "Reviving sickness lifts her languid head;
> Life flows afresh; and young-eyed Health exalts
> The whole creation round. Contentment walks
> The sunny glade, and feels an inward bliss
> Spring o'er his mind, beyond the power of kings
> To purchase."

The San Antonio river affords most delightful bathing at all seasons of the year, and at all hours of the day and night parties of both sexes may be seen enjoying this luxury, of which they seem never to be tired. Those who bathe here have all impurities washed away and never die, but like the lotus flower mingle with the surrounding atmosphere when they disappear from earth, and contribute by their songs and breath to make it purer and more healthful.

"Bathe thee, maiden, bathe thee here
In this river, cool and clear;
Bathe, till every fleshly blot—
Earthly stain and carnal spot—
And each remnant of decay
Shall for aye be washed away;
For she that doth her members lave,
In this unsullied lustral wave,
Ne'er shall sink into the grave,
But live for aye, a deathless fay."

The Alamo, now familiar to everyone, is a military outpost near the city, established by the Spanish government in 1718 as a place of refuge and defence from the Indians. It is a quadrangular enclosure of, perhaps, half an acre of land, with walls of mud and freestone, about fifteen or twenty feet in height, and four or five in thickness, having barracks, &c. within the walls; and a church without of great architectural strength and beauty, with a chime of three bells, and several statues of saints and the apostles, &c. of exquisite chiselling, and worthy of Athens in her best days. They are now, alas! a heap of ruins, having been destroyed by the Mexicans at the last storming of the Alamo in 1836. The church and fortress are now as desolate as the dwellings of Morna. The flowers around seem to languish, and the birds sing less gaily, but the spirits of Bowie, and Travis, and Crockett, will hallow the scene for ever, and render it dear to the pilgrim of liberty, and an object of interest to all ramblers, who, like myself, have been curious to learn the legends of this sunny land.

The river, which bursts from its fountains three or four miles above San Antonio, glides rapidly through it and waters every portion of the city. This affords the best water power, probably, in the world, and under the magic wand of some enterprising Yankee, another Lowell or Rochester could be made to start into being, as it were, in a moment. We unhesitatingly say that no spot in America offers such inducements to capitalists, or affords such local and general advantages for manufactures of all sorts as *San Antonio de Bexar.* With the most enchanting country around it, and the most salubrious climate in the world—the finest cotton and wheat district on earth, with myriads of fine cattle and sheep grazing upon the hills—nothing, we say, can surpass it. The raw material is all upon the spot—cotton, wool, hemp, and silk, if you please, while the labor required to work the machinery, and manufactures, may be had from countless Mexican men, women, and children, for a song, and a permanent home market for every article of cotton, linen, woollen, silk, iron, &c, &c, that could be manufactured, would be had at the door. The whole of Mexico, including the Californias and Oregon, might be supplied from this single fountain—this Lowell, this Rochester, this Sheffield, this Manchester, as it might be of the far west! While the wealth of the Mexican gold and silver mines would be concentrated and brought here in exchange for commodities which are ever needed, and now annually imported some thousands of miles distant from a foreign land!

The water power and privileges here are as far superior to Lowell as possible, and if $10,000,000 of capital can be employed there, why may not an equal or greater amount be profitably invested at San Antonio? and considering the facility of obtaining the raw material, and bread-stuffs, and the water power, and the labor, and the market, and above all, the salubrity of the climate, it must some day or other take precedence of all manufacturing cities, and in time acquire a power and wealth unprecedented in the history of America. It remains to be seen who is to set the ball in motion—what village Whitney—what Arkwright—is to erect here a monument of wealth and fame for himself and his posterity.

Here both manufactures and agriculture may profitably engage the attention of the settlers. The water-power, as we have remarked, is unlimited, and agriculture of every description may be brought into successful operation. The cultivation of the vine and olive, especially—wheat, maize, rye, barley, and all the small grains, indeed, as well as cotton, sugar, tobacco, hemp, and upland rice, will reward the husbandman indefinitely for his toil. The raising of horses and mules, and cattle, and hogs, is accomplished without labor, while the raising of sheep, as fine as those which feed upon the mountains of Arcadia, or fat pastures of Sicily, and the growing of wool and the manufactures of silk and wine, will become the legitimate business of the European emigrant, and reward him seven fold for his labor, and his flocks, and his herds.

> "Lo, here the world is bliss; so here the end
> To which all men do aim, rich to be made."

The region of country about Bexar and the San Antonio river is regarded by all travellers as the El Dorado of the new world. "To the most salubrious climate it unites the most varied and enchanting scenery of hill and dale, watered by large springs, which furnish abundant supplies for irrigation. The winters are very mild and hardly felt, and two yearly crops of corn and grain are the regular tribute of husbandry. The sugar-cane lasts or *ratoons* for eight years, and a certain species of cotton without planting, and the quality is far superior to that of Louisiana or Mississippi. To these advantages is to be added the facility of raising cattle; the buffalo clover and wild grass, or muskeet, as it is called, being so excellent and abundant, that they 'increase and multiply, and replenish the earth,' without any care on the part of the owners. And then the fruits! From the fig, and quince, and peach, and orange, and lemon, and chirimoya of the south, to the pear and apple of the northern climate, the immense variety of Ceres' and Pomona's realms embellishes the land, and enriches the husbandman. The most delightful districts of the south of France, with all the wealth and refinement which ages of civilization have accumulated, cannot be compared with this blessed spot, such as it is even now, when its natural resources have hardly begun to be developed; nor could the island of Calypso itself, in the fabled description of Fenelon, or the happy valley of Rasselas, enter into competition."

The country west of San Antonio, along the valleys of the Medina, San Miguel, Frio, and Nueces, is the same earthly paradise, and most of the soldiers of the Texan army who hold government claims, and are entitled to bounty lands, have located them in this region. The climate is absolutely enchanting. "There is a mild radiance in the sunbeams, a balsamic serenity in the air, which infuses a voluptuous listlessness, that desire of remaining imparadised in one delightful spot, which in classic fiction was supposed to render those who tasted the lotus, forgetful of country, of friends, and of every tie; they loathed the idea of moving away."

"Here, if thou lovest a clime
Where health may flourish—rankling care decrease,

And beauteous nature smoothe thy stream of time—
Here repose, and feast thy soul with scene sublime.

The sunbeam shall not smite thee, for the sea
Tempers its fervor; Winter's kindly ray

Shall never chill thee, for the myrtle-tree,
Pomegranate, palm, and citron, shade the land

With fruit and foliage; nature's face shall be
Thy book and mirror—one long summer day."

San Antonio in 1846 by Josiah Gregg

INTRODUCTION TO DOCUMENT

Josiah Gregg became one of the most noted chroniclers of the early American West. In 1831 the twenty-five-year-old Gregg headed west to Missouri where he embarked on a ten-year-long career as a trader on the Santa Fe-Chihuahua Trail. An amateur naturalist as well as a merchant, in 1844 Gregg published his experiences on the Great Plains and in northern Mexico in a work called *Commerce of the Prairies*. His vivid descriptions of the life and land he saw cemented his reputation as an expert on the region.

Gregg was advised at the outbreak of the Mexican War in 1846 to travel to San Antonio where he could find work with the United States Army as an interpreter and guide. However, General John E. Wool, the officer selected to lead an American column from San Antonio to Chihuahua City disliked Gregg and turned down is services. Gregg chose to accompany the column as a civilian anyway, again chronicling his experiences as he went.

While in San Antonio Gregg visited various sites about the town. He noted that his father, Harmon Gregg, had once visited San Antonio. [See San Antonio de Béxar in 1828 by J. C. Clopper.] He was stuck by the toll that decades of conflict had taken on the town.

DOCUMENT[36]

I was certainly very greatly disappointed at my first view of, and debut into, the town of San Antonio de Bexar. I did not, it is true, expect to see any considerable grandeur of elegance, either in architecture or fashion; yet I must confess that I did not expect to see so poor and wretched a looking place. There were many stone houses; yet these are about as shabby looking as those of *adobe*, of which the larger portion of the better houses are built. Like the dwelling of all of interior Mexico they are generally but one story high and a large portion, flat dirt roofs or *azoteas*. Yet there are a considerable number of *jacales*, or picket-huts, which are thatched with a short of bulrush. Then, there are now many shingle and board roofs, introduced by the Americans. Though there are numerous detached rooms, yet the best houses are built on a square enclosing a *patio* or court, and a corral, or back yard. The streets are dirty, crooked, and narrow—no sort of pavement or even sidewalks; I believe none of

Mounted Béxarenos ride past an assortment of typica architectural styles, from the stone and stucco house on the left to the jacale and adobe on the right. Circa 1840s. Daughters of the Republic of Texas Collection at Texas A&M University-San Antonio.

the streets even have names. The populations, including the village of the Alamo does not I think pass 2,000 souls, though some contend for 2,500 to 3,000, while others reduce it to 1,500. Old Don José de la Garza (who is one of the most respectable Mexican sages and has been a member of Congress) says that in 1812 the population was at least 3 or 4 times greater than at present; other intelligent persons (especially Bustillo) say it never exceeded 3 or 4 thousand; there is little doubt however that 30 or 40 years ago it was in a much more flourishing condition than at present. My father visited this region (and this town) in 1822 [1828], and I have often heard him speak of its thriving condition than at that period, though it had been visited by civil wars, etc. Yet it has since been scenes of continual warfare—both revolutionary and Indian.

It was taken in 1813 by the revolutionary patriots, following the declaration of Hidalgo. But it was soon re-taken by the Spaniards; taken and re-taken by the same in 1817; after which it remained in procession of the Spaniards until the victory of Iturbide, and the establishment of Mexican Independence. In 1835 the town was taken from Gen. Cos by the Texans and re-taken early by Gen. Santa Anna. It was again evacuated by the Mexicans and re-occupied by the Texans, after the defeat of San Jacinto in April 1836. It was re-taken again in 1842 by Gen. Vazquez but soon abandoned. Taken again in Sept. 1842 by Gen. Woll—retreated soon after, taking 58 prisoners to the Castle of Perote, besides 13 taken at Salado [Dawson Massacre]. In this battle a detachment under Capt. Morgan was cut off while attempting to join Col. Caldwell and upwards of 30 killed, besides the 13 above mentioned taken prisoner— only one or two escaped.

During the period of wars—taking and retaking—there have been several serious battles in the town. I boarded in the house where Gen. Milam was killed, known as the "Berimendi House", his remains now buried in a spot covered with a heap of firewood, in the back yard."

Besides the general dilapidated condition of the buildings they show considerable marks of these wars, with their ball-scathed walls, doors, windows, church steeples, etc., as well from cannon and musket shots.

In these wars, the gardens, orchards, and trees of ornament also suffered.

A Kentucky Volunteer in San Antonio, 1846

INTRODUCTION TO DOCUMENT

A major obstacle to Texas annexation to the United States was the fear that the act would bring on a war with Mexico. This prediction came true when Mexican and U.S. forces clashed on the Rio Grande in April 1846. At President James K. Polk's urging, the U.S. Congress declared war on Mexico on May 13, 1846.

San Antonio served as a marshalling point for American troops headed to Mexico. By September 1846, 3,000 United States volunteers and regular soldiers had assembled outside town, soon to be on their way to northern Mexico. While here, these eager young men flocked to town to see the local sights, especially the Alamo.

One such American who came to see where Crockett and Bowie had died was Kentucky volunteer officer, Captain Jefferson Peak. Peak had the opportunity to meet Erasmo Seguín. The encounter shows the distain exhibited by Anglos towards Tejanos, even a man as well accomplished and respected as Seguín.

DOCUMENT[37]

[*September 16, 1846*]   The Alamo of fort at this place where Crocket and Boey was in when murded was a Strong fort but it was almost completely demolished before they finally [were] overpowered and put to deth. after these two hearoes were crually put to dethe ther bodies were burned on a Large fier.

I remained in Sanantone by request of Genl Wool until the 19 as he wished to take time to consider whether he would take our Redigement which him to Chewawa or Sent it on to Genl Taylor. Mager John P. Gain[e]s arrived at this place on the morning of the 19 as I was about to Start and wished me to stay until evening and go with him but I refsed to Stay and put of[f] and Left him which he did not like.

The distance from Sananton to the Gulf is cald 175 miles.

[*September 19, 1846*]   Left Sanantonio Debexar ½ past 10 oclock for Port Lavaca where our Regiment was stationed and past Mishion Conception 3 miles, also Mishon St. Hosey (very fine and when refused admitance I drew my pistol and he opnd door) 5 miles to Mishion St. Whan 8 miles to Mishon St. Spathers or Spaid 10 miles to past a Saw and grist mill all on the Sanantone River and in a lovely and beautiful country and thence on to Cantrones Ranch 25 miles. Her I staid all knight at the house of a Dr. [Horace Alsbury] from Lexington his wife Was a Spanish woman [who] could Speak English. Hur husband the Dr. was gon to the Rio grnde. this lady gave me a full detale of the massacre of Colanels Crocket and Boey. She was in the prisen [the Alamo] with them during the seag and Colonel Boey married the Ladies cousin whilst in the Alamo. [This Alamo survivor was Juana Gertrudis Navarro, the wife of Dr. Alsbury.]

[*Sept. 20, 1846*]   Traveled 8 miles to breckfast to old Mr. [Erasmo] Segeans [Seguin's]. This is the father of Colonel [Juan] Sagean [Seguin] who joined the Texians and befrended them and was a member of the Texian Congress and finaly became dissatisfyed with Texas and thought him Self badly treted and is at this time in the Mexican army afighting aganst the americans. this family of Mexicans Shows a considerable Smartness and a good deal of dislike to the americans particular the old lady, the mother of the Colonel and his father is very old as well as his mother. He has an awful countinence as well as the old Lady. they have 3 grone daughters living with them all fine lookin girls for Mexicans and apper intelligent and not one of the family presant but the youngest daughter could Speak a word of English and she could Speak very plain. her I cald for breckfast and after a short time they sat 2 small earthen boals on a bench Each containg about ½ cups of bad tasted Coffee (G. W.

Crawford being with me). I asked if that was all that we could get for Bkfast and the girl that could Speak English Replied yes that was all they had. I told Hur I wanted moor Coffee and better and Some I said that is meat. She Spoke to her muther and they all had quite a jabering and finally she replied that they had non for us. I told her I wanted a giean [gallina] then that is chicken. She spoke in Spanish to her mother what I said and I Saw that the old hag had the old billy in hur big enoug. for the daughter turned very sudden from her with a mortifyed countinance and Remarke that they had no gieans. I pointed I think to the finest looking gang of chickins I think I Ever Saw and Remarked that ther was plenty and that I wanted one and would have it and for them to kill and prepar it at once. the old lady positively refused. I had found out by this time that the old man and 3 daughters all wanted me to have it. our horses had been fed and it was almost imposible for Crawford to keepe the chickins from Eating the greater part of the corn from the horses. I stept out into the yard wher the chickens was and I sheld a litle corn and they gatherd around like flyes to a Saucer of molases. I in a second caught one of the finest pulets by the neck and in another Second I gave it a Sling and its body fell to the ground whilst its hed stuck to my hand. the old lady looking on and in a second or 2 she came ataring and the old man and three daughters and of all the scremes and shreak that I ever heard from a fiend this old lady beat all. She danced and ran around me three or four Times and semed as tho she could not keepe her hands off and it was all that old man and 3 daughters could do to Silence hur. there were 4 or 5 Mexican men Standing of and lisened to and Saw all that pased but never said one word to eithir of us. I had a pr of side pistols belted on and my sword and a pair in my holsters on one arm. Finally the old woman picked up the chickin and the 3 daughters Laid hold and fixed us a good mexican breckfast and brot out a botle of muscal (whisky) for us to drink I paid them liberal for our Bkfast and horses and all parted in the finest humer and to all appearences the best of friends (but only from teeth outwards with them) Thence on to the ranch on the Sea Willow [Cibolo] 25 miles. here we got some Beef. Traveled on 10 miles. Hear encamped in the woods. 35 miles.

PART 4: Early Statehood

A German Scientist Attends a Fandango, 1847

INTRODUCTION TO DOCUMENT

By the mid-1840s, German immigrants began to arrive in Texas in large numbers. Many settled in the Texas Hill Country, establishing the towns of Fredericksburg and New Braunfels. By the 1850s, the number of Germans who chose to settle in San Antonio formed the basis for the town's increasingly significant German population.

Dr. Ferdinand von Roemer, who earned his doctorate in paleontology at the University of Berlin in 1842, traveled through Texas. Roemer visited the newly established German settlements, taking notes for a published account of his 1845–1847 trip. Like many Americans and Europeans who visited Texas, he travelled to San Antonio. His account of a fandango provides a description of what had become an entrenched tradition throughout Mexico that still was practiced in San Antonio.

DOCUMENT[38]

Presently we saw the city some distance before us. It lies in a broad, almost level plain. Already from the distance the sight of the city has somewhat of a foreign appearance, altogether dissimilar to any other Texas city. The cupola of a large stone building especially drew our attention, since it is an unusual sight in Texas. This foreign appearance became more pronounced when we entered the city itself. After passing a few miserable huts whose walls were constructed by ramming poles perpendicularly into the ground and binding them with strips of raw oxhide, we came a street with stone houses. This street led us to a rather large square from which several streets diverged at right angles. The square was surrounded on three sides by one-story, stone houses with flat roofs; the fourth side was occupied by a church built in Spanish style with a low tower above the entrance and a flat-arched cupola over the chancel.

The entire place gave the impression of decay, and apparently at one time had seen better and more brilliant days. . . .

We lodged at a hotel, which was formerly the home of the Spanish governor. It was built of stone and was rather roomy, which high ceilings. It had few windows and while these had blinds, they contained no window panes. The walls were plain white and the beams upon which the roof rested were visible. Small cedar boards were laid across these, then followed first a layer of mortar and then a layer of dirt. All the roofs

Fandangos were a common feature of life in early San Antonio. Daughters of the Republic of Texas Collection at Texas A&M University-San Antonio.

of the Mexican houses in San Antonio were constructed in the same manner. Most of the rooms had a small fireplace which appeared tiny in comparison to those found in the houses of the colonists in which can be burned trunks of trees several feet long.

Our host was an American and all the arrangements in the hotel were according to American style. We found no shelter for our horses at the hotel, but were obliged to take them to a livery stable where horses were kept for hire. We paid one dollar per day for their keep. After supper we took a walk through the city, in order to view the night life which begins at the approach of darkness. I had heard much about the fandangos or dancing amusements of San Antonio as being something unusual; we decided, therefore, if possible to learn more about them. The tones of a fiddle or miserable violin, coming from a house on the square near the church, left no room for doubt where to go in order to satisfy our curiosity. We entered, a long, narrow room, level with the ground, in which two or three wax candles, fastened to the walls, dimly lighted the place. A number of young women, dressed in their best apparel, sat on benches at the end of the room, waiting for the invitation to the dance. They were, however, as little noticed for the time being by the men present, as were the violin players who, without interruption, played one and the same monotonous piece of dance music over and over again. At the other end of the room stood a few tables at which games of chance were being played. A motely mixture of Mexicans and Americans crowded around these tables. They were playing Monte, a game of cards to which the Mexican is passionately addicted. The Americans, who are almost equally interested in all games of chance, displayed the same eager interest as did the Mexicans. The piles of Spanish dollars and even gold pieces, lying in heaps on the tables, formed a notable contrast to the miserable appearance of the place and the shabby dress of some of the Mexicans. At one table, an old Mexican woman was banker.

Now and then the play was interrupted, as some of the spectators and a few of the players, usually Americans, turned to the dance. The patiently waiting "beauties," among who were (to be honest) only a few beautiful faces, although several of them had fiery black eyes and comely figures, were asked for a dance, and the various couples arranged themselves in the proper dance order. The dance which now followed was not a fandango, as one would assume from the name which is applied to these evening gatherings, but a peculiar contradance which moved in rather slow tempo, but despite its simplicity was not an unpleasant sight.

The dancers who, as has already been remarked, were mainly young Americans, indeed sought earnestly to act gracefully toward their partners, but in comparison with the natural charm and grace of their companions, the contrast was very obvious. The national difference was still more apparent when, as happened very seldom, also Mexicans took part in the dancing. In contrast to the dignified movement, peculiar even to the lowest of them, and the charm which is enhanced by the becoming dress, the movements of the Americans seemed clumsy and awkward.

When the dance ended, every dancer led his partner to a table near the gambling tables. It contained refreshments of the simplest kind, namely a kind of small cake which was sold by an old Mexican woman. Every girl would select some of the pastry and her dancing partner would pay for it. However, as a rule the refreshments were not eaten by the girls, but tied in a cloth which evidently had been brought along for this purpose. Each new dance added another piece to the supply and at the end of the dance, all was carried home, which, after all, was the real reason for attending the dance.

It should also be mentioned here that these fandangos are visited only by Mexican women of the poorer and uneducated families. The women of the few educated Mexican families who still live in San Antonio, visit these public dance halls as little as do the resident American women.

After watching these particular performances for some time, we left the house, for we had learned in the meantime that fandangos were in progress at two other places, and wanted to see those also. We, indeed, soon found the house pointed out to us. The rooms in which the gambling took place, the gambling tables, the black-eyed senoritas and the long, clumsy frames of their American partners, in short, the whole performance was so similar to the one we had just seen, that we did not gain much by the change and, therefore, returned to our hotel toward midnight.

Such fandangos take place every night God permits to return and some of the resident Americans have not missed any of them for years. Who furnishes the rooms for these amusements is not clear to me, since the guests do not purchase anything and every one can enter and leave without paying. However, I presume that the Mexican bankers of the gambling tables find their business lucrative enough to furnish two or three thin wax candles to illuminate the rooms. Another point was not clear to me at first: How can these games of chance flourish here so openly, since the American laws in general, and the laws of Texas in particular, prohibit them under heavy penalties. An American living here for quite some number of years gave me a satisfactory explanation to my query in an unabashed manner which seemed plausible to me after having seen these things with my own eyes. He said, "In San Antonio everybody gambles and naturally there are no accusers and judges, therefore, who are inclined to prosecute." I learned, furthermore, that when the circuit court which periodically holds its session at different places in a certain district, and especially also the grand jury which is compelled under oath to report all knowledge of lawlessness, come to San Antonio, the professional gamblers seek safety by leaving town and do not return until the court sessions are over.

Recommendation to Use Parts of the Alamo as Military Depot, 1847

INTRODUCTION TO DOCUMENT

Two dates stand in importance in the sage of Texas's annexation. On December 29, 1845, U.S. President John Tyler signed into law a joint resolution of Congress that admitted Texas as the twenty-eighth state in the Union. On February 19, 1845, Texas President Anson Jones ordered the flag of the Republic of Texas lowered in a ceremony in Austin that signified acceptance of statehood.

With Texas now part of the Union, U.S. troops began arriving on the Texas coast at Corpus Christi in July 1845. In spring 1846, President James K. Polk ordered the army to march to the Rio Grande, the boundary Texas claimed as its border during it nine years existence as an independent Republic. On April 26, Mexican troops on the north side of the river attacked two companies of U.S. Dragoons, killing 11 and capturing the rest. The following month, Polk announced that "American blood has been shed on American soil" and asked Congress to declare war on Mexico.

Armed with a declaration of war, Polk and the War Department launch a three-pronged land campaign against Mexico. General Zachary Taylor, already on the Rio Grande was ordered into northern Mexico. General Stephen W. Kearney was charged with leading a column from Fort Leavenworth with the goal of capturing New Mexico and California. A third column under General John E.

Wool, was slated to depart from San Antonio and link up with troops traveling with Kearney to capture Chihuahua. Wool's column was later ordered to join Taylor's command halfway during its march and never made it to Chihuahua.

The Mexican War transformed San Antonio forever even though the town for once was hundreds of miles from the actual fighting. As noted by earlier Spanish and Mexican commentators on the town's economic woes, the biggest problem was the lack of a market for goods and services. The arrival of the United Stated Army changed that situation.

San Antonio quickly became a staging area for the war. With supplies pouring into town, the army's Quartermaster Department rushed to lease existing property where equipment and provisions could be safely stored out of the weather. According to the annexation treaty all Texas forts were to be turned over to the U.S. Army. With its well-known history as a military barracks and fortress, the officers of the Quartermaster Department assumed that the former structures of former Mission Valero, or the Alamo, was theirs to use. By the time they learned that the property still belonged to the Catholic Church, plans were under way to occupy the old convent or Long Barrack.

DOCUMENT[39]

Quarter Masters Office
San Antonio, February 20,1847

Sir

I have the honor to submit to you an estimate for the improvement of the most material parts of the Alamo at this place & of soliciting your approbation of the expenditures therein contemplated.

The reasons for making the expenditures & improvements are numerous & cogent unless it shall be the policy of the Department to abandon this as a military depot.

The Quartermasters stores, Ordnance & Ordnance stores at this place are much exposed, as well to the depredations of incendiaries as to the action of the elements. They are deposited in store houses the best to be had, but were not wholly protected from the storms and its doors and walls are not sufficient to protect them from thieves or incendiaries—and as the town is generally crowded with Indians & Mexicans, not residents, I do not consider the property secure. The store houses are scattered over every part of the town & cannot be guarded without very great expense. The expense of house rent is too great for the accommodation afforded it being now 570$ per month & I do not know how it can be reduced without repairing & appropriating the Alamo to public use.

I herewith enclose a ground plan of the Alamo with the Chapel & yard. It was built by the Spaniards, occupied by the Mexicans and subsequently by the Texians, as a military fortress. It therefore by virtue of the compact of Annexation, with all its outposts, became the property of the United States—I have it in possession & use such parts if it as may be used in its present dilapidated state for Mechanic Shops, forage houses & the yard as a Waggon Yard; & adjoining it I have erected a shed & mangers for the accommodation of the Public Animals.

By the expenditure proposed the whole of the Quarter Masters Stores and Ordnance Stores at this Post could be concentrated & the entire property in charge of the Officers on duty in this Department may be subject to his daily & personal supervision, adding increased facilities to the public service, security to the public property & greatly reducing the expenses.

The Chapel adjoining the Alamo, an estimate for the improvement of which I also enclose, is somewhat differently situated. It was built at a more recent period. The workmanship is better & the walls stand firmer.

By an act of the Texas Congress approved on the 18th January, 1841 it was granted to the use of the Catholic Church. The terms of the grant are ambiguous & it may be doubtful whether it did not also pass to the United States by the act of annexation. But supposing it not proper to make improvements on property led by a doubtful tenure I would propose the purchase of it from the Bishop of Texas. I think it can be had on favorable terms. It would make a good & spacious Commissaries Store.

If it should be contemplated by the War Department to establish permanent posts along these frontiers to give protection against Mexican Robbers & Hostile Indians this may selected as a general depot from which to furnish supplies; in such event the improvement of the Alamo might become a subject of some importance.

I have the honor to be, Sir,

Respectfully,

Your Obt. Servt.

J. H. Ralston Capt.

A.A.Q.M. USA

Estimate of the Expenses of Roofing the principal building at the Alamo, San Antonio de Bexar

190 feet by 20

10700	feet Lumber	@ 6c per feet	645.96
42000	Shingles	@ 10$ per 1000	420.00
500	lbs. nails	@ 8$ per 100	40.00
	Labour		300.00
	Contingencies		150.00
			1555.96

Expences of Roofing the Alamo Chapel

13552	feet Lumber	@ 6c per feet	818.12
400000	Shingles	@ 10$ per 1000	400.00
500	lbs. nails	@ 8$ per 100	40.00
	Labor		300.00
	Contingencies		150.00
			1703.12

General Thomas S. Jessup

Quarter Master General

U.S. Army

San Antonio As Reported In *The Alamo Star*, 1854

INTRODUCTION TO DOCUMENT

The years immediately following the Mexican War brought San Antonio a level of peace and prosperity it had always sought. Not only was the ever-present threat of invasion from Mexico ended, a new line of army forts located west and north of the town formed a protective barrier against the Comanche. San Antonians began to think of their community as a place of commerce and enlightenment.

James P. Newcomb, a Canadian immigrant to Texas, became a major promoter of the notion that San Antonio had become a modern city worthy of adulation by the rest of the world. In 1854, seventeen-year-old Newcomb and a partner started a newspaper in San Antonio called *The Alamo Star* which lasted for a two-year run. Newcomb was later involved in other local papers, but left town in 1861 due to his pro-Union stance. He later returned and became a major figure in Reconstruction politics.

Newcomb's paper initially mirrors the format of other literary publicans which relied heavily on serialized version of short stories mixed with poetry and song lyrics. Within a short time, however, the editors began including news of events and people of the day. Politically, Newcomb flirted with the nativist Know Nothing Party, a seemingly odd thing for an immigrant to do. Nevertheless, *The Alamo Star* presents a clear vision of San Antonio as it struggled to shed its status as an isolated frontier outpost.

DOCUMENT[40]

March 25, 1854, Page 2: Inaugural Issue

Our paper will not be neutral in any-thing, but our columns open at all times to discuss any and every subject, as long as personal or abusive language is not used.

We shall endeavor to give the news of the day, both local and foreign, trying at all times to write and select, that which may amuse and, interest our readers.

Newspaper reading is the most improving thing at which a person can spend their leisure moments; every event which occurs within the bounds of civilization, is laid before you, and at evening, when the family is gathered around the centre table, you can sit quietly down and enjoy one of the greatest blessing conferred on the human race.

Our name in itself ought to be enough to insure us a liberal patronage; the Alamo!—a name at which the world grows pale to think what happened withing its walls, and when we look back to that period of struggle and strife, and compare the present condition of our growing, beautiful and time honored city to when it was invaded, taken, and re-taken, time and again during the Texas Revolution we see with surprise, the greatest change that ever happened—from poverty and oppression, to opulence and freedom, and we ought to be thankful to the Almighty Being, who thus guides and rules over the destinies of nations.

In Commencing the *Star*, we labor under many disadvantages, neither of us ever before attempted to pen an article for a paper, and as yet, we have had to depended on volunteers to assist us in our undertaking, [and] you must not expect too much of us.

April 8, 1854, Page 3

DOGS! DOGS!

Mr. Editors: There are hundreds of un-licensed dogs in our small city—a regular nuisance. There is such a barking and howling kept up at all times of night that it is the next thing to an impossibility to obtain a moment's rest. Our city contains dogs of all descriptions from the lazy New-Foundland, down to the insignificant little fice.

It has hereto fore been the case, that as soon as any one starts on a tour of the city, for the purpose of ridding us of these petty pests, the Old Cathedral bells are tolled, which is kind of pre-concocted signal for the Mexicans to hustle their dogs under the bed, until such a time as the *diablo*—as they term the perpetrator of dog-murder—passes by. This matter should be investigated and a dog-slayer appointed who will do his duty. Bill.

May 13, 1854, Page 3

SAN ANTONIO.

What a strange change has taken place in the condition of San Antonio, we have to look back but a few years to see a time when the citizens were in constant dread of the savage and his scalping knife; but aside from the warfare of savages, it has been drenched with the blood of contending armies. Who can contemplate without the most chivatric emotions, the scenes that have taken place in SAN ANTONIO! When TRAVIS with his Spartan few defended the ALAMO against the combined army of SANTA ANNA; but were at last overpowered by overwhelming forces, and *all* except one or two, were murdered by the inhuman command of Santa Anna.

> "And together lay in a shroud of blood!
> The coward and the brave."

What a different appearance SAN ANTONIO now presents, she is now making rapid strides in every thing that pertains to the advancement of civilization, there are many beautiful buildings going up in our city, both private and mercantile. This spirit of endeavor is diffusing itself among the people and we now have very good schools, but we need a College, and when we get it, we will have every facility for education. And we may look to the time when SAN ANTONIO will be the QUEEN of the WEST.

May 27, 1854, Page 3

Messrs Editors: It is with delight that I every evening take a walk up Flores street and view those beautiful gardens which our German and American friends cultivate, there

BOWEN'S BEND, SAN ANTONIO RIVER.

This 1850s scene shows one of the main fords of the San Antonio River and captures the garden-like appeal of the town. The Briscoe Museum of Western Art is on this site today. Daughters of the Republic of Texas Collection at Texas A&M University-San Antonio.

you can find all sorts of vegetables which are needed for table use, and of the finest quality, but it is not the only part of the town where there are fine gardens. You can go down Flores street and meet with the same view, go to the Alamo, and you will see as far as the eye can reach, a perfect carpet of green, and it is so all through and around town, and in every direction. It gives me pleasure, Messrs Editors to see all this—it looks civilized and not like it did some twelve years ago, without any of these beautiful spots to meet your gaze, nothing but the wild chaparral. But how different the scene now? Houses and gardens occupy that space where the chaparral stood, and which was made sacred by the blood of our fathers, who fought and bled there for their's and our freedom. Every where you go you can see buildings going up, all of which are of good material. Every now and then, when I come across an ancient Mexican building which has stood the storm of time and past revolutions, and which has not been replaced by finer ones, it brings to my mind recollections of the past, when TRAVIS, with his handful was massacred at the ALAMO, and MILAM, following his brother soldiers, also died within the walls of one of the ancient buildings, (the one which your printing establishment now occupies,) [Veramendi House] where his remains were buried and some six or eight years ago were taken up and re-buried near the old Catholic graveyard. I am sorry to say that since then his remains have been neglected, there was not even a stone placed there to point where he was buried; I do not think there is a person in this place who can point to his grave and I dare say there are now over one hundred persons in this place who attended his remains to the grave. I was one of the number, and have a good recollection of things which passed, and often have gone there afraid to point out the place to strangers and never yet have found it. It is a real shame on this community. They should have looked to this long since. Why not take up his remains if they can be found, and place them by the side of those brother patriots, WALKER and GILLESPIE, who are buried at [near] the Alamo, and erect a monument to him similar to those erected to them. I call upon the people to do this one act of patriotism, as they owe it to his memory. In conclusion, Mrssrs Editors, I refer you to the importance of the subject and sincerely hope that through the influence of your valuable sheet our citizens will aid you to do this work which has been left undone for too long. AN OLD TEXAN.

June 3, 1854, Page 2

San Antonio presents at the present time more [unclear word] life appearance that any other city in the state. There are upwards of fifty stores; three large drug stores, twenty shoe makers shops, about the same number of tailor shops, two tin shops, six blacksmith's shops, an innumerable number of carpenter and cabinet maker shops; two large hotels, twelve restaurants besides a number of private boarding houses; fifteen or twenty grogshops, and three livery stables. The employments of our city are too numerous to mention here. There is also four churches and three Sunday schools, which show that San Antonio is moral as well as immoral. Six schools besides the nunnery and [unclear word] one Debating Society and one theater, and four city papers. Its citizens are composed of every civilized nation on the globe. The streets are continually jammed with carts, wagons, carriages, horses and people; in fact they are too narrow (which is now beyond remedy,) for the business of the city. And without exception San Antonio is the most beautiful and flourishing city in Texas. Nature has done everything, art little. It is situated on the San Antonio river, a stream which for beauty or scenery and clearness of water, is not surpassed by any in the world. Although it is not navigable, which is of little consequences, as a railroad is the best and quickest conveyance to the Gulf, it possesses the greatest water power in the world, and on its banks will one day be a second Lowell or Manchester. There is upwards of a hundred houses in process of erection, and imigrants are continually pouring in from every part of the globe.

A railroad is also in contemplation between this place and the gulf, which will, to a moral certainty, be built before three years has rolled over our heads, although it is so strenuously opposed by *some*.

June 17, 1854, Page 2.

THE NEW BRIDGE.
The structure is now almost finished, which is a great acquisition to the city in the way of improvement and convenience. It is beautifully situated, the tall cottonwoods that border along the banks of the river, (green monuments of olden times,) casts

a romantic touch on the surrounding scenery, and at evening it is visited by those who wish to enjoy the cool breeze that sweeps over the rippling surface of the [fold in page].

June 24, 1854, Page 2.

[First sentence of this article is unclear but refers to the city's need for a better meat market.] Upwards of ten thousand human beings rely on it for existence. The market house consists of a shed fifteen feet wide and fifty feet long, its stalls are slabs placed on course frames. With two or three rows of hooks fastened above to hang the meat on. Beef is about the only article that is sold in this market, mutton, pork and other meat is rarely found there, while outside this shelter the place is literally jammed with Dutch gardners peddling vegtables of all description. A sickly fume is continually rising from this meat deposit, and in muddy weather, it is a perfect quagmire, which is enough to create pestilence. This looks like the market place of some half-civilized and indolent people, instead of an enlightened and free people, surrounded by every comfort, execept a good market house, and why can't we have one? Surely the most populous, wealthiest and oldest city in Texas can afford a decent market house. We say these few words so as to call the attention of our City *Fathers* to the state of affairs in that quarter, and urge upon them the stringent necessity of immediately erecting a good and comfortable market house.

July 1, 54, Page 2.

Our Citizens Becoming Fashionable.
The hard times havd disappeared, fasionable society has eclipsed the old pioneering habits of the original settlers. This once dreary and gloomy looking city is a gay and lively one now. Our streets, where once the comanche trained his wild mustang and reveled with pleasure, now fine carriages dash along filled with the rich and gay and our pavements are paraded by fair ladies. But what gives our city such fashionable appearance is its theater, conducted in a very creditable manner by some of our citizens, assisted by the best actors in the United States. At the theater you may see a specimen of San Antonio aristocracy, the leading menbers of fashionable society

appear on the stage; we think a revolution is taking place in the fashionable circle. On last Saturday night they played to a large crowded and delighted house; the theater is attended by the beautiful and wealthy, giving it a splendid appearance.

They perform again to-night, when the thrilling five act tragedy of "Douglas" will be enacted, in which Mrs. H. Lewis takes the part of young Douglas. They will also play the Tragiuco, Melo-dramatico, Farcio, Burlesque piece of Bombastes Furioso. It is at the request of many friends that they perform the latter piece.

July 8, 1854, Page.

FOURTH OF JULY.

Day dawned, and the rising sun was greeted by the roar of cannon, which echoed and re-echoed on the still morning air, rousing the freeman from his couch, reminding him of the seventy-eighth anniversary of the Declaration of Independence.

The city was in a perfect bustle from 5 o'clock till 10, A.M; troups of horsemen and vehicles of every description filled with pleasure seekers dashed through every part of our city.

About 10 o'clock we joined in with a party of juveniles who were on their way up the river to take a swim, abundantly supplied with melons. Proceeding to a secluded woodland place on the river we had a glorious swim, and comfortable repast, which by common consent the party proceeded to the head of San Pedro, where the Germans had prepared to have a kind of public celebration. Arriving at the place where the doings was to come off and finding nothing going on, we adjourned to the springs where we quinched our thirst with the cool waters the gushed from the rock, and threw ourselves down in the shade of the tall pecan trees that grew around the place. The scene was a pleasing one and of a romantic character, on every side were gushing streams of crystal waters dancing and gurgling along over the pebble bottom, and formed into a lake below, a variety of tiny warblers fluttered through the trees, singing sweet songs, as if they knew it were our Independence day.

About 3 o'clock we walked up to the house where the people had already begun gathering: at each end of the house was a bar where the dizzy multitude emptied glass after glass of intoxicating liquors, dull eyes and giddy heads were a general thing—tables were scattered in every direction through the woods, which surrounded both the gay of both sex. There was no public dinner, but refreshment could be had at a very exorbitant price.

By 5 o'clock a great concourse of people had gatherted, principally Germans, impatient to hear the oration to be delivered by J. A. Wilcox. . . .

Mr. Wilcox arrived about 6 o'clock, on whose arrival thirty-one guns were fired. Mr. Wilcox immediately took the stand. In the first part of his address he particularised the sons of every nation and congratulated them on the happy choice of this county as their home. His oration was adapted to the occasion and the audience. In speaking of our country and its institutions he very properly alluded to the constitution, and protested against any change, which was good and to the point. . . .

July 8, 1854, Page 2.

A Dancing Master Come at last.
Our readers may see by an advertisement in another column that a dancing master sure enough, has arrived in our city. Mr. J. C. Dever, had been raised to this art, and we advise out young friends to avail themselves of this opportunity of learning the necessary and beautiful accomplishment.

July 15, 1854, Page 3.

Messers. Editors: What has become of Bill? I have not seen any of his communications in your paper for some time, which is truly regretted by the readers of the Star, as he always kept them informed of all the dog fights that occurred in the city. He excited the marshalls to their duty in destroying those petty pests, we think the marshalls need Bill to urge them on for there seems to be a double supply now raising.

This morning as I was talking my walk, my attention was directed towards the Alamo by a rising crowd of dust, I hastened to the spot, and there to my surprise were fifty to sixty unlicenced dogs, all gamboling and sporting about the Alamo square, as if all the dog slayers had died off. Timothy.

July 22, 1854, Page 3.

Messers. Editors: Having read one of your sheets, I was struck with the appearance and zeal with which it is conducted. It is well adapted to improve the morals of the youth of the State, and being one of the craft, I like to give such an enterprise an encourgage[ment.] I think the young men of San Antonio, set an example to the State, as far as the improvement of the young men's mind is concerned. You have a Debating Club, which I see by your paper is well attended.

There is a Temperence Association here, which meets once a month. Viz: its regular meetings. It meets once a week, now, and will continue till the August election is over.

Times are tolerably brisk here now. The town is rapidly improving. Capt. Grumbles is putting up a steam mill on the river. He has a splendid engine, which will be in operation in about two weeks. ROLLA.

July 22, 1854, Page 4.

BATH HOUSE.
The subscriber respectfully announces to the citizens of San Antonio, that he has fitted up a new bathing house and is ready to accommodate the public. Subscribers will be entitled to the use of towels and soap. The terms for bathing can be had by applying to his barber shop on Solidad street. NACO DUVAL.

August 26, 1854, Page 2.

San Antonio can now boast of as many neewspapers as any city in the State. It has five; viz: The Western Texan; Houston & Smith proprietors; San Antonio Ledger, West & Bourke proprietors; San Antonio Zeitung, ------- proprieters; Alamo Star, Newcomb & Lambert, proprietors; San Antonio Weekly Reporter, Frank M. Whitemond, proprietor.

Septemper 2, 1854, Page 4.

FEMALE DISSIPATION.
"The drink, the drink, Cassio"
O' how revolting it is to every sense of refinement and morality, to see a woman intoxicated. We have lately witnessed two cases of this nature near the bridge on Commerece street, and we could not help from shuddering at such a striking evidence of the miserable and degraded state of some portions of society, and the proneness of man's nature to a mean low station where education and refinement never enter. But thank heavens, the source from whence this misery and degradation comes is to be closed, that is the liquor shops.

Septemper 2, 1854, Page 4.

A STRANGE FREAK OF A MEXICAN.
A few days since, a Mexican went into the Mission San Juan and with a club commenced to demolish all the picture[s], saints and wooden Jesus. He was, however, prevented by the timely interference of some señoritas, one of which came near having her arm broken in the melee. When questioned as to his conduct, he said the Mexican Gods could neither eat, walk or talk, and were no Gods at all, consequently he wanted to put them out of the way. This same man said that "if the Mexicans had worshipped the true and only God, the 'gringos' could never have taken Texas."

September 16, 1854, Page 2.

On Monday evening last, two strangers arrived in our city on horseback, and after riding up to the Plaza House they dismounted and ordered their horses to be put up. After registering their names they called for a room so they might go straight to sleep, which was accordingly given to them. Mr. Wilcox, upon looking over the register immediately saw that they were the murderers of William Byrd of Austin and he immediately started out in search of a marshall. After finding one he returned and had them arrested and they are now safe in jail.

September 16, 1854, Page 2.

EMIGRATION.

To all new countries emigration directs its course, at first it is composed of the hardy yeomanry of the plow, the true pioneers of civilization but as it settles up and the "hard times" begin to fade away, the polished and educated are seen flocking to it for the purpose of realizing better fortunes, or from a love of change, novelty or adventure.

Texas has passed through all vicissitudes of a newly settled country and has fairly recovered from the effects of a bloody but successful revolution and is settling up with astonishing rapidity.

San Antonio, where occurred the most trying times of the TEXAS revolution, and where was enacted the noblest and most daring feats of Texian heroism, is now the largest and most oppulent city of TEXAS. It is continually filled with genteel and respectable strangers, which show that its emigration is not only composed of the poor and uneducated, but the educated and wealthy. We clip the following from the "Lavaca Commercial."

"The travel from here westward is now considerable. On last Thursday morning, three coaches, loaded down with passengers left here for San Antonio.

Nearly every stranger that visits TEXAS strikes for San Antonio fancying no doubt that they will not 'see TEXAS,' unless they visit that old and war-torn city."

San Antonio bids fair of being the most flourishing part of the South.

September 23, 1854, Page 2.

ROBBERY.

We learn that a Mexican, in the employ of Captain Beck, while on his way to his farm was attacked by two men a short distance on this side of the Salado. He was struck at, one by, with a large bowie knife, which fortunately missed him; the other robber then commenced drawing a pistol, but the Mexican sprang from the mule and made his escape in the chaparral before they had time to fire at him. The two thieves took all that he left behind on the mule, together with the saddle and bridle. The are the same fellows no doubt, that chased the gentleman which we noticed last week.

September 30, 1854, Page 2.

DISTRICT COURT.

The District Court is still in session—Judge Devine presiding—and the criminal docket on hand. The three Mexicans, Antonio Gomez, M. de Luna and Ignacio Peres, who murdered Graham on the Medina, were found not guilty; Claudio Garcia, for abduction of slaves, was sentenced to the penitentiary for twelve years; Wm. Gibson, for assault with intent to kill , one year; A. Pena, same offence, four years; John Farrel, same offence, one year; John Monroe, grand larceny, one year; John Fisher, horse stealing, two years; José A. Garcia, larceny, one year; Francisco Menchelli, same offence, one year. There are two or more cases to be tried yet, all of which, will go to the Huntsville Hotel.

October 9, 1854, Page 2.

FRIDAY NIGHT.

On last Friday evening the Vauxhall Gardens were enlivened by a scene not common to this old rendezvous of the pleasure seeking Germans. Our Teutonic friends had a private ball at that place, and from the sweet music and splindid manner in which it was lighted up, it must have been a joyous affair.

Also in another quarter of our city there burst forth a sound of music and merry voices, a private party gotten up by some of our gents came off at the residence of Mr. Navarro on the east side of the San Pedro. There reigned supremely the fair, gay, dancing daughters of old Castile.

The Youth's Debating Club also held forth on this memorable night. Quite a large number of the members present, the society was reorganized on proper and different systems from the one it is heretofore carried on by, and bids fair of being an inexorable source of instructive enjoyment to our youth during the coming session.

We are also informed that a wedding came off some where or other. This is becoming such common occurances now-a-days, that we are getting used to them.

These cool, romantic, moon-light nights are productive of more ball, parties, and wedding than any other cause.

October 16, 1854, Page 2.

THE CITY.

Our city for the past week has been enlivened by several important changes. Marriages are common events, while congratulations on happy unions are passed around on every hand; such occurances make one believe that the happy time is coming when every man shall have his mate and society shall work on a different and happier plan, and mankind shall glide into the shades another world, without regret for his life in this.

New goods are daily arriving from below in proof of which, our readers may be informed through the medium of the Star.

Sickness is very rare and it is such an uncommon thing to see the funeral of some poor mortal winding along our streets to man's final resting place, the grave, that it cast a melancholy look over our city, when at other times it would be scarcely noticed.

Very sultry, cloudy weather, during thd last few days, sometimes we have mist, and sometimes rain, following which we have the hottest kind of weather. Roads are bad in every direction, and mails irregular.

Nothing but the ringing of the blacksmith's anvil and the clattering of the carpenter's hammer, greet our ears.

October 16, 1854, Page 2.

A WAGON LOAD OF CRIMINALS.

We witnessed a scene the other day that spoke volumes of meaning, and presented a striking picture of human depravity. On Thursday a wagon load of criminals, strongly guarded, started for Huntsville, (the fruits of the labors of Judge, Jury, and Lawyers, for five long tedious weeks,) there to toll away days and years, for the crimes probably of a minute, what a warning to all evil inclined individuals. As they neared the skirts of town, from some cause or other the wagon stoped, when a crowd of Mexicans gathered round some through curiosity and others for the purpose of taking leave of a friend; the inmates were principlly Mexicans, numbering ten. Among the spectators we noticed a shabby dressed woman with a babe in her arms and a little boy clinging to her hand, tears coursing down her cheeks a husband was one of the doomed. One Mexican was very liveley, shaking hands with every one, telling his countrymen that the poor Mexicans were sadly persecuted; we don't blame him, his sentence was twelve years hard labor; another of the inmates commenced quarreling with a person standing outside the wagon about some property belonging to him, which the individual had in his possession, but he was hurried away before he could justify his claims. As the vehicle moved away we walked off, thinking to ourselves, "the way of the transgressor is hard."

October 21, 1854, Page 2.

STABBED.
A Frenchman, by profession a fencing master, has been going about our city, sometimes with his sword buckled about him creating disturbances at the grogshops and other places of "worship," most of his time slightly inebriated, got into a row with a young German bar keeper in a grogshop near the market, on Friday night and vilely stabbed him while he was unsuspecting it, and fled endeavoring to conceal himself. The young man who was stabbed, is now lying at the ploint of death, with very feint hopes of his recovery; the Frenchman is now in jail, and if the statements are as we hear them, he may have to pass the remainder of his days within the walls of the Huntsville Penitentiary.

October 30, 1854, Page 2.

A small Mexican boy got shot accidentally in the hip on last Wednesday, on the following day his leg was amuptated by Dr. Cupples, aided by several other distinguished Medical Gentlemen; the patient died a short time after the operation was performed.

The bones of a very small child were found in one corner of an apartment of the Verimenda House which Mr. Casiano is having repaired, it was buried about half foot deep under the ground, it must have lain there for years from the appearance of the bones.

October 30, 1854, Page 2.

INDIANS! INDIANS!
AN UNFORTUNATE AFFAIR!!!

Lamochina Hill, Medina River, Oct. 30th, 1854.

Mr. H. Williams was killed by the Indians on Sunday last, he went to haul a barrel of water and his wife heard him holler and ran to see what was the matter, on arriving near by, she saw six Indians, who had just finished the brutal murder of her husband, and were on their way to her camp, where they took every thing they wanted, also her three children, after which they went a short distance off and sat down to eat; when she went to them and begged from them her two youngest children; the Indians took her oldest child Fanny, and the horse and left. Mrs. Williams in making her way to Caruther's got lost and did not find the house until day-light this morning.

Yours, F. J. Forest.

By the politeness of a friend we were handed the above letter for publication.

Can our citizens longer bear to hear the every day details of cold blooded Indian massacre within short distance of the most populous city in the State, almost within our very sight and hearing? If the widow's moan and orphan's cry is not sufficient to create some resentment from our citizens for the repeated wrongs they have received from the Indians, what is? The rangers are recalled, and where shall our frontiers look for defence against their depredations, if our citizens don't afford it?

There should be steps taken immediately to raise some men and go in pursuit of the Indians.

November 13, 1854, Page 2.

OUR THEATER.
Old Winter with its hoary locks is advancing in the distance, and already a change is coming over all, the maidens and the woods are donning darker dresses, and as the cold North whistles round the house and through the key hole, we begin to

contemplate and dream of winter pleasures, and how we will pass the long winter evenings. Visions of bright blazing fires and happy family groups gathered round them, engaged in reading book and papers, or telling stories pass before our minds; this is certainly one of the sweetest pleasures winter affords, but we live in a city, yes a city in the full sense of the word, and we want something that will stimulate, amuse, instruct and throw off the cares of business; this is embodied in our Little Theater. Here citizens can huddle together on winter evenings and truly enjoy themselves.

True it is not large and splendid, nor do the best actors in the world play in it, but it is small and comfortable and has first rate performers. This institution was got up by some of our most worthy and entergetic citizens for the city's benefit not to speculate or make money like the transient shows and circuses that sometimes visit our city, get all the money they can and *vamose*. What it makes it spends in our midst and for this and other reasons it certainly commands and deserves the patronage of all, which is all it asks for.

We consider it an ornament to our city and a necessary institution to society and therefore offer our might to its support.

November 21, 1854, Page 4.

NEW GOODS,
New Firm and New Stand!!
ON COMMERCE STREET, 3d DOOR from Main Plaza. CROSBY & Co., manufacturer, Wholesale and Retail Dealers in

New and Fashionable Stock,
Consisitng in part of Ladies, Misses and childrens Shoes, such a Gaiters, Buckskins, Ties and Slippers, Walking Shoes, etc. A full assoctment of

Men's Fine Calf Sewed Boots;
Also, Mens', Boys, and Youth' Calf Pegged Boots and brogans, Mens' patent leather, calf and cloth Congress shoes, both sewed and pegged. Also a good assortment of mens' hunting

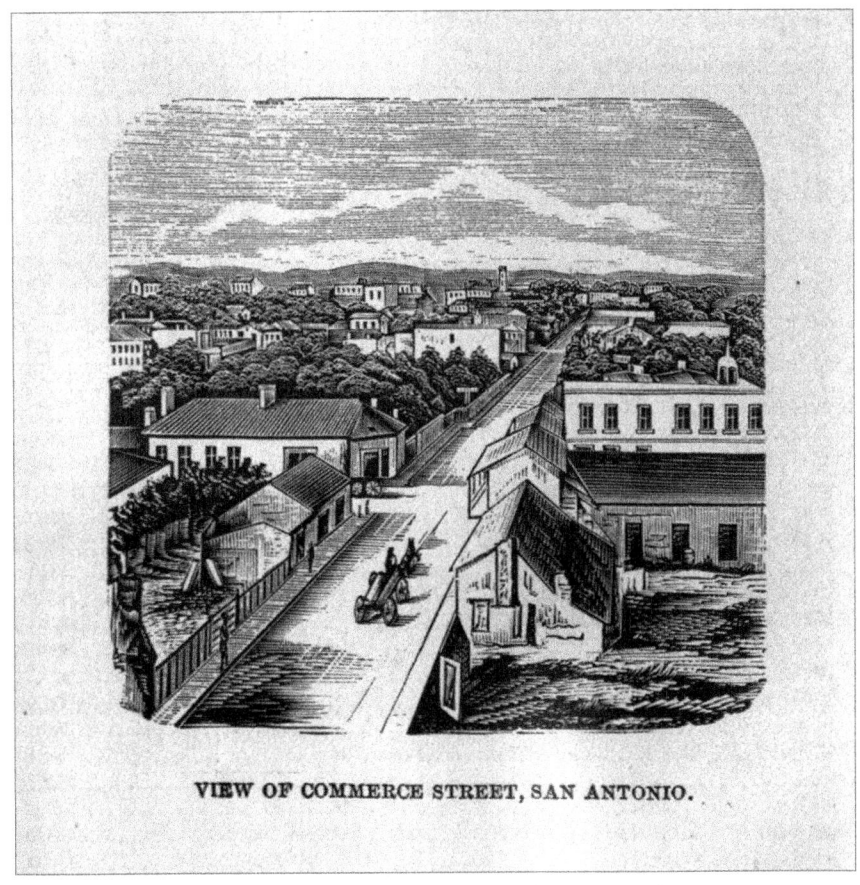

VIEW OF COMMERCE STREET, SAN ANTONIO.

An 1850s stylized image of one of the main thoroughfares in San Antonio shows a quiet but prosperous town. Daughters of the Republic of Texas Collection at Texas A&M University-San Antonio.

Water-Proof and Mud Boots,

And brogans, etc. A general assoctment of

Hats and Caps,

Consisting of Brown Beaver, Black Warrior, Hunting and WIDE AWAKE Hats and Hippodrome Capes, etc. etc., all of which will be offered low for CASH! The subscribers offer

Great Inducements to County Merchants,
Being connected with the largest Man[ufacturing]-establishments in the east, they flatter themselves that they can furnish them at a

Small Advance from New York Prices.
All persons are respectfully invited to

Call and Examine
Our stock of Goods, as we are confident that we can offer superior articles in our line, at cheap rates. CROSBY & Co.

December 4, 1854, Page 2.

THANKSGIVING DAY.
"Praise God from where all blessings flow."

On last Thursday, the 30th, the day appointed by the Governor to be kept with prayer and thanksgiving, was observed with proper solemnity by our citizens. Merchants closed their stores, by request of the Mayor; and the clerks took advantage of their leisure time to cut a dash on horseback; and in buggies, no doubt they would like thanksgiving days to come often. From outward appearances the day seemed to pass off pleasantly and quietly, every one seemed to feel the solemnity that attended the keeping of the day. Sumptuous dinners were served up and consumed by hungry beings, we hope with thankfulness, and that they felt their dependence on God for life and its necessities. Prayers ascended from the humble home circle, thanking God for the blessings he bestowed on them and their country and beseeching him to continue his goodness. But no churches were opened for divine worship, no pealing organs or choirs, sent forth anthems of praise to God, on that day.

This is one of the days that humblers men of every station to one common grade, the statesman and the common laborer feel alike their dependence on God.

December 4, 1854, Page 2.

A DESPERATE AFFAIR.

On last Friday morning an affair took place in our city that makes our blood run cold at the very thought of it. A man named Gillespie, who has been in our city a few days, being at a fandango on Thursday night, became rather boisterous when Mr. Stephens, the city marshall interrupted him and was compelled to draw a revolver to keep the peace. Next morning, (Friday) Mr. Gillespie assaulted Mr. Stephens in the market place striking him across the face with his revolver. Mr. Stephens obtaining the aid of Mr. Nicks proceeded immediately to arrest Mr. Gillespie, a scuffle took place in the vicinity of the Bowling Saloon, Mr. Gillespie drew his revolver and shot at Mr. Nicks hitting him in the arm, inflicting a severe wound, Mr. Nicks shot at Gillespie hitting him in the back, but the wound was slight. Mr. Stephens in attempting to arrest Gillespie was shot at by him and was compelled to shoot Gillespie in self defence, the ball entering his right breast killing him immediately. It is supposed that several shots were fired from the Bowling Saloon at Stephens and Nicks by the comrades of the deceased.

The above particulars attending this unfortunate affair, we receive from a reliable source, but we have heard it originated over a game of cards, but how true it may be we know not, and it matters little. Mrs. Stephens and Nicks were examined before a court of justice and cleared.

We hope our city will soon take measures to prevent these tragical scenes. An ordinance preventing the wearing of fire arms about the street should be enacted and enforced; the ordinance now in existence preventing indigence should be strictly enforced; the late liquor law, which by trial has been found applicable, should be daily enforced; until every grog shop the originators of all crime, was closed. Until this is done we can expect no reform.

It is a mistake about there being shots fired from Bowling Saloon.

December 4, 1854, Page 2.

FROM THE RANGERS.

Mr. William Pratt came in from the Ranging camp on Wednesday. He brings the annexed news.

Capt. Travis returned from his scout eight days since, without having discovered any Indians.

David Dean, a member of Capt. Travis' company killed Mr. Kirk, a messmate of his, on Monday evening last in Fredericksburg. The murder was dastard and cold-blooded. He managed to disarm Kirk and then blew his brains out. The exertion of Capt. Travis alone, saved him from the summary vengeance by the men. The excitement was intense, but was happily restrained. Dean was in custody—strictly guarded by fifteen men. His Committing trial was to take place on Thursday.

Capt. Walker after returning from the San Saba, made a reconnaissance on the head of the Guadalupe. He encountered a party of Indians—killed several and recaptured nineteen American horses. The particulars of the engagement were not given to Mr. Pratt.

Capt. Henry is still out. He is reported to have drawn supplies for a month and purposes finding Indians if possible.

Col. Waite was in the vicinity, and the companies of Walker, Travis, Henry and Rogers were to have mustered into the United States service Thursday. Two of the companies are to be sent to Fort Clarke and to Fort Chadbourne.—*Austin Times*.

December 11, 1854, Page 2.

Captains Walker's, Roger's and Henry's companies of Rangers are to be mustered into service in our city. These rangers are all Americans, healthy, fine looking men, well mounted and equipped, a more formidable and gallant looking set of men we never saw before; they are able to keep the Indians in subjection, but what can they do when they are placed away out of ther reach of the Indians? General Smith is determined they shall do no good by placing them on the outer skirts of Texas, hundreds of miles from here, when massacres and horse thieving have been commited within the last month twenty and thirty miles from our city.

December 16, 1854, Page 2.

GAMBLING HOUSES.

We have in our city establishments that will truly come under the above caption. Yes these hellish holes have a place within the very heart of our city, and send forth a stream of poisonous influence upon the honest, industrious and moral world around. Crime raises it fiendish head above the gaming tables, and men destitute of every little feeling and sentiment, pledge themselves to Mamon, their God. Here the young and promising are hurled headlong into the grave of poverty and degradation. Here religion, morality and honor find a common grave. Yes they are [word unclear] in a community, poisoning, corupting and destroying all that is good.

We visited one of these establishments not long since, and there saw gambling carried on in all its hideous forms. In one room was a faro bank, which seemed to be the head and principal gambling stand of all; on a table was a glittering pile of gold and silver we suppose over a thousand dollars as an enticement to the foolish better who in hopes of betting his fortune looses his all, around this table was gathered a crowd of anxious men. In other apartments there were different species of gambling, the roulet, monte bank and chuchage[?] that caught all the same change that came along.

We do not wish to injure any man's business or profession, but professing to be an advocate of morality, and devoted to the true welfare of society, we feel in duty bound to denouce such establishments.

Gambling houses are the abodes of prostitutes and swindlers, and if it be possible, eradicate them from our and every community.

U.S. Inspector General's Inspection Report, 1856

INTRODUCTION TO DOCUMENT

San Antonio continued to serve the United States military as a staging area as it had done under the Spanish, Mexican, and Texian forces. Its location now made it a gateway to the west as the U.S. Army pushed a second line of forts hundreds of miles out into what was traditionally the Comanche home range. To support these forts, supplies were brought to San Antonio from the coast and housed at the Alamo. From there they were again loaded onto wagons and escorted to their final destination as places like Fort Inge, Fort McKavett, Fort Lancaster, Fort Clark, and various other forts and temporary camps.

DOCUMENT[41]

"It is beyond dispute that San Antonio is the best position for the Head Quarters of this Department being the most central and convenient to all the other posts.... From this depot all posts beyond San Antonio are readily supplied."

>Colonel J. K. F. Mansfield's Report of the Inspection of the Department of Texas in 1856.

EARLY STATEHOOD

DOCUMENT[42]

"From its resources and position in regard to the Rio Grande and Indian frontiers, [San Antonio] possesses advantages which seem to point it out as the proper place for Department Head Quarters and the offices of the Chiefs of the several branches of the Staff attached thereto."

"W. G. Freeman's Report on the Eighth Military Department."

"This branch of the San Antonio Depot, now and for some time past under the charge of Bvt. Maj. James Belger, Asst. Quarter master, occupies the extensive pile known as the 'Alamo buildings,' and an adjoining lot of ground. The title to the former is in dispute, but the property was leased from Bishop Odin of the Roman Catholic Church, at a rent of $150 per month, January 1, 1850, to continue in force during the pleasure of the United States; when given up, the improvements to revert to the lessor. The lot is rented from S. A. Maverick of San Antonio, at $20 per month, for ten years from Oct. 1, 1851, 'should the Government require it that length of time.' The terms of these two leases are considered highly favorable. The buildings and premises are admirably adapted to their purposes; the storage for supplies is ample and secure, and by the workshops, stables, storerooms and offices, being thus brought together, a stricter vigilance can be exercised over the public interests by the officer in charge (whose own residence adjoins the establishment) than it would be possible for him to exert under a less compact arrangement."

"W. G. Freeman's Report on the Eighth Military Department."

Frederick Law Olmstead on San Antonio, ca. 1857

INTRODUCTION TO DOCUMENT

Frederick Law Olmstead is best known as the landscape architect who designed New York City's Central Park. During the 1850s, though, Olmstead made several journeys throughout the American South which he chronicled in a number of books. Like other authors before him, he introduced his reader to a world beyond their communities that many would never visit. In A *Journey Through Texas*, Olmstead gave his impressions of San Antonio, which the New England intellectual found picturesque but somewhat lacking in refinement.

DOCUMENT[43]

The town of San Antonio was founded in 1730 by a colony of twelve families of pure Spanish blood, from the Canary islands. The names of the settlers are perpetuated to this day, by existing families, which have descended from each, such as Garcia, Flores, Navarro, Garza, Yturri, Rodriquez. The original mission and fort of San Antonio de Valero dates from 1715, when Spain established her occupancy of Texas.

THE MISSIONS.
Not far from the city, along the river, are these celebrated religious establishments. They are of a similar character to the many scattered here and there over the plains

of Northern Mexico and California, and bear a solid testimony to the strangely patient courage and zeal of the old Spanish fathers. They pushed off alone into the heart of a savage and unknown country, converted the cruel brutes that occupied it, not only to nominal Christianity, but to actual hard labor, and persuaded and compelled them to construct these ponderous but rudely splendid edifices, serving, at the same time, for the glory of the faith, and for the defense of the faithful.

The Alamo was one of the earliest of these establishments. It is now within the town, and in extent, probably, a mere wreck of its former grandeur. It consists of a few irregular stuccoed buildings, huddled against the old church, in a large court surrounded by a rude wall; the whole used as an arsenal by the U. S. quartermaster. The church-door opens on the square, and is meagerly decorated by stucco mouldings, all hacked and battered in the battles it has seen. Since the heroic defense of Travis and his handful of men, in '36, it has been a monument, not so much to faith as to courage.

The Mission of Concepcion is not far from the town, upon the left of the river. Further down are three others, San Juan, San José, and La Espada. On one of them is said to have been visible, not long ago, the date, "1725." They are in different stages of decay, but all are real ruins, beyond any connection with the present—weird remains out of the silent past.

They are of various magnificence, but all upon a common model, and of the same materials—rough blocks of limestone, cemented with a strong gray stucco. Each has its church, its convent, or celled house for the fathers, and its farm-buildings, arranged around a large court, entered only at a single point. Surrounding each was a large farm, irrigated at a great outlay of labor by aqueducts from the river.

The decorations of the doors and windows may be still examined. They are of stucco, and are rude heads of saints, and mouldings, usually without grace, corresponding to those described as at present occupying similar positions in Mexican churches. One of the missions is a complete ruin, the others afford shelter to Mexican occupants, who ply their trades, and herd their cattle and sheep in the old cells and courts. Many is the picturesque sketch offered to the pencil by such intrusion upon falling dome, tower, and cloister.

THE ENVIRONS.

The system of aqueducts, for artificial irrigation, extends for many miles around San Antonio, and affords some justification for the Mexican tradition, that the town, not long ago, contained a very much larger population. Most of these lived by agriculture, returning at evening to a crowded home in the city. These water-courses still retain their old Spanish name, "acequias." A large part of them are abandoned, but in the immediate neighborhood of the city they are still in use, so that every garden-patch may be flowed at will.

In the outskirts of the town are many good residences, recently erected by Americans. They are mostly of the creamy limestone, which is found in abundance nearby. It is of a very agreeable shade, readily sawed and cut, sufficiently durable, and can be procured at a moderate cost. When the grounds around them shall have been put in correspondence with the style of these houses, they will make enviable homes.

THE SAN ANTONIO SPRING.

There are, besides the missions, several pleasant points for excursions in the neighborhood, particularly those to the San Antonio and San Pedro Springs. The latter is a wooded spot of great beauty, but a mile or two from the town, and boasts a restaurant and beer-garden beyond its natural attractions. The San Antonio Spring may be classed as of the first water among the gems of the natural world. The whole river gushes up in one sparkling burst from the earth. It has all the beautiful accompaniments of a smaller spring, moss, pebbles, seclusion, sparkling sunbeams, and dense overhanging luxuriant foliage. The effect is overpowering. It is beyond your possible conceptions of a spring. You cannot believe your eyes, and almost shrink from sudden metamorphosis by invaded nymphdom.

BATHING.

The temperature of the river is of just that agreeable elevation that makes you loth to leave a bath, and the color is the ideal blue. Few cities have such a luxury. It remains throughout the year without perceptible change of temperature, and never varies in height or volume. The streets are laid out in such a way that a great number of houses have a garden extending to the bank, and so a bathing-house, which is in constant use. The Mexicans seem half the time about the water. Their plump women, especially, are excellent swimmers, and fond of displaying their luxurious buoyancy. The fall of the river is such as to furnish abundant water-power, which is now used but for a single corn-mill. Several springs add their current to its volume above the town, and that from the San Pedro below. It unites, near the Gulf, with the Guadalupe, and empties into Espiritu Santo Bay, watering a rich, and, as yet, but little-settled country.

The soil, in the neighborhood of the city, is heavy, and sometimes mixed with drifts of limestone pebbles, and deposits of shell, but is everywhere black, and appears of inexhaustible fertility, if well cultivated and supplied with moisture. The market-gardens, belonging to Germans, which we saw later in the season, are most luxuriant. The prices of milk, butter, and vegetables are very high, and the gains of the small German market-farmers must be rapidly accumulating.

TOWN LIFE.

The street-life of San Antonio is more varied than might be supposed. Hardly a day passes without some noise. If there be no personal affray to arouse talk, there is some Government train to be seen, with its hundred of mules, on its way from the coast to a fort above; or a Mexican ox-train from the coast, with an interesting supply of ice, or flour, or matches, or of whatever the shops find themselves short. A Government express clatters off, or news arrives from some exposed outpost, or from New Mexico. An Indian in his finery appears on a shaggy horse, in search of blankets, powder, and ball. Or at the least, a stagecoach with the "States," or the Austin, mail, rolls into the plaza and discharges its load of passengers and newspapers.

The street affrays are numerous and characteristic. I have seen, for a year or more, a San Antonio weekly, and hardly a number fails to have its fight or its murder. More often than otherwise, the parties meet upon the plaza by chance, and each, on catching sight of his enemy, draws a revolver, and fires away. As the actors are under more or less excitement, their aim is not apt to be of the most careful and sure, consequently it is, not seldom, the passers-by who suffer. Sometimes it is a young man at a quiet dinner in a restaurant, who receives a ball in the head; sometimes an old negro woman, returning from market, who gets winged. After disposing of all their lead, the parties close, to try their steel, but as this species of metallic amusement is

EARLY STATEHOOD

A typical cantina in early San Antonio. Daughters of the Republic of Texas Collection at Texas A&M University-San Antonio.

less popular, they generally contrive to be separated ("Hold me! Hold me!") by friends before the wounds are mortal. If neither is seriously injured, they are brought to drink together on the following day, and the town waits for the next excitement.

Where borderers and idle soldiers are hanging about drinking places, and where different races mingle on unequal terms, assassinations must be expected. Murders, from avarice or revenge, are common here. Most are charged upon the Mexicans, whose passionate motives are not rare, and to whom escape over the border is easiest and most natural.

The town amusements of a less exciting character are not many. There is a permanent company of Mexican mountebanks, who give performances of agility and buffoonery two or three times a week, parading, before night, in their spangled tights with drum and trombone through the principal streets. They draw a crowd of whatever little Mexicans can get adrift, and this attracts a few sellers of whisky, *tortillas,* and *tamaules* (corn slap-jacks and hashed meat in corn-shucks), all by the light of torches making a ruddily picturesque evening group.

The more grave Americans are served with tragedy by a thin local company, who are death on horrors and despair, long rapiers, and well oiled hair, and for lack of a better place to flirt with passing officers, the city belles may sometimes be seen looking on. The national background of peanuts and yells, is not, of course, wanting.

A day or two after our arrival, there was the hanging of a Mexican. The whole population left the town to see. Family parties, including the grandmother and the little negroes, came from all the plantations and farms within reach, and little ones were held up high to get their share of warning. The Mexicans looked on imperturbable.

San Antonio, excluding Galveston, is much the largest city of Texas. After the Revolution, it was half deserted by its Mexican population, who did not care to come under Anglo-Saxon rule. Since then its growth has been rapid and steady. At the census of 1850, it numbered 3,500; in 1853, its population was 6,000; and in 1856, it is estimated at 10,500. Of these, about 4,000 are Mexicans, 3,000 Germans, and 3,500 Americans. The money-capital is in the hands of the Americans, as well as the officers and the Government. Most of the mechanics and the smaller shopkeepers are German. The Mexicans appear to have almost no other business than that of carting goods. Almost the entire transportation of the country is carried on by them, with oxen and two-wheeled carts. Some of them have small shops, for the supply of their own countrymen, and some live upon the produce of farms and cattle-ranches owned in the neighborhood. Their livelihood is, for the most part, exceedingly meagre, made up chiefly of corn and beans.

Inspector General Report for San Antonio in 1861

INTRODUCTION TO DOCUMENT

By 1861 San Antonio was at the center of an extended network system that forwarded supplies, munitions, and men to the U.S. Army forts and camps pushing the frontier line west. A view of the U.S. Army's operation in San Antonio was provided by Colonel Joseph K. F. Mansfield, an inspector who toured the department just before the outbreak of the Civil War. Texas had already seceded and state officials had seized the federal installations in San Antonio by the time he submitted his report.

DOCUMENT[44]

Col. Joseph K. F. Mansfield
Inspector General
San Antonio, Texas
February 22, 1861

Quartermaster Department

Maj. David H. Vinton assumed command as chief of this department, 5th Jan. 1857, when he relieved Bvt. Lt. Col. A. C. Myers. He supplies all the posts of this department with funds & quartermaster stores either directly or indirectly thro' the various subordinates. There is an officer at each military post in Texas acting as assistant quartermaster. All contracts are approved or made by him. He occupies 1 1/2 rooms in the Brick Block for offices and keeps two clerks at 100 & 75 dolls per month respectively, and one messenger at 25 dolls, and the three receive in addition a ration each. His books, papers, & accounts are all properly kept, and duly forwarded. There was due the U.S. on the 31st last, 30,615.29 dolls, and due at date, 29,609.29 dolls. Of this sum 14,634.5 dolls is in Assistant Treasury at N. Orleans & 13,691.64 dolls in the Assist. Treasury at New York & 23,303.13 dolls in cash.

His expenditures for the year 1860 amounted to 531,673.32 dolls. This almount includes the transfers of funds to subordinates of the department, as the amount actually disbursed by him was 4787.38 dolls in that period.

In this office is kept the books of the estimates for clothing, requisitions, inspections, & boards of surveys, abstracts, accounts & summary statements of subordinate posts, and the contracts for transportation & for rents, &c, &c, throughout the Department of Texas.

It appears that a new system for transporting supplies has been adopted, and a new contract entered into accordingly. The depot at Indianola has been broken up and the property ordered to be sold and the government supplies are all received under the new contract (with James Duff) at New Orleans for the year 1861 and shipped to Indianola & transported by him to all the posts at the following rates, to wit. From N. Orleans to Indianola, 87 cents the barrel of 5 cubic feet and 75 cts. for 100 lbs. for 100 miles to San Antonio. Thence to Forts Inge, Clark, Wood, Hudson, Duncan, Lancaster, Stockton, Verde, Mason, Chadbourne, Colorado, Cooper, 92 cts. for 100 lbs. for 100 miles. Thence to Forts Davis, &c, 100 cts. For 100 lbs. for 100 miles. Thence Forts Quitman, Bliss, Fillmore, 122 cts. for 100 lbs. for 100 miles. The contractor to receive on one days notice to San Antonio not exceeding 20,000 lbs. & an 10 days notice not exceeding 200,000 lbs., & 20 days notice not exceeding 500,000 lbs. He is to receive and store at Indianola all articles for which he is to be paid 17 cts. The barrel of 5 cubic feet, and to keep at Indianola all supplies and feed & forage sufficient to meet the wants of the quartermaster's department and to be paid the market price for them. In the transportation ox teams are to make 12 miles a day and mules 18 miles a day.

The amount paid to 13 individuals in San Antonio for rent for building accounts to 1038 dolls per month, or to 12,436 dolls per annum. Of this 7500 is paid to Vance & Brother for the use of the Brick Block, &c, of a square. I think about 1500 dolls too much is paid to this concern. Six thousand per annum would pay them well in my opinion. There is also 9060 dolls per annum paid for the hire of sites for military posts to 13 individuals for land in this state, that otherwise would not yield anything at all. Of this amount, a new lease was made, 30th April 1860, with Geo. T. Howard for land at the rate of 600 dolls per annum for a new post near Fort Inge which should never be built for a school of artillery practice. This I consider a superfluity & should be cut off'.

A subordinate branch of this department is here under the command of Capt. A. W. Reynolds, assistant quartermaster. This is indispensable for the current service. Capt. Reynolds relieved Capt. E. E. McClean on 1st April 1860 in this duty. The means of transportation, and the change of the quartermaster's workshops, &c, are under his immediate orders. He occupies the building & locality called the Alamo. The first floor of the Alamo is used as a granary and the second floor by the military store keeper (see plan herewith*). The building fronting the common is two stories and used for offices, storerooms, packing rooms, saddler's shop, harness room, & wagon shed. On the east side of the street is the corral for wagons & the carpenter's shop and smith's shop & hay yard. About 4 miles out of the city on the river is another corral where all the supernumerary trains, g[oing] & c[oming], not in use are kept & the mules grazed. These arrangements seem to be all proper & correct.

There are the following persons employed, one clerk at 91.66 dolls, 1 at 83.33 dolls per month, 1 store-keeper 75 dolls per month, 1 assistant military store-keeper at 66.66 dolls per month, 1 messenger at 25 dolls per month, 4 store-house laborers at 25 dolls, 5 wheelwrights one at 50 dolls & 4 at 40 dolls per month, 3 smiths at 50, 40, & 35 dolls per month, 3 saddlers at 50, 45 & 40 dolls per month, 1 yard master at 40 dolls per month , 3 watchmen at 18 dolls per month, 1 cook for mechanics & teamsters at 18 dolls per month, 1 overseer in charge of all the mules at the corral at 40 dolls per month, 3 wagon masters at 58.60 dolls per month, 72 teamsters at 20 dolls per month, 1 cart driver & 9 laborers & ostlers [stablemen] at 18 dolls per month, 1 chief herder at 35 dolls per month, 12 herders at 18 dolls per month, 1 forage master at 58.60

per month. The above named employees, with the exception of the assistant military store-keeper & the wagon masters, all receive a ration each.

One wagon & forage master appointed by the quartermaster genl. under the law of Congress at 89.54 dolls per month. One express man to Camp Colorado with the mail & one wagon & two mules per contract 248.95 dolls per month. This contract is not to be renewed unless ordered.

He keeps 1 horse, 820 mules, 192 wagons, 1 hospital ambulance, 3 carts, 2 spring wagons.

Under the present contract for forwarding supplies to the posts, the number of employees here seem to me unnecessarily large. It appears to me the assistant mail store keeper might be dispensed with, also 2 wheelwrights, 1 smith, 1 saddler, 5 laborers & ostlers [stablemen] & 6 herders, as the teamsters should herd the animals & the duty of forage & yard master might I think be done by one person. The number of mules & teamsters appear to me very large, as the posts have their regular teams, & there is no great change of troops contemplated.

Capt. Reynold's books & records are all in order and his quarterly returns of property to the 30th Sept. have been forwarded & the like returns of the 31st Dec. will be forwarded within a month. The summary statement & all monthly papers to the 31st Dec. have been forwarded, showed a balance due the U.S. of 4585.72 dolls at that date. And his quarterly accounts to the 31st Dec. will be forwarded to the 25th instant. He received from Major Vinton in January, 9539.35 dolls & expended in January, 8743.05 dolls, leaving a balance due the U.S. at date, 5382.02 dolls. Of this amount there is in the Assistant treasury, New York 139.85 dolls and in the Assist. Quartermaster Lieut. M. L. Davis on the Assist Treasury of New Orleans, 904.97 dolls, and in a check of Paymaster Van Ness, 5.32 dolls. The residue, 4317.38 dolls, was in cash, which was counted out of several little bags in his safe in small amounts. He pays for hay 12.47 dolls the ton and has about 60 tons on hand, 2 dolls the bushel for corn of which he has about 2090 bushels on hand.

Connected with this department is the military store keeper R. M. Potter.** He has charge of the camp & garrison & clothing stores & occupies the second story of the Alamo and two store rooms on the square of the Brick Block. These store rooms are generally full and contain at least one year's supply for five regiments. His books are properly kept & his property returns to the 31st Dec. made out complete for forwarding except the fair copy.

A large amount of property having been destroyed by fire not long since. The department is now provided with a fire engine.

*No plan included with report.

**Reuben Marmaduke Potter published the first history of the Alamo battle in 1860 entitled The Fall of the Alamo.

PART 5: SAN ANTONIO IN THE CIVIL WAR

General Twiggs Surrenders San Antonio to the State of Texas, 1861

INTRODUCTION TO DOCUMENT

By 1861, Texas had amassed a variety of grievances with the national government in addition to the contentious issue of slavery. Some Texans were still vexed over what they perceived as the forced cession of a large section of New Mexico claimed by the Republic of Texas to help push through the Compromise of 1850. Additionally, federal army troops stationed along two lines of forts had failed to protect settlers on the frontier from Comanche raiding parties. More recently, a candidate—Abraham Lincoln—had been elected president of the United States when his name had not even appeared on ballots in Texas or other southern states. Secession seemed an action that would restore control of their affairs. For many Texans initially, secession promised to revive Mirabeau B. Lamar's vision of a great western empire stretching clear to the Pacific Ocean.

South Carolina's December announcement that it had left the Union increased Texas secessionist sentiment. To the displeasure of the state's secessionists, Governor Sam Houston, who strongly opposed the idea, refused to call the state legislature into session hoping cooler heads would prevail. The legislators, however, backed the plan to hold a session convention to determine the will of the state's citizens. Delegates to the meeting, held January 28–February 1, 1861, voted 166 to 8 in favor of disunion. Although the question still had to be presented to the public in a plebiscite, Texas's course was set.

The secession of Texas in 1861 was felt first in San Antonio. This image shows Texas state troops occupying the main plaza. Daughters of the Republic of Texas Collection at Texas A&M University-San Antonio.

State officials immediate turned their attention to the large number of federal forts and their garrisons located throughout Texas. Negotiations were begun with the commander of the military district comprising Texas, Major General David E. Twiggs, about plans for his troops to leave the state. Additionally, Texas officials demanded that Twiggs turn over all public property managed by the army to the state. After Samuel A. Maverick, acting in the role of commissioner, reported that Twiggs appeared to be delaying the transfer of power, the state's newly formed Committee of Public Safety asked three well-known veterans of the former republic's conflicts—Benjamin McCulloch, Henry McCulloch, and John S. Ford—to raise a volunteer force to seize San Antonio. As the headquarters of the military district, its warehouses and arsenal were too important a prize to let slip away. One thousand volunteers reportedly followed the McCulloch brothers and "Rip" Ford into town early on the morning of February 16. Later that day federal forces surrendered the town in what became known as Twiggs's Surrender.

Twiggs, a Georgian and a national hero for his service in Florida against the Seminole Indians and in the battles in Mexico, stated publicly and privately that he turned over the town without a fight because he could not bring himself to shed the blood of fellow Americans. In a move mirroring Cos's surrender of the town in 1835, Twiggs's men were allowed to march away under arms. The general resigned his commission after George left the Union and was award a generalship in the Confederate Army.

DOCUMENT[45]

Headquarters Department of Texas,
San Antonio, Texas, February 18, 1861.

GENTLEMEN: Your communication of the 17th instant, which you say is a reply to mine written yesterday, the 17th instant, was received last night. I consent to the conditions that the troops shall leave Texas by the way of the coast, with the provision expressed in my communication of yesterday.

As to the condition of surrendering the guns of the light batteries, that, you must see, would be an act which would cast a lasting disgrace upon the arms of the United States, and under no circumstances can I believe that the State of Texas would demand such a sacrifice at my hands, and more particularly so, after I have yielded so much to meet what I deemed to be due to the State, and to avoid any unnecessary collision between the Federal and State troops. In this view of the case, I am sure you will not insist in a demand which, you must see, I am not at liberty to grant.

Very respectfully, your obedient servant,

D. E. TWIGGS,
Brevet Major-General, U. S. Army, Comdg. Dept.
Messers. Thos. J. Devine,
S. A. Maverick,
P. N. Luckett,
Commissioners on behalf of the Convention of the People of Texas.

SAN ANTONIO, *February 18, 1861.*

SIR: In reply to your communication of this date, we have to say that we accept the terms therein stated, viz, that the two batteries of light artillery, with the arms for the infantry and cavalry, shall be *retained* by the troops under your command; all other public property, as set forth in our previous communications, to be delivered up to agents authorized to receive it.

We remain, respectfully, your obedient servants,

Thos. J. Devine,
S. A. Maverick.
P. N. Luckett,
Commissioners on behalf of the Convention of the People of Texas.

CAMP SAN PEDRO, *February 23, 1861.*

COLONEL: In compliance with instruction that I should report such information as I possess on the subject of the events which transpired in San Antonio on the 16th instant, I have the honor to state as follows:

For several days previous to the 16th there were many rumors of the formation of forces to take possession of the public property at the depots. They were not generally credited until the 14th, when more reliable information was received that a strong force of citizens was collecting from the counties to the east and northeast. This was confirmed on the 15th, and it was general understood that several hundred men would enter the city the next morning. The orders given to the guard were, that they should not resist a large organized force, but to preserve the public property from depredations by individuals or any mob, as usual. The troops consisted of Company I of the First, and A of the Eighth Infantry, were to form at quarters and await further orders in case of the approach of any considerable force.

At fifteen minutes of 4 o'clock on the morning of the 16th, I received a message from the officer of the day that a large armed force was entering the city. Repairing to my company quarters, a low, one-story building, marked B on the accompanying plot,* [*plot omitted] situated in the yard used as a depot for ordinance, the men were formed, and ordered to remain at their quarters. I then proceeded to the Army offices in the building marked A, where officers were awaiting developments rather than orders, it being understood that no resistance would be made. A few minutes after, some eighty armed citizens took position across the street at point C, and another eighty in the lot at H. Returning towards my company quarters, I found a strong party on the street leading to the plaza, some of them ascending the stairs to the second story of the ordinance building, D. Approaching them, I was accosted by two persons, who seemed surprised at being observed. One of them was announced as Colonel McCulloch. I informed him that the house on the corner was occupied by soldiers. He said he could not help that. I asked, perhaps you will tell me what you intend to do, to which he replied that his force was in commanding positions, and would take possession of all the public property, after which, if anything was wanted, it would have to be asked of the commissioners, and that the persons of my men were secure, and would not be molested. During the conversation he gave me to understand that the force on the east side of the river served to prevent my company and that of the First Infantry at F from uniting. In the mean time his people were mounting to the roof of the ordinance building, of the house adjoining on the south, and of the Masonic Hall at G. About one hour after this conversation, having heard that it was intended to demand the arms in the hands of our men, I sought Colonel McCulloch, and asked him if I had understood him rightly that the persons of the soldiers would not be molested. He answered, "Yes." I stated that they would consider their persons very much molested if their arms were interfered with. He replied, "That is a question for the commissioners to determine." I added that such an attempt would be followed by serious consequences, which would be painful to all concerned, and suggested that he would confer with his commissioners on the subject if he had not been instructed upon it. He signified his intention to obey their instructions, whatever they might be, at any cost, and added: "Some of you had better arrange this matter quickly, or my men will do it for you," thus intimating that they might not be controlled.

Near 7 o'clock Colonel McCulloch came to me with a letter, addressed to the commander of the Department of Texas. I informed him that I was not that officer, and referred him to you as commanding the post.

At 10 o'clock I particularly reported the situation of my company, in contracted quarters, and so completely surrounded and commanded by the citizens' force that no man could move without having several hundred guns pointed at him, at the options of that force, and that they had been in this situation nearly six hours. You notified the department commander of this. It seems to be of consequence, in yielding to the Texas commissioners, that *these two companies* should leave the State "by the way of the coast." On this point you are better informed than I am; my knowledge of it is incomplete. I understood, however, that our troops would not be permitted to leave their quarters if this demand was not acceded to, and that it was the one measure to restore quiet.

About 11 o'clock the order was given to prepare to go into camp, and at 3 p.m. the two companies marched out of the city, and formed their camp at this place [San Pedro Springs].

I am, very respectfully, your obedient servant,

LARKIN SMITH
Major by Brevet, Captain, Eighth Infantry
Lieut. Col. WILLIAM HOFFMAN.
Eight Infantry, Commanding San Antonio Barracks.

Federal Surrender of San Antonio from a Texan's View, 1861

INTRODUCTION TO DOCUMENT

Texans had been ready to march on the federal facilities in December 1860 but had to wait until state officials were prepared to act. On February 3, 1861, the Committee Public Safety commissioned Ben McCulloch, a hero of the Mexican War and strong advocate of frontier defense, to raise a force to seize the Alamo and other properties occupied by the U.S. Army if necessary. McCulloch's force ultimately numbered about one thousand Texan secessionists who were organized into military companies. Although they lacked uniforms and carried an assortment of arms, McCulloch's force rode into town under the cover of darkness and took up positions commanding the federal facilities.

Twenty-two-year old Morgan Wolfe Merrick, a immigrant whose family arrived in San Antonio in 1851, participated in the takeover of federal facilities. Although initially from the North, Merrick had joined the local castle or lodge of the Knights of the Golden Circle. Although an eclectic speller, Merrick nevertheless recorded his personal experience of Twiggs's Surrender.

DOCUMENT[46]

Feb. 1861. The Castle council [of the Knights of the Golden Circle] at their military meeting appointed a committee of two, Dr. Geo. Cupples & Judge Jacob Welder, to wait on Genl Twigs, Comd of U.S. troops of the Dept or Texas and request of him arms and accouterments for one company of infantry. On visiting Genl Twigs and making known their business; the Gnl granted them their request and gave them an order on the ordnance Dept.

The Ordinance Officer Capt Whightly on receiving the order, wanted the Comt to receive a lot of old obsolete guns that had been used in the Mexican war. Which they promptly refused to receive, and the Comt returned to Gnl Twigs and reported the case. The Genl then issued an order to the Ordinance Officer to issue the new Spring Field Rifle with everything compleat which was promptly done. And turned over to me as Ordinance Officer of the K.G.C. I received them at a place on Market St. at a little house formerly occupied by Braden as a Bakery, next to the Hotel, the hall of which the K.G.C. used as a lodge room & drill hall.

And it was in this hall on the night of Feb 15th. that the company went into actual service. There was a detail made out for that night and a volunteer squad to keep an Eye on the U.S. soldiers Quarters and their movements.

I had selected the verimendi hous for my post, as from the roof I could have a commanding view of the arsenal grounds. The U.S. Soldiers were prepared for an atacke and on the defensive. The rumors that had been going the rounds had caused them to prepare for emergency as they had about one or two milion in government property to look after and rumor had a large body of Texans were coming to seize all government property.

It is tru they were coming to tak possession peacefully if possible, by forse if necessary. Our one company could not have taken the place alone. It is true there was a Militia company here, but it was generally believed they were Unionists. And I don't know now where they stood on the question.

Well as I mentioned before I took my stand on the verimendi house after dark sometime. it was not so dark but I could look down on the arsenal grounds and see what was going on. They had placed a howitzer in position to cover the bridg that spans the river at the N.E. corner of the arsinal yard and one at the big gate or main entrance, both guns were charged & the [port] fires were in readiness and the sentinal's walking their beats by them. This looked very much like business.

Well every thing went smoothly, I had been down to the hall several times during the night. It was now about 2 A.M. when I got back to my place on the roof, and had been sitting there some time when I herd the tramp of cavalry along Main St. moving in the direction of the plaza. out side of the sound of the horses feet I could here nothing they were moving quietly. I was about going down to the hall again, when a slight nois attracted my attention to the top of the arsenal building where against the Star lit sky I could see figures in a stooping posture gliding along to the rear of the building, a place that would controle the arsenal yard, by whoever occupied it. now the U.S. soldiers were Quartered on the lower floor, and from the inside had access to the roof. Now the question in my mind was, are they taking position? Or has our people found away by means of laders to occupy the place, if so the must have done their work very nice, for I have heard no nois apart from that which called my attention to the roof. Hence I concluded it was those occupying the building, and was on the point of going to report when a member of the company Max Niemdorff came up to me. I was about to tell him what was taking place: That is alright said he, those are our men. I came up to tell you, and more by day light we will have them cut off from each other that is those occupying ther Vance property on the E. side of the river. the Alamo & the Vance house are already surrounded. McCullough & Baylor have a larg force in town. This was about 4 A.M. Max returned to the hall. Shortly after his going, Jack Barkeeper for Tager who kept a saloon in the Verimendi House, opened up and stated a fire, and as I had left my coat at the hall and being out all night I felt chilly so I go over and takes a seat on the chimney with my legs hanging down inside; and was in this position when Genl Ben McClloch stuck his head over the parapet. I droped my pistol on him, Halt, against orders for anyone to come up! All right. Sir! good boy I'll go see the officer of the day. by this time, the cook for the U.S. soldier had started his fire in the arsenal yard right against the North Wall of the Verimendi House.

I sneeked over to that side to take a peep. The cook was a big Jolly Irishman. he had not noticed me looking down on him. I droped a peble into the camp kettle he was making coffee in. He jerked his head up, Exclaiming! Good mor'n! Son Good morn! ye must be cauld up thare? Somewhat said I! Would yes have a pot of coffee, I don't know, said he. It will warm yes up. All right said I (at the same time thinking my God shoot a man that treats you like that) He went and brought a string fastened one end to a quart cup, the other end to a stone and cast it up. I pulled up the coffee, and as I did, he threw up a loaf of bread. Remarking, if they go to shooting niver ye moind them, drink your coffee in pace, it is no manner of Gentlemen that would be enterrupting a gentlemen when he do be taken his ta! I'll keep my eye on yes that no haram comes to yes.

All right said I. They had better leave this job to me & you. I think we could fix it! Sure and you are after spaken me own mind. we could thot in the whif of a poif and both schmoken at the same time.

While the coffee drinking and talk was going on it had become day light and I could see a larg body of men drawn up in line on Houston St in front of the Vance Hous or Head Quarters of the U.S. Troop and an other body of men on St. Mary's St in front of the U.S. Barracks while the roof of the arsenal was occupied by an other body of men. My Co was lined up on Soledad St just across from Houston. I came down and rejoined my company.

Every thing remained about as I've described it until about 9. A.M. when we was ordered back to the hall and the other troops were withdrawn from the streets. Giving us to understand that every thing would be surrendered at 4. P.M.

At 6. P.M. about the company was ordered to take up quarters at the arsenal and occupy the building just vacated by the U.S. troops they having marched out to the San Pedro Springs & camped. So we went on duty immediately, on our arrival on the grounds a guard detail was made out

Roster of the guard   Feb 16th 1861

Officer of the day	Ed Stevens	
" " " guard	S.W. McCallister	
Sgt. " " "	M.W. Merrick	
Corpl " " "	Wm Breece	
Privates " " "	S. Childers	P. Eagen
Pady White	Pady Brady	I Kening
John Whickham	-- Denis	Smith
Wm Moore	A gagen	

Life in San Antonio during the Civil War

INTRODUCTION TO DOCUMENT

San Antonio served that same purpose for the State of Texas as it had for all governments before. Confederate and state government alike counted on the stragtegically located city as a marshalling point for troops on their way to the front. In addition, its proximity to the Gulf Coast and the Mexican border ensured its involvement with trade and commerce. Although shielded from actually fighting, the war still affected the towns whose residents sent relative and friends off to battle.

The Maverick family once again was once again swept up by historic events. Samuel A. Maverick, who had acted as a commissioner for the secession convention, served as San Antonio mayor from 1862–1863. Three of their sons, Samuel Maverick, Jr., Lewis Maverick, and George M. Maverick, served in the Confederate Army. Another son, fourteen-year-old William, attended boarding school before later joining his brother Lewis at the front. Three other children, Mary B., Albert, and Elizabeth remained at home. Ever the diarist, Mary Maverick recorded events she witnessed happening around her.

This early 1860s photo shows San Antonio transitioning from a frontier village into an important American transportation and commercial center. Daughters of the Republic of Texas Collection at Texas A&M University-San Antonio.

DOCUMENT[47]

Mary Brown Maverick to Her Father, Samuel A. Maverick

December 15, 1861

I am yet going to school to Miss Lewis she has a great many scholars, I like her very much she is a very nice young lady. There was a flag presented to young Mr. Maclin which you know is a capt yesterday afternoon and there was a great many people there it was at the Military plaza. Mis Martha Vance made a speech and it was a very good one too. It (the flag) was made at the sewing society. Brother Sam has been here a short time he went away Wednesday morning expecting to go to Austin. I hope you will come home before Christmas. We are all in fine health I hope you are too. I hope that brother Lewis will be home too at the same time. We all send you our love.

Mary Adams Maverick to Her Son, Willie Maverick

March 6, 1864

. . . Judge Stribbing had gone off to the Yankees, so has Fisk, and Broom Anderson. Judge Devine has got back from Mexico & the Rio Grande ports are open again. The papers tell us that old Sherman has taken Jackson Miss—bad news, but I hope we will soon whip them back again. We got the catalogue you sent us, and a monthly report last week & glad to see how high you stand in your lessons & in your conduct which is very important to a boy who intends to be a gentleman. We have 3 cows & begin to make butter now. Prince is going to plant the Rancho in corn and potatoes this year. Austin was going along the other day bending under the weight of a bag of flour, when someone holl[er]ed out to him—"Hello, Austin, why don't you get a cart?" "O Sir," he answers, "the carts charge specie & I'm to good a southerner to give it!"

March 6 [& 7], 1864

It is a beautiful day of warm sunshine & Pa is grafting grapes & Franklin digging holes for cuttings. Most of our grapes, except the black Spanish, have been killed by the cold & Pa intends to graft the wild vines with the black Spanish & try to get enough grapes that will bear regularly every year. Old Mrs. Dignowitty has, I hear, married a young fellow named McLure. I don't know how she will manage about old Dig—but she [said?] he was an old Yankee & she never wanted to see him again. I reckon she is anything that is mean herself.

Don't let anybody vaccinate you, Willie, because the Yankees have got poison scattered all thro[ugh] the country of "vaccine virus," and many people have arms so rotten from it that it is feared they will have to be amputated. Lewis says 70 of Wood's & 160 of Brown's regt's are vaccinated with it. And all of Mrs. Peck's beautiful girls have it, Mr. Menefee tells me. I do hope George is not, but L didn't say.

Do you think your shirts will last until June? I hope you keep well and are not troubles by the jayhawkers.

April 7, 1864

... I have not had very late a letter from Lewis or George—but hope I will tomorrow. Col. Robinson sent to George a Cap[tain's] Commission, and cousin Joe sent him an offer to exchange into his Company if he liked it. I do not like the idea of his going into the swamps of Louisiana. It is so sickly there. Lt. Col Robinson of Terry's brigade is going into Arizona & New Mexico. Did you see anything of Issac's [sic] knife?

The Catholic ladies here are getting up a fair for Sister Felicita to come off tonight, and I have just cut and sent them a large pan of splendid roses & honeysuckles & am baking some cakes for it. Sisters Felicita's orphans get more than their share, I think, in these hard times, but nobody likes to refuse. The Aid store has had new goods again & sold out at high prices. I got 2 bolts of cloth for the negroes, three calico drepes [sic], some candles & a pr of shoes & had to pay over $700.

Our garden looks very well. The figs are not all killed, but most of them are. The frost has left a considerable number of peaches & we have plenty of grapes. We have radish and lettuce now.

An 1849 image of San Antonio's main plaza by local artist William G. M. Samuel. Loose dogs fighting, balky cattle, and a stagecoach full of passengers give a sense of the daily hustle and bustle on the growing town. Daughters of the Republic of Texas Collection at Texas A&M University-San Antonio.

May 8, 1864

... The S. S.'s [Sons of the South] had a concert last night to make money for poor soldier families. The Casino was crowded, $20 a ticket. We all, but Allie, went. The performance [was] very good. It looked as if 500 people were there. The schools here all give July and August for vacation. George says Frank Conrad had [a] ball to tear his coat and shirt sleeve & never graze him. We have lost heavily in officers. N.Y. papers say Banks lost 14,000 men! Next we will whip them out of Miss. & take New Orleans where the noble ladies are so true to the South.

We are all right well. Some cases of bloody flux in town. Maj. Griffin died last week of cramps suddenly.

June 12, 1864

... The rains and floods have been great. Last Monday night 7th the San Antonio rose very suddenly 12 or 15 feet—washed down 4 houses & caused others to be undermined or to crumble partly down. It was pitchy dark & the rains incessant—yet only one negro woman was entirely drowned. Waelder's, Lee's, Story's, & Coffee's houses turned to mud, and most of their furniture & clothing were swept away. Waelder's family [was] rescued with great difficulty. John Elliot was conspicuous for swimming when others drew back—but he made fast to a large rope & took out one family. [Sol?] Childress & Tom were active & had 40 carried to his house and dried, the water came into his basement & 4 ½ feet into the commissary building, destroying valuable stores, munitions, and medicines.

August 7, 1864

... When will the war end, Lewis? Everybody is predicting that the hardest fighting is all over & the war to end right away. How is it? Do they only hope so? Or is it that these prophets are at a safe distance and want to bolster up the poor soldiers and their anxious friends to stand it as long as possible? ...

The streets of S.A. are always crowded, the stores full of goods & plenty of melons & peaches for sale on the plaza. The place is actually flourishing & silver abounds.

Strangers from the east who visit here tell us we know nothing of the war. But this is a mockery. Are not our dearest ones in the war, suffering and daring everything? I am thankful for quiet home & all its comforts, but it is no less true that we are in the war too—our hearts are there. And these foreign speculators & sneaks such as Bob Duff, McCarthy, & plenty of others under official seals are fattening upon our county's wants. I hope they will get their deserts and be made to stand aside when brave men and true come home.

A U.S. Cavalryman's View of San Antonio, 1866

INTRODUCTION TO TEXAS

The end of the Civil War meant the return of the United States Army to Texas. During the period known as Reconstruction, which lasted from 1865 until 1870, federal troops acted as an occupying force sent to support the newly installed pro-Union state government, protect freed slaves as they transitioned to life as free men and women, and restore order to the Indian frontier.

H. H. McConnell, a recent recruit to the U.S. Cavalry, journeyed to Texas with his unit as they headed back to Fort Richardson located near the Texas border with Indian Territory or modern-day Oklahoma. Like previous visitors to San Antonio, McConnell found the city different from any other he had seen, noting its antiquity while commenting on its thriving trade despite the lack of a railroad. Expressing a concern that others would soon voice, McConnell lamented the fact that no monument marked the famous struggle that had taken place at the Alamo.

DOCUMENT[48]

The whole face of the country was covered with mesquite, and cactus a thousand different shapes were seen, some of a huge growth. I had never seen cactus before, outside of a conservatory, and then only of a smaller size. The fruit borne by it, known as the prickly pear, is sometimes used as food, and in small quantities is wholesome and palatable. The leaves, when submitted to the action of fire in order to burn off the sharp stickers, are used as food for cattle, and in very drouthy seasons, when grass is short, are of great value. I had imagined this section of Texas to be a broad expanse of prairie, but such was not the case, and nowhere in Texas have I seen any "prairie" that is worthy of the name—that is to say, nothing like those of Illinois or Iowa. The prairies of Texas are all more or less dotted with groves of timber, which add to the beauty of the landscape, and afford a grateful shade to the traveler.

On December 1st I had a refreshing bath in the San Antonio river, and the next day came in sight of the city, lying in a shallow basin, surrounded by a low range of hills, far up on the side of which a ruin was pointed out as the remains of one of the old Jesuit missions, established by those pioneers of Christianity fifty years before the Pilgrims set foot on Plymouth Rock.

Entering the city of San Antonio, we felt at once that we were in a strange country, or at least among a strange people. The town is one of the oldest in the Union, contemporary with San Augustine and Santa Fe, and its old cathedral church of San Philip de Bexar dates away back, having been built by the generation immediately succeeding the men who were fellow adventurers with Cortez. The streets seemed narrow but clean, and the more modern portion filled with handsome business houses and lighted with gas. The town is well watered, and many of the streets had little streams or ditches on each side filled with clear running water, fed by, or tributary to, the San Antonio and San Pedro rivers, both of which meander through it, and are crossed by several bridges.

There are three plazas or public squares, the Main plaza, the Military plaza and the Alamo plaza, on the latter of which stood the ruins of what may be considered, or should be, the Mecca of Texas, the historic building known as the Alamo. Here Crockett, Bonham, Travis, Bowie and some three hundred other heroes fought the legions of Santa Anna for days, finally retreating and fighting from room to room; at last, after their ammunition was exhausted, in a hand-to-hand contest, with their rifles clubbed, the last one fell, but Texas was free. Well might it be said of such a place:

> "Such spots as these are pilgrim shrines,
> Shrines to no code nor creed confined;

> The Delphic groves—the Palestines—
> The Meccas of the mind."

To the everlasting disgrace of Texas, no noble monument marks the spot; in fact, when I first saw it, it was part of a livery stable.

The plazas were often filled with immense Chihuahua wagons, all the way from Monterey and San Luis Potosi, many of them with fourteen and eighteen mules hitched four abreast, and the shops filled with Mexican saddles and Navajo blankets and other Mexican commodities.

At this time San Antonio was far from any railroad, and enjoyed an immense trade from Mexico, all of it transacted by these great wagon trains. The circulating medium was entirely in silver dollars; when our greenbacks were presented, the merchant invariably discounted them, all prices being in coin; this discounting of paper money, by the way, was kept up in Texas long after specie payments had been resumed elsewhere.

The United States arsenal was in an unfinished condition, having been captured by the South when Texas seceded, and was not yet completed; in fact, much of the importance of San Antonio, aside from its trade with Mexico and the Rio Grande, is due to its having been military headquarters for Texas ever since the close of the Mexican war in 1848. We tramped along through the streets to the San Pedro Springs, where we went into camp near some companies of United States cavalry stationed here.

The weather, although in December, had up to this time been very beautiful—just such balmy days and delightful nights as back home we were accustomed to in the late summer and early fall; but during this first night at San Antonio I experienced my first "norther." These "cold waves," which are more or less prevalent from November until April, constitute most of the really cold weather felt in this latitude. Of course, Texas is an empire in extent, and when you speak of such or such a peculiarity of soil or climate, in referring to Texas, you must indicate the *portion* of the State, for in Northern Texas, at Jacksboro, I have seen the mercury 13° below zero more than once. It is the suddenness with which the norther comes up (or down), and the consequent rapid fall in the mercury, often from 80° or 85° to the freezing point, or several degrees below it, that makes them so piercing. Generally before the advent of one it is rather more still and sultry than usual; as evening approaches, a dull, dark bank begins to rise on the

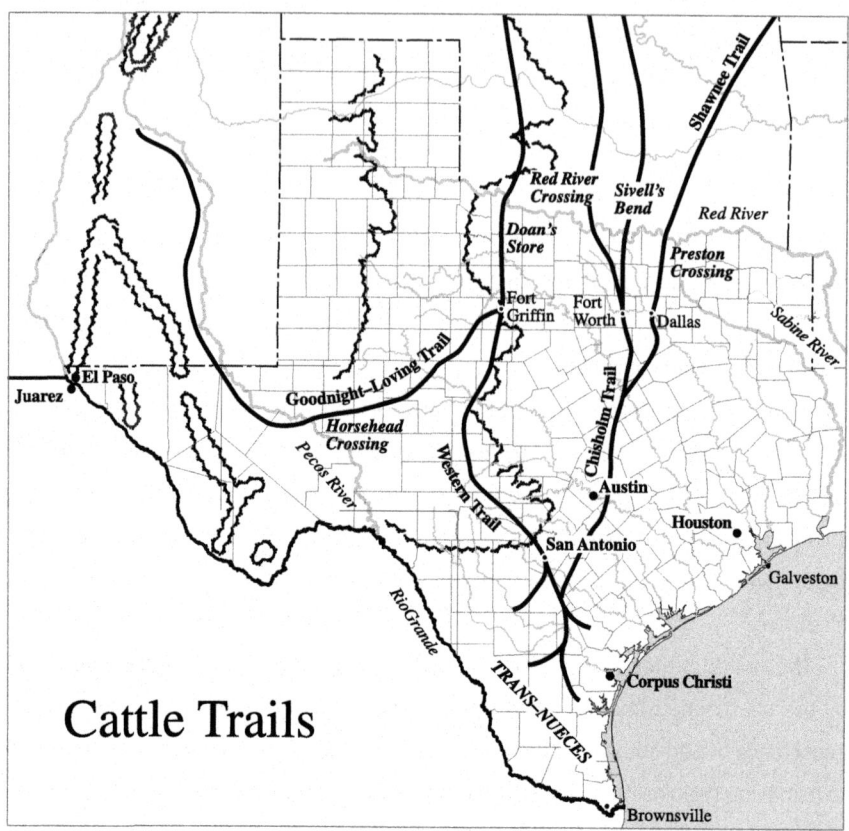

Cattle Trails

northern horizon, and about sundown the "cold wave" comes, often accompanied by a wind with a velocity of thirty to forty miles an hour. Their force is usually expended in about twelve hours, but sometimes they continue to blow for two or even three days.

The climate of the part of Texas so far seen by me had taken fast hold on my mind as approaching the ideal. Many of the early impressions, written down for these sketches at the time, subsequent experience and observation have caused me to modify, but the following verbatim entry in my diary, written in December, 1866, on the climate, I have never yet seen fit to alter: "Beyond doubt, the balmy and glorious climate, the gorgeous skies, the glowing sunsets, the pure and bracing atmosphere, the splendid landscapes, cannot be surpassed on the continent; and in the near future, when the railroad shall have traversed its immense distances, and the six-shooter and bowie shall have been replaced by the plow and school-house, no portion of our vast heritage will present so many attractions to the emigrant, the tourist, or the invalid, as the Empire State of the Southwest."

After remaining in camp a few days, we drew clothing for such of the men as needed it, replenished our supply of rations, and having exchanged our Mexican train for government mule teams, set out for Austin, about ninety or one hundred miles distant in a northeasterly direction.

Sidney Lanier Visits San Antonio, 1873

INTRODUCTION TO DOCUMENT

A native of Georgia, Sidney Lanier developed a reputation as a poet and popular author. He supported his family by selling poems and stories to various national publications, becoming well-known for his works that often dealt with the poor whites and blacks of the South. Towards the end of his life, he secured a position as a professor of literature on the faculty of John Hopkins University.

San Antonio attracted artists, writers, and other sculptors much the way that Santa Fé, New Mexico, did in the early twentieth century. Lanier, who visited San Antonio in 1873, penned a brief history of the town which ended with his impressions of the town when he saw it. After his death from tuberculosis, which he contracted while a incarcerated in a Union prison during the Civil War, his wife edited a volume of unpublished essays which appeared in 1890.

DOCUMENT[49]

San Antonio is at an altitude of 564 feet above the level of the sea, in latitude 29° 28', longitude 98° 24'. It is placed just in the edge of a belt of country one hundred and fifty miles ride, reaching to the Rio Grande, and principally devoted to cattle-raising. One can sit on one's horse, in the western suburbs of the city and mark where the line of the rude Mexican *jacals* (huts) abruptly breaks off, and yields place to the vast mesquit-covered plain, over which the eye ranges for great lonely distances without detecting any traces of the occupancy of man. No gardens, pastures, scattered houses, or the like are there to break the sudden transition: it is the city, then the plain; it is home cheek by jowl with desert. Inside, the location of the city is no less picturesque. Two streams, the San Antonio and San Pedro river, run in a direction generally parallel, though specially as far from parallelism as capricious crookedness can make itself, through the entire town. The San Antonio is about sixty feet wide; its water is usually of a lovely milky-green. The stranger strolling on a mild sunny day through the streets often finds himself suddenly on a bridge, and is half startled with the winding visa of sweet lawns running down to the water, of weeping-willows kissing its surface, of summer-houses on its banks, and of the swift yet smooth-shining stream meandering this way and that, actually combing the long sea-green locks of a trailing water-grass which sends its waving tresses down the centre of the current for hundreds of feet, and murmuring the while with a palpable Spanish lisping which floats up among the rude noises of traffic along the rock-paved sheet, as it were some dove-voiced Spanish nun out of the convent yonder, praying heaven's mitigation of the wild battle of trade. Leaving this bridge, walking down the main ("Commerce") street, across the Main Plaza, then past the San Fernando Cathedral, then across the Military Plaza one comes presently to the San Pedro, a small stream ten or fifteen feet in width, up which the gazing stroller finds no romance but mostly strict use; for there squat the Mexican women on their haunches, by their flat stones, washing the family garments, in a position the very recollection of which gives one simultaneous stitches of lumbago and sciatica, yet which they appear to maintain for hours without detriment. If it had been summer-time we would most likely have seen, before we left the bridge over the San Antonio, the black-locked heads of these same ladies bobbing up and down the surface of the river; for they love to lave themselves in this tepid water, these sleek, plump, black-eyed, olive-cheeked *Mexicanas*.

Crossing the San Pedro we are among the *jacals*. Here is surely the very first step Architecture made when she came out of the cave. A row of stakes is driven into the ground, in and out between these mesquit-twigs are wattled, a roof of trigs and straw is fastened on somehow, anyhow, and there you are. Not only you, but your family

This image from the late 1860s shows the renovations to San Fernando Cathedral which fundamentally changes the appearance of one of the city's most famous landmarks. Daughters of the Republic of Texas Collection at Texas A&M University-San Antonio.

of astonishing numbers are there, all huddled into this kennel whose door has to be crawled into. Of course typhus-fevers and small-pox are to be found amoug such layers of humanity. People are not sardines.

Now we come to a step in advance in the matter of houses. A row of stakes is put down, this is enclosed by another row leaving a space between of about a foot's width, which is filled in with stones and mud, a thatched roof of straw is then put on, and the house is complete. Still more pretentious dwellings are built of *adobes*, or sun-dried brick. The majority of the substantial houses of the town are constructed of a whitish limestone, so soft when first quarried that it can be cut with a knife, but quickly hardening by exposure into a very durable building material. The prevailing style of dwelling houses is low, windows are few and balconies scarce, though in the more pretentious two-storied dwellings there are some very good Moorish effects of projecting stone and lattice-work.

By far the finest and largest architectural example in the town is the San Fernando Cathedral, which presents a broad, varied, and imposing facade upon the western side of the Main Plaza. Entering this building one's pleasure in its exterior gives way to curious surprise; for one finds inside the old stone church built here more than a century ago, standing, a church within a church, almost untouched save that parts of some projecting pediments have been knocked away by the builders. In this inner church services are still regularly held, the outer one not being yet quite completed. The curious dome, surrounded by a high wall over which its topmost slit-windows just peer—an evident relic of ancient Moorish architecture, which one finds in the rear of most of the old Spanish religious edifices in Texas—has been preserved, and still adjoins the queer priests' dormitories, which constitute the rear end of the cathedral building.

There are other notable religious edifices in town. Going back to Commerce Street, one can see a fine large church just being completed for the German Catholics (San Fernando Cathedral is Mexican Catholic).

Crossing a graceful iron foot-bridge, down an alley that turns off to the north from Commerce Street, one glances up and down the stream, which here flows between heavy and costly abutments of stone to protect the rear of the large stores whose fronts are on the Main Street, and whose rear doors open almost immediately over the water. Across the bridge the alley widens into a street, and here in this odd nook of the steam is St. Mary's, the American Catholic Church, its rear adjoining a long three-storied stone convent building, and its yard sloping down to the water. Strolling up the river a quarter of a mile, one comes upon a long white stone building which has evidently had much trouble to accommodate itself to the site upon which it is built, and whose line is broken into four or five abrupt angles, while its roof is varied with dormer-windows and sharp projections and spires and quaint clock-faces, and its rear is mysterious with lattice-covered balconies and half-hidden corners and corridors. This is the Ursuline Convent; and standing as it does on a rocky and steep (steep for Texas plain) bank of the river, whose course its broken line follows, and down to which its long stern-looking wall descends, it is an edifice at once piquant and sombre, and one cannot resist figuring Mr. James' horseman spurring his charger up the white limestone road that winds alongside the wall, in the early twilight, when dreams come whispering down the current among the willow-sprays.

There are notable places about the town which the stranger must visit. He may ride two miles along a level road between market gardens which are vitalized by a long *acequia*, or ditch, fed from the river, and come presently upon the quaint gray towers

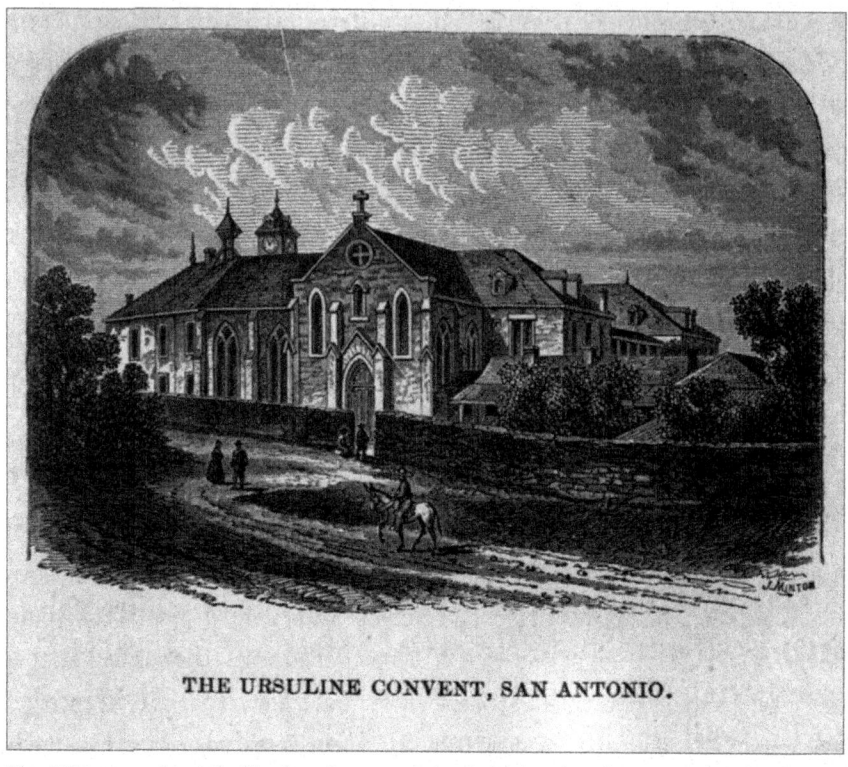

THE URSULINE CONVENT, SAN ANTONIO.

This 1850s image shows the Ursuline Convent, and early landmark in San Antonio. Today it houses the Southwestern School of Art. Daughters of the Republic of Texas Collection at Texas A&M University-San Antonio.

of the old Mission Concepcion whose early location had been incidentally mentioned in the foregoing history. The old church, with its high-walled dome in the rear, is in a good state of preservation, and traces of the singular many-colored frescoes on its front are still plainly visible. Climbing a very shaky ladder, one gets upon the roof of a long stone corridor running off from the church building, and, taking good heed of the sharp-thorned cactus which abounds up there, looks over upon a quaint complication of wall-angles, nooks, and small-windowed rooms. The place ceased to be used for religious purposes some years ago, and is now occupied by a German with his family, his Mexican laborers and his farm animals. This German tills the fertile mission lands. Heaven send him better luck with his crops than he had with his English!

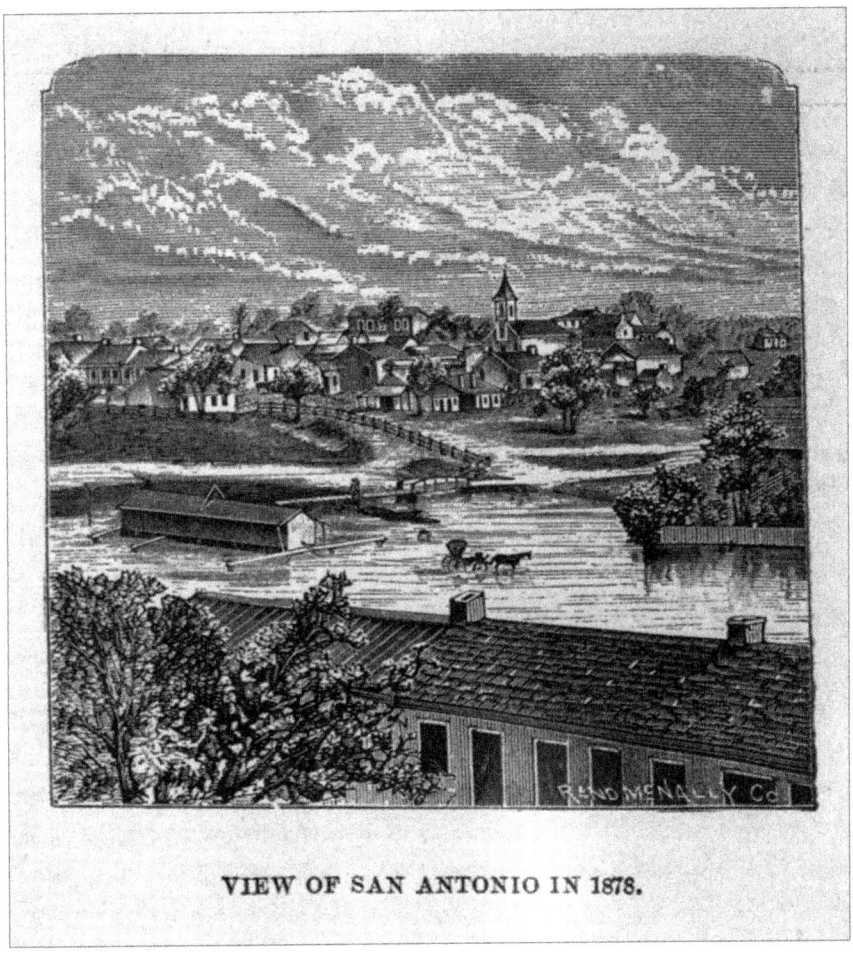

VIEW OF SAN ANTONIO IN 1878.

By the late 1870s, San Antonio looks and feels like an American town. The river, shown here out of its banks, is still the focus of the community. Daughters of the Republic of Texas Collection at Texas A&M University-San Antonio.

Further down the river a couple of miles one comes to the *Mission San José de Aguayo*. This is more elaborate and on a larger scale than the buildings of the first Mission, and is still very beautiful. Religious services are regularly conducted here; and one can do worse things than to steal out here from town on some wonderfully calm Sunday morning and hear a mass, and dream back the century and a half of strange, lonesome, devout, hymn-haunted and Indian-haunted years that have trailed past these walls. Five or six miles further down the river are the ruins of the Mission San Juan, in much dilapidation.

Or the visitor may stroll off to the eastward, climb the hill, wander about among the graves of heroes in the large cemetery on the crest of the ridge, and please himself with the noble reaches of country east and west and with the perfect view of the city which from here seems "sown" like Tennyson's, "in a monstrous wrinkle of the" prairie. Or, being in search of lions, one may see the actual animal by a stroll to the "San Pedro Springs Park" a mile or so to the northward. Here, from under a white-ledged rocky hill, burst forth three crystalline springs, which quickly unite and form the San Pedro. Herr Dürler, in charge, has taken admirable advantage of the ground, and what with spreading water oaks, rustic pleasure buildings, promenades along smooth shaded avenues between concentric artificial lakes, a race-course, an aviary, a fine Mexican lion whom burly Herr Dürler scratches on the head, but who does not seem to appreciate similar advances from other persons, a bear-pit in which are an emerald-eyed blind cinnamon-bear, a large black bear, a wolf and a *coyote*, and other attractions, this is a very green spot indeed in the waste prairies. Or one may drive five miles to northward and see the romantic spot where the San Antonio River is forever being born, leaping forth from the mountain, complete, *totus*, even as Minerva from the head of Jove. Or one may take one's stand on the Commerce Street bridge and involve oneself in the life that goes by this way and that. Yonder comes a long train of enormous blue-bodied, canvas-covered wagons, built high and square in the stern, much like a fleet of Dutch galleons, and lumbering in a ponderous way that suggests cargoes of silver and gold. These are drawn by fourteen mules each, who are harnessed in four tiers, the three front tiers of four mules each, and that next the wagon of two. The "lead" mules are wee fellows, veritable mulekins; the next tier larger, and so on to the two wheel-mules, who are always as large as can be procured. Yonder fares slowly another train of wagons, drawn by great wide-horned oxen, whose evident tendency to run to hump and fore-shoulder irresistibly persuades one of their cousinship to the buffalo.

Here, now, comes somewhat that shows as if Birnam Wood had been cut into fagots and was advancing with tipsy swagger upon Dunsinane. Presently one's gazing eye receives a sensation of hair, then of enormous ears, and then the legs appear, of the little roan-gray *bourras*, or asses, upon whose backs that Mexican walking behind has managed to pile a mass of mesquit firewood that is simply astonishing. This mesquit is a species of acacia, whose roots and body form the principal fuel here. It yields, by exudation, a gum which is quite equal to gum arabic, when the tannin in it is extracted. It appears to have spread over this portion of Texas within the last twenty-five years, perhaps less time. The old settlers account for its appearance by the theory that the Indians—and after them the stock-raisers were formerly in the habit of burning off the prairie-grass annually and that these great fires rendered it impossible for the mesquit shrub to obtain a foothold; but that now the departure of the Indians, and the transfer of most of the large cattle-raising business to points further westward, have resulted in leaving the soil free for the occupation of the mesquit. It has certainly taken advantage of the opportunity. It covers the prairie thickly in many directions, as far as the eye can reach, growing to a pretty uniform height of four or five feet—though occasionally much larger—and presenting, with its tough branches and innumerable formidable thorns, a singular appearance. The wood when dry is exceedingly hard and durable, and of a rich walnut color. This recent overspread of foliage on the plains is supposed by many persons to be the cause of the quite remarkable increase of moisture in the climate of San Antonio which has been observed of late years. The phenomena—of the coincident increase of moisture and of mesquit—are unquestionable; but whether they bear the relation of cause and effect, is a question upon which the unscientific lingerers on this bridge may be permitted to hold themselves in reserve.

But while we are discussing the mesquit, do but notice yonder Mexican in gorgeous array, promenading, intent upon instant subjugation of all his countrywomen in eye-shot! His black trowsers with silver buttons down the seams; his jaunty hussar-jacket; his six-inch brimmed felt *sombrero*, with marvelous silver filigree upon all available spaces of it, save those occupied by the hat-band, which is like two silver snakes tied parallel round the crown; his red sash, serving at once to support the trowsers and to inflate the full white shirt-bosom—what *Mexicana* can resist these things? And—if it [should] happen to be Sunday afternoon—yonder comes the German *Turnverein*, marching in from the San Pedro Springs Park, where they have been twisting themselves among the bars, and playing leap-frog and other honest games what time they emptied a cask of beer. Walking too, as tired men will walk, one sees sundry sportsmen returning from the prairies, where they have been popping away at quail and donkey-rabbits all this blessed Sunday. In especial notice that old German walking lustily in the middle of the street. He has a rusty gun on his shoulder; his game-bag is bloody and full; his long white beard and white moustache float about a face determined, strong, yet jovial. It is Rip Van Winkle in person. "But where is Schneider?" said one, the day we saw this man—"what a pity he hasn't Schneider with him!" "By Jove, there *is* Schneider!" in a moment cried another of the party; and veritably there he was. He came dashing round the corner, and ran and trotted behind his grizzled master, bearing an enormous donkey-rabbit tied by its legs around his neck.

And now as we leave the bridge in the gathering twilight and loiter down the street, we pass all manner of odd personages and "characters." Here bobbles an old Mexican who looks like old Father Time in reduced circumstances, his feet, his body, his head all swathed in rags, his face a blur of wrinkles, his beard gray-grizzle—a picture of eld such as one will rarely find. There goes a little German boy who was captured a year or two ago by Indians within three miles of San Antonio, and has just been retaken and sent home a few days ago. Do you see that poor Mexican without any hands? A few months ago a wagon-train was captured by Indians at Howard's Wells; the teamsters, of whom he was one, were tied to the wagons and these set on fire, and this poor fellow was released by the flames burning off his hands, the rest all perishing save two. Here is a great Indian-fighter who will show you what he calls his "vouchers," being scalps of the red braves he has slain; there a gentleman who blew up his store here in '44 to keep the incoming Mexicans from benefiting by his goods, and who afterwards spent a weary imprisonment in that stern castle of Perote away down in Mexico, where the Mier prisoners (and who ever thinks now-a-days of that strange, bloody Mier Expedition?) were confined; there a portly, handsome, buccaneer-looking captain who led the Texans against Cortina in '59; there a small, intelligent-looking gentleman who at twenty was first Secretary of War of the young Texan Republic, and who is said to know the history of everything that has been done in Texas from that time to this minutely; and so on through a perfect gauntlet of people who have odd histories, odd natures, or odd appearances, we reach our hotel. It is time, for the dogs—there are far more dogs here than in Constantinople—have begun to howl, and night has closed in upon San Antonio de Bexar. 1873.

PART 6: SAN ANTONIO COMES OF AGE

Description of San Antonio in the Late Nineteenth Century by a Resident

INTRODUCTION TO DOCUMENT

Prosperity allowed San Antonians to reflect on the city's history as hardships faded away. A growing number of books presented a nostalgic view of the town's past to both residents and visitors who increasingly flocked to the city. One such 1890 publication, William Conner's *San Antonio de Béxar*, presented short essays and documents expounding on the town's Spanish origins up through its development into a modern city. So popular was Corner's work that other author's began relying on it as a source of information for their own books.

DOCUMENT[50]

CHAPTER XIV.

*MODERN SAN ANTONIO**

A "Live" Town—The Coming of the French and Germans—Stage Coach Days—The "Bat Cave"—The Plazas—The Cortina War—"La Ley de Mondragon"—Early Commercial Interests—The "Battle of Flowers."

[The major portion of the facts as given in this chapter were furnished by a historical and statistical calendar outlined in William Conner's "San Antonio de Bexar".]

Improvement was immediately manifest at San Antonio after annexation: the town became a base of supplies for Chihuahua and other neighboring Mexican states, as well as for the frontier army stationed at a long line of forts established by the United States government. Many expeditions were made in connection with requisite supply and transportation, thus contributing materially to the town which—soon became the "livest" city in the southwest.

In an address to the people dated January 15th, 1849, the newly-elected mayor, J. N. Devine, urged very forcibly the question of education, peace, law and order. His action produced the effect of a "Sunday Closing" ordinance, April 5th, for the closing of Bar Rooms, Workshops, etc., after 9 a. m. on Sunday. It is said that the tide thus set in changed San Antonio from a blood-stained border town to a progressive modern city. However, even as late as the early '80's, it was the home of certain questionable amusements, sports and pastimes,—real bull fights and games of roulette and faro, where "only the sky was the limit."

The atmosphere was indeed spectacular. One could eat a dish of chili, listen to the twang of a guitar, view the obstreperous Punch, the dancing bear, or had he an ear for

Even with modern progress sweeping the city, it was still a town in transition. Horses, Oxen, and donkeys were still the main forms of transportation. This side street scene is in sharp contrast to the more commercial parts of town. Daughters of the Republic of Texas Collection at Texas A&M University-San Antonio.

SAN ANTONIO COMES OF AGE

sounds tinged with the commercial, could turn it toward the harangue of the patent-medicine man, splendid in coat studded with five-dollar gold piece buttons.

In the meantime, foreign emigration under the auspices of various societies, had become directed toward Texas. This was one of the most important sources from which the State, and naturally its metropolis, received its impetus through increasing population. The first French settlers of San Antonio came out from Alsace (then a French province) with the members of the Castro Colony in April, 1844. An important member of this colony was Dr. George Cupples, who had served as Staff Assistant Surgeon to the British Legion In Spain, going there during the first Carlist War in 1836. He afterwards returned to Paris where he met Henri Castro who induced him to emigrate to Texas. It was Dr. Cupples who all unwittingly; located the present town of Castroville. He, together with others of the colonists, soon after settled permanently in San Antonio.

It was during the years from 1845 to 1850, that most of the German colonists came to Texas. In 1845 the "Association of German Princes for the Protection of German Emigrants in Texas" sent its first colonists to the State under Prince Carl of Solms Braunfels. Landing at Port Lavaca, they started inland, he traveling in princely style, while they walked or rode in ox-wagons. Becoming tired and discouraged they went into camp at Victoria, while Prince Solms passed on to San Antonio. Here he purchased, on March 14th, 1845, a tract of land from Rafael Garza and wife, Maria Antonio Veramendi, upon which the colonists were soon after settled and the town of New Braunfels begun. Prince Carl had with him a man named Bluecher, a relative of the noted Prussian general. He afterwards became a surveyor and surveyed most of the lands in this section.

Among the colonies joining "The Association Comal County, of German Princes" in settling Texas, was a Socialist Society formed in northern Germany by about forty highly educated young men who had created quite a stir when their intentions of emigrating to Wisconsin, U. S. A., became known. "The Association" persuaded to come to Texas instead. They landed at the west Texas port of Indianola the latter part of August, 1847, and settled about 200 miles west of San Antonio on the Llano River. These colonists, headed by Dr. Ferdinand Herff of Hesse-Darmstadt, who had preceded them, suffered more of hardships and privations than any of the German settlers, being surrounded by hostile Indians and most distant from other habitations and traffic. Dr. Herff treated the Indians for wounds and sickness and was never molested by them as were most of the colonists. The Society had expected to reap profits, but failed and in the end came to nothing, the colonists for the most part scattering, many going to San Antonio. Dr. Herff returned to Germany, there married, and in 1850 with his wife emigrated to San Antonio, where they continued to reside. For many years Dr. Herff was the Nestor of the medical fraternity in Texas.

In 1849 occurred San Antonio's second cholera epidemic, lasting a month or more, the first of this order having been in 1833. Many people fled from the city in ox-carts, some going to the mountains where they died of the disease that broke out among them and which was communicated to the Indians who attacked the camps and themselves fell victims to the dreadful scourge. One Sunday in 1849 was called "Black Sunday," twenty-nine people having died that night. Many noble women, members of prominent San Antonio families—as well as of poorer ones—proved their heroism at this time, some dying while nursing patients thus afflicted. Dr. Cupples did much humanitarian practice during those days of panic, disease and death. Many of his patients were so poor as not to be able to afford lights, so the doctor always carried a candle in his pockets to be available in such homes.

Late in the '40's a stage route covering 680 miles was established between San Antonio and El Paso. Changes of animals were made at "stations" built of rock and adobe, every twenty-five to forty miles, or whenever a stream, spring, or water-hole could be found. From El Paso the "Butterfield Daily Mail" soon extended its route to San Francisco, and later to San Diego. On October 5th, 1857, the mail from San Antonio arrived at San Diego, California, having made the trip in twenty-six and a half days, the fastest time on record, and demonstrating the complete triumph of the southern route. This route was afterwards followed by the Southern Pacific Railroad. Later, however, it made much better time. These coaches, besides carrying mail, also accommodated a few passengers. They were always accompanied by an armed escort for protection against hostile Indians. As late as October, 1867, a coach was attacked by them enroute from San Antonio, and two of the escort killed. On October 26th, 1868, the fastest stage record from El Paso was made—the journey occupying but six days to San Antonio.

SAN ANTONIO COMES OF AGE

In 1854, under Governor Pease, a permanent public school system was established for Texas. In San Antonio the convent was also permitted to draw part of the school fund. Although well started in their operations when the Civil War broke out, nearly all schools were soon closed. In the latter part of 1858, a German-English school was established in San Antonio, which in 1870 was enlarged to accommodate five hundred pupils. To show the increase of the population in the city, in 1856 it was reported by the assessor as being 7,142, while in March, 1860, it was estimated at between 10,000 and 12,000.

The "Bat Cave" was commenced at the northwest corner of Military Plaza in 1850. This nickname was given to the combined city hall and city and county jail which stood at this place until torn down when the present city hall in the center was erected. In Spanish and Mexican times entries on the west side of the "Plaza de Armas" were closed at nightfall by rawhides hung on chains stretched tightly across the narrow roads. Behind this settlers in the Plaza enclosure were safe from surprises by Indians and their arrows, rawhides being arrow-proof. In later years this plaza became the center of display of a unique Mexican feature of out-door life—the chili stand. At night

By the 1880s, San Antonio's main plaza had taken on the trappings of a modern city. Daughters of the Republic of Texas Collection at Texas A&M University-San Antonio.

it would be dimly lighted as to municipal illumination, but ablaze with small camp fires and flaming lamps, picturesque booths would spring up as if by magic, and odors of garlic and onions fill the air. Chili and chili con carne, tamales, tortillas, enchiladas, frijoles and "sopa de arroz," would be dispensed to the curious and expectant tourist. Under the brilliant modern electric light, which has hunted these al fresco restauranteurs from plaza to plaza, the scene could never be reproduced, could never serve to hold echoes of such a characteristic past.

On March 23rd, 1857, appeared the first issue of the San Antonio Daily Herald, the oldest daily newspaper in Texas. The Weekly had appeared three years before. In 1858 the Vance brothers gave one lot of land for the erection of a place of worship for St. Mark's congregation. Mr. S. A. Maverick also donated four city lots for church purposes. On October 3rd, 1874, the bell for St. Mark's arrived from Troy, New York. It was cast from an old cannon ball dug up in the Alamo, and the expense of the casting was paid by S. A. Maverick. [Note: The bell is now believed to have been cast by melting down the famous "Come and Take It" cannon which had been brought to San Antonio during the revolution. The cannon was later found on the Maverick's property located on Alamo Plaza.] The present cathedral was consecrated April 25th, 1881, the corner-stone being laid December, 1859, under Rev. Lucius A. Jones, rector. The Civil War interrupted the progress of building and not until 1873 was the work resumed, this was under Rev. W. R. Richardson, who became rector of the parish in June, 1868. In 1859 the first wool was bought and warehoused in San Antonio, which was thus made a home market for this product. In 1875,—600,000 pounds were marketed. Berg's old mill for washing wool, near San Juan Mission, is now a noted landmark.

A San Antonio citizen, Captain William Tobin, later my host of the Vance House, greatly distinguished himself in what was called the "Cortina War". Juan Nepomuceno Cortina, heir of the original grantee of what is called the Espirito Santo tract on which Brownsville is located, but who lived at Matamoras, Mexico, just across the river, raided Brownsville in 1859, with some fifty or sixty followers, apparently for plunder, but as a matter of fact, five people were killed, they being those against whom the Mexicans had grudges. Cortina seems to have been a bandit who operated on the Rio Grande border all the way from Brownsville to Laredo, stealing stock and terrorizing the people. The whole of San Antonio was in great excitement because of the Brownsville invasion, and Captain Tobin, with a company consisting of sixty men, hastened in

November to relieve the frontier of the Cortina aggressions. Colonel "Rip" Ford, the noted Indian fighter, with Captain Tobin had charge of the Texas forces who met and defeated Cortina in battle near Brownsville, December 27th. The following February, Colonel Robert E. Lee was ordered to follow Cortina into Mexico if necessary. But the bandit had evidently decided to cease his aggressions, history being silent regarding any further disturbance on his part.

Among the volunteers who came to San Antonio in September, 1861, to join the Sibley expedition to clear New Mexico of the Union forces, was a certain Bob Augustin, who with others of his ilk, arrived from Gonzales. He was soon after arrested for disorderly conduct, having upset and over-ridden the chili stands on Main Plaza. He was released by the mayor, but immediately after taken in charge by a mass of determined citizens, which resulted in one of the most excited hangings in the history of the city, performed by the Vigilant Committee, and with the unanimous consent of a large number of citizens. The tree at the southeast corner of Main Plaza on which he was hung, was soon called "La Ley de Mondragon," and a popular ballad made to fit the theme.

On the 18th of March, 1861, many of the citizens of San Antonio swore allegiance to the Confederate States under District Judge Devine. Thomas J. Devine, Samuel A. Maverick, and P. N. Luckett were the three Confederate commissioners who received the property surrendered to San Antonio by General Twiggs two months before. Soon after the close of hostilities between the North and South in 1865, soldiers arrived at San Antonio, as at other important cities of Texas and of the South, and "reconstruction" began.

The only communication between San Antonio and Laredo on the Rio Grande, even later than 1866, was by means of four trips per month made by a mail rider. In the early '70's ox-carts—carretas—were seeing their great day. The old-fashioned freighters, or prairie schooners, were still largely in evidence. Commerce Street was crowded with such trains, each wagon drawn by from eight to sixteen mules with bells dangling from their collars, loading goods for Mexico, as well as Texas points, or bringing merchandise from the former. It required three months for goods to reach San Antonio from Cuero, Yorktown, and Powder Horn (one of the names by which Indianola was designated). After torrential rains—which were frequent—Commerce Street, as well as Main Plaza, were almost impassable. Vehicles stuck in the mud for days. In the old days

Market day on military plaze, circa 1880s, brought with it a panorama of sights, smells, and sounds. Daughters of the Republic of Texas Collection at Texas A&M University-San Antonio.

mules in charge of a Mexican who held on to the bell mule. Failing in this the Indians shot the man with arrows which were afterward gathered and handed to General Carleton.

The first industry in Texas to gain commercial importance was cattle-raising; wire fences were then unknown and the broad prairies furnished "free grass" to vast herds of "long horns." In the early '70's the cattle trail to Kansas was in constant public use. Ten years later fence-cutting and burning becoming rampant. Governor Ireland issued a proclamation of severe character against fence-cutters, and also against persons unlawfully enclosing land by fences. In December, 1883, an indignation meeting of citizens at San Antonio was held strongly condemning wire cutting. At the Cattlemen's Convention held in that city in December, 1884, the principal topic discussed was that the National Cattle Trail would have to go "before the land grabbers and the railroads." In February of the following year the Maverick Ranch fence on the Bandera road was cut. By 1890 railroad connection between Texas and northern markets caused the disuse of the old trail.

Another commercial enterprise, one which affected all the markets of Texas, came

SAN ANTONIO COMES OF AGE

An early photograph of the the rear of San Fernando Cathedral. Notice the carretas and vendors in the foreground. Daughters of the Republic of Texas Collection at Texas A&M University-San Antonio.

through the slaughtering of the buffalo in West Texas. An advertisement in a San Antonio paper of May 24th, 1874, called attention to "dry buffalo meat for sale, just from the plains." In January, 1877, buffalo hides and meat were being received in large quantities "from the frontier"—a few months later ten loads of buffalo hides had been brought to town from "out west." The bleaching bones of the slaughtered buffalo later made San Antonio one of the shipping points for this great fertilizer.

Stage, ambulance, and the government telegraph were the only means of communication between San Antonio and the outside world until the coming of its first railroad, "The Sunset" or the G. S. F. & S. A. On the night of February 19th, 1877, a torchlight procession, 8000 strong, celebrated the event. From that time San Antonio

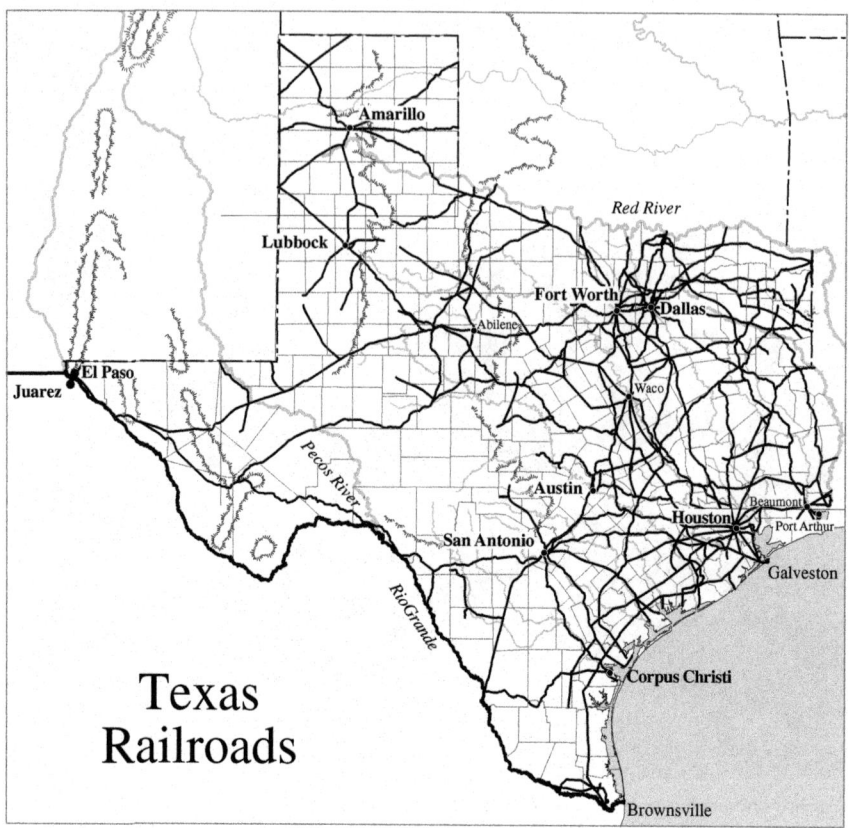

Main Plaza was one of the most important parts of the town. Stockmen and country folks would gather there for miles around at which time it was a treeless market. It was on February 27th, 1870, that a Committee on Public Improvement reported favorably on the planting of trees on this plaza. In ante-Independence days that portion of the city around Market Street from Main Plaza was outside of the thickly settled limits. It was called the "Potrero," or place for horses, all horses of travelers being put there for the night.

The Indians continuing troublesome near San Antonio, a mass meeting, which proved ineffective, was held in 1868 to devise means for removing the Kickapoos from Texas and the Mexican border. In the following January, Judge George H. Noonan's special court was dispersed at Uvalde by Indians of this tribe. On February 17th, 1870, a band of Lipans only nine miles out from San Antonio, tried to stampede a bunch of ceased to be a frontier town and began to put on city ways. (On December 5, 1883, the abandoned wires of the Military Telegraph were purchased by the Erie Telephone & Telegraph Company.)

In 1891, when President Harrison was making his Southern tour, with the members of his cabinet, San Antonio, in trying to out-do all other towns in cordiality and the novelty of entertainment, decided upon a "Battle of Flowers." By a happy chance the date of his visit fell on April 21st, San Jacinto Day, and upon this memorable anniversary, the "battle" was given; but instead of the whizzing of bullets and shrieking of shells, there was a scene of revelry—no more deadly guns, cannons and sabres—flowers became the only missies used. Because of the initial success of the one day's fete, it was later lengthened into a week of carnival. Since 1915, King Antonio of San Antonio de Bexar the order of Quivira has come to usher in the fetes of Fiesta San Jacinto, which has become a patriotic and social annual festival of San Antonio. One of the founders of this "Flower Battle," and for some time president of the organization, was Mrs. Duncan C. Ogden, who as Elizabeth Cox, came to Texas from Lexington, Kentucky, in 1832, and lived under five of its flags. She was one of the bravest of the State's pioneer women, passing heroically through all the privations, hardships and terrors incident to those times that tried men's souls. Her husband, Captain D. C. Ogden came to San Antonio in 1838 from New York, and took an active part in the making of early Texas during the days of the Republic and the era following. He was among those carried captive to Perote prison, escaped as did John Twohig and others, but was captured and returned to incarceration to be later released through the efforts of Henry Clay. He was soldier, patriot, and orator, his wife a worthy help-mate.

President William McKinley Visits San Antonio, 1901

INTRODUCTION TO DOCUMENT

In May 1901 President William McKinley toured Texas by rail, crossing the state in four days. His official stops included Houston (May 3), Austin (May 4), San Antonio (May 5), and El Paso (May 6). In addition, his party made short stops along the route where he addressed crowds from the back of the train. At each of the major stops he was met by state and local political figures and dignitaries. Mckinley was shown the best that city had to offer.

Public speeches by the president and others stressed the theme of reunification and unity. The recent Spanish American War had given Southern states the opportunity to show their support and loyalty during a national emergency. The speakers made the point that although once foes, they were all Americans now.

DOCUMENT[51]

The *San Antonio Express* of May 5th said:

William McKinley, President of the American Republic, and Commander-in-Chief of the Army and Navy of the Nation, was the guest of San Antonio Saturday, and his reception and entertainment here was a credit to the Alamo City. The people with one

This 1901 stereoscope image of William McKinley shows him speaking in front of The Alamo in May. The visit of a sitting president sent a clear signal to the world that San Antonio was coming into its own. He would be felled by an assassin's bullet just a few months later. Daughters of the Republic of Texas Collection at Texas A&M University-San Antonio.

accord, and with but one purpose, turned out to do honor to the people's President and the distinguishes party who accompany him on his tour from ocean to ocean.

The scene in San Antonio was a grand one and one that will be long remembered by those who witnessed it. Men, women, and children of all colors and all nationalities thronged the streets to get a sight of the President. It was not a political but a public demonstration, and the character of it was a credit to the people of this city, which for the second time in its history has been honored by the presence of the head of the government.

The decorations of the city were numerous and beautiful, but the grandest sight of all was the ten thousand school children on Travis Park Square, and it was a sight that gave particular pleasure to the presidential party. The arrangement of the reception and its management were perfect and everything passed off without a hitch and without an unpleasant incident.

Besides the people of San Antonio prominent in the reception of the President here, there came from the State capital Governor Jos. D. Sayers, Attorney General Charles K. Bell, United States District Judge E. R. Meek, United States Internal Revenue Collector Webster Flanagan, Hon. Jeff McLemore, Hon. Joe Lee Jameson, and Dr. B. M. Worsham.

The line of march included a visit to Fort Sam Houston, where the Second Battery Field Artillery, under Capt. Clermont L. Best, fired a president's salute. The main exercises were held in Alamo Plaza, where a grandstand had been erected. On the stand Governor Sayers was seated to the right and Mayor Marshall Hicks to the left of the President. Mayor Hicks delivered the adddress of welcome. He described the successful struggle of Texas for independence in 1835–1836, the fall of the Alamo, and the growth of the commonwealth, the quota of men furnished by San Antonio for the War with Spain, and in the course of his remarks he said:

"At the exact spot upon which the stand is erected the eccentric but daring David Crockett yielded up his life. * * * The spirit of its heroes lives in the heart of Texas. * * * Upon this spot we welcome you and pledge on the behalf of our people, to the Union and its preservation the same loyalty, devotion, sacrifice that were exhibited by these patriotic Texans more than sixty-five years ago.

"The veterans in Blue and Gray are with us today, sitting side by side. They are one. We of the South love our past, revere its heroes, and cherish its memories, but, with loyal hearts and patriotic emotions, we hail the flag of the Union, and we welcome you here and bid you Godspeed in your journey across the continent."

The President's speech in reply was well received. "You," said he in conclusion, "have everything—strong men, fair women, and your fields are full of fruits waiting the uses aid cultivation of men. I congratulate you upon this splendid heritage, and I join with your honorable mayor in saving that we stand today, one in heart, one in faith, one in liberty, one in destiny, the freest republic beneath the sun, a republic which the living and those who are to come after will pass along to the ages and to the centuries to come."

When the President finished, Governor Sayers arose and presented him, in behalf of the Business Men's Club, with a picture of the Alamo, painted by Verner White, a local artist. The President said in reply: "The people of San Antonio could have selected nothing which I will prize more highly and cherish longer than this picture of this great historic place, and I beg you, in my name, to thank them all."

The Governor then turned to the people on the plaza and repeated the thanks of the President, which were received with enthusiastic applause.

This concluded the speech-making, and President McKinley and party visited the Alamo and entered their names on the visitors' register.

The San Antonio International Fair, ca. 1901

INTRODUCTION TO DOCUMENT

By the dawn of the twentieth century San Antonio had finally earned the reputation as a model modern city. Paved streets, electricity and gas, public water works enhanced the quality of municipal life. Most of the old Spanish and Mexican structures that had made the town so picturesque yet so ancient disappeared, often replaced by multistoried commercial buildings and frame house for residents. Connected to the world by a network of railroads, what was once a frontier out post had been transformed into Texas' foremost metropolis. Many of the civic traditions originated in this period when San Antonio proudly announced it had come of age.

DOCUMENT[52]

The picturesque city of San Antonio, cosmopolitan and aggressive, and, at the same time, invested with all the quaint charm pertaining to an old Spanish community rich in architectural memorials left by a vanished civilization, has steadily grown in favor for a decade or more past as a winter resort for people of wealth from the Northern and Eastern States. It is, also, headquarters for the United States military department of Texas, and has one of the best equipped posts (Fort Sam Houston) in the Southwest. As a manufacturing and trade center it is a city of first importance.

The people are noted equally for business enterprise and energy, and for hospitality and that love of pleasure that, in a wider arena, have made Paris, the capital of France, the most brilliant and popular metropolis in the world, and one of the most prosperous as well.

The annual "Battle of Flowers" at San Antonio draws thousands of people from all parts of Texas and neighboring States, but the greatest attraction is the fair held each year by the "San Antonio International Fair Association."

In reply to a letter requesting information regarding this organization Mr. J. M. Vance, secretary of the Association, writes:

"The officers of the association are: Vories P. Brown, president; Jno. W. Kokernot, vice-president; T. C. Frost, treasurer; and J. M. Vance, secretary. The fair was organized in January, 1899, and was incorporated under the laws of Texas with a capital stock of $50,000 divided into 5000 non-assessable shares at $10 a share. The capital stock was increased to $75,000 in 1901.

By the late Nineteenth Century, San Antonio was a very cosmopolitan city. Notice the Drug Store sign advertises in three languages—English, German, and Spanish. This is a scene from West Commerce Street. Daughters of the Republic of Texas Collection at Texas A&M University-San Antonio.

"The following parties organized the fair association: Geo. W. Brackenridge, T. C. Frost, Chas. Hugo, H. D. Kampmann, Otto Wahrmund, Frank Arnold, J. D. Straus, Frank Grice, F. A. Piper, J. M. Vance, V. P. Brown, Jno. W. Kokernot, and W. Wiess.

"We have held three successful fairs. The first, October 28, to November 8, 1899; paid attendance 67,177; receipts, including subscription to stock, $66,249; expenditures, $63,567, most of which was put into permanent improvements on the grounds.

"The second fair was held October 20 to November 2, 1900; paid attendance about 72,000; receipts, $66,055; expenditures, about $69,000.

"The third fair was held October 19 to October 30, 1901. This was our most successful fair. Attendance about 80,000; receipts, $55,292; expenditures, $51,885. The receipts for the first two years were larger than the last on account of subscriptions made by shareholders, amounting to nearly $60,000.

"Our exhibits included everything usually shown at fairs in the way of live stock, agricultural products, art and ladies textile and culinary work. Our live stock show last year was the largest ever held in the South, there being over 2000 head of registered stock on the grounds. Our poultry show was as large as any ever held in the State. We had an extensive fish and game exhibit from the coast, which was shown in our large refrigerator operated by our cold storage plant. We also had a very fine exhibit furnished by the Mexican government.

"The dates for the fair of 1902 have not yet been set, but very likely will be October 18th to 19th, inclusive. We intended this year to have a much larger fair and better than we have held before. Our premiums will be larger and we will also endeavor to secure a much larger exhibit from the Mexican government and make this one of the leading features of our fair.

"Our association is in a very prosperous condition. We have assets to the amount of $108,000, including the land and improvements, all paid for with the exception of $15,000 due on the land. This has three years to run at five per cent. interest, but we expect to wipe this debt this year if possible."

"San Antonio," said the announcement for 1901, "is most favorably situated for holding a large annual fair, as all the county east and north of this city is good farming country, and the vast scope of country south and west of San Antonio is the best stock raising and stock farming country in the world. * * *"

Endnotes

1. Hoffman, Fritz, ed. "The Mezquía Diary of the Alarcon Expedition into Texas, 1718," *Southwestern Historical Quarterly* Vol. 41, No. 4 (April 1938), 312-323.
2. Leutenegger, Fr. Benedict, ed. and trans. *Guidelines for a Texas Mission: Instructions for the Missionary of Mission Concepción in San Antonio, ca. 1760.* San Antonio: Old Spanish Mission Historical Research Library at San José Mission, 1976.
3. Conner, William, ed. *San Antonio de Béxar: A Guide and History.* (San Antonio: Bainbridge Press, 1890), 126.
4. Leutenegger, Benedict and Benito Fernández. "Memorial of Father Benito Fernández Concerning the Canary Islanders, 1741," *Southwestern Historical Quarterly*, Vol. 82, No. 3 (January 1979), 273-276.
5. Leutenegger, Benedict and Benito Fernández. "Memorial of Father Benito Fernández Concerning the Canary Islanders, 1741," *Southwestern Historical Quarterly*, Vol. 82, No. 3 (January 1979), 277-296.
6. Magnaghi, Russell M. "Texas as Seen by Governor Winthuysen, 1741-1744," *Southwestern Historical Quarterly*, Vol. 88, No. 2 (October 1984), 173-174.
7. Brickerhoff, Sidney, and Odie B. Faulk. *Lancers for the King: A Study of the Frontier Military System of Northern New Spain, with a translation of the Royal Regulations of 1772.* (Phoenix: Arizona Historical Foundation, 1965), 15, 17, 49, 59-60.
8. Briscoe Center for American History, Bexar Archives, Translation of Croix to Ripperdá, enclosing ordinances and by-laws concerning the government of Texas and the establishment and management of mesteñas fund, January 11, 1778. Digital Archives: *https://www.cah.utexas.edu/projects/bexar/gallery_doc.php?doc=e_bx_002652.*
9. Leutenegger, Benedict. "Report on San Antonio Mission in 1792," *Southwestern Historical Quarterly.* Vol. 77, No. 4 (April 1974), 490-491, 494-498.
10. Faulk, Odie, ed. "A Description of Texas in 1803: Report of Governor Don Juan Bautista Elguézabal." *Southwestern Historical Quarterly.* Vol. 66, No. 4 (April 1963), 513-515.
11. Coues, Elliot, ed. *The Expeditions of Zebulon Montgomery Pike.* (2 Vols.; New York: Dover Publications, Inc., 1987), Vol. 2, 697-699, 704, 783-784.

12. Hunter, John Warren. "Some Early Tragedies of San Antonio: The Autobiography of Carlos Beltran," *Frontier Times*. Bandera, Texas. Vol. 18, No. 3; 117-121, 122-123, 139-141.
13. Cox, Wayne. *Field Survey and Archival Research for the Rosillo Creek Battleground Area, Southeast of San Antonio, Texas*. Appendix by Dora Guerra. (San Antonio: Center for Archeological Research, The University of Texas at San Antonio, Archeological Survey Report, No. 177), 38.
14. Austin, Stephen F. "Journal of Stephen F. Austin on His First Trip to Texas in 1821," *Quarterly of the Texas State Historical Association*, Vol. 7, No. 4 (April 1904), 296.
15. Jack Jackson, ed., *Texas by Terán: The Diary Kept by General Manuel de Mier y Terán on His 1828 Inspection of Texas*. (Austin: University of Texas Press, 2000, 15-18.
16. _____, *Texas by Terán*, 19-20. Castañeda, Carlos E., ed. and trans., "A Trip to Texas in 1828, *Southwestern Historical Quarterly*, Vol. 24, No. 4 (April 1926), 257.
17. _____, *Texas by Terán*, 34-37.
18. Clopper, J. C. "J. C. Clopper's Journal and Book of Memoranda for 1828 for the Province of Texas." *Southwestern Historical* Quarterly. Volume 13; No. 1; section on San Antonio de Béxar, 69-76.
19. Cruz, Gilbert R., ed. "San Antonio City Ordinances, 1829," in *Catholic Southwest: A Journal of History and Culture*. Vol. 20, 2009, 83-97.
20. Benjamin Lundy. *The Life, Travels, and Opinions of Benjamin Lundy*. (Philadelphia: William D. Parrish, 1847), 47-56.
21. Sons of Dewitt Colony Texas Web Site. " Juan Almonte's Report on Texas, Spring/ Summer 1834, Published in 1835," https://www.sonsofdewittcolony.org/almonterep.htm. Juan N. Almonte's full report on the Department of Bexar can be found in Jackson, Jack, ed., *Almonte's Texas: Juan N. Almonte's 1834 Inspection Report & Role in the 1836 Campaign*. John Wheat, trans. (Austin: Texas State Historical Association, 2003), 233-244.
22. Sons of Dewitt Colony Texas Web Site. "Account of the Siege and Battle of Bexar From Within Bexar From the Diary of Samuel A. Maverick," http://www.sonsofdewittcolony.org/dewitt.htm.
23. Wallace O. Chariton. *100 Days in Texas: The Alamo Letters*. (Plano: Wordware Publishing, Inc., 1990), 203-204.
24. _____, *The Alamo Letters*, 225-226.
25. _____, *The Alamo Letters*, 226-227.
26. Carlos Casteñeda, ed. and trans. *The Mexican Side of the Texas Revolution*. (Washington, D.C.: Documentary Publications, 1971), 12-13.
27. Timothy M. Matovina, ed. *The Alamo Remembered: Tejano Accounts and Perspectives*. (Austin: University of Texas Press, 1995), 54-57.
28. Jenkins, John H., ed. *Papers of the Texas Revolution*. (10 Vol.; Austin: Presidial Press, 1973), 7:244.
29. Green, Rena M. *The Diary of Mary A. Maverick*. (San Antonio: Alamo Printing Co., 1921), 21-26.
30. _____, *Mary A. Maverick Diary*, 31-34.
31. _____, *Mary A. Maverick Diary*, 53-54.
32. Texas State Library and Archives, 5th Congress, General Laws, Texas Digital Archives, https://tsl.access.preservica.com/uncategorized/IO_a7a3e14f-4c48-481e-8cea-00b72fe9f50d/.

33 Sanchez Lamego, Gen. Miguel A. *The Second Mexican-Texas War, 1841-1843*. Hillsboro: Hill Junior College, 1972), 82.
34 Nance, Joseph Milton. "Brigadier General Adrian Woll's Report of His Expedition into Texas in 1842." *Southwestern Historical Quarterly*. Vol. 58, No. 4 (April 1955), 528-31.
35 [Page, Frederic Benjamin]. Prairiedom: Rambles and Scrambles in Texas or New Estrémadura. By A Suthron. (New York: Paine and Burgess, 1845). 124-135.
36 Gregg, Josiah, *Diary & Letters of Josiah Gregg*. Edited by Maurice Garland Fulton. (2 Vols.; Norman: University of Oklahoma Press, 1941), Vol 1, 236-238.
37 Edith Rydell Roberts, ed., *The Mexican War Logbook & Letters of Captain Jefferson Peak*. (Richardson: A Publication of the Descendants of Mexican War Veterans, 1996), 9-10.
38 Romer, Dr. Ferdinand. *Texas: With Particular Reference to German Immigration and The Physical Appearance of the Country*. Oswald Mueller, trans. and ed. (San Antonio: Standard Printing Company, 1935), 119-124.
39 Quartermaster Records from National Archives in the Office of Alamo Curator.
40 *Alamo Star*, San Antonio, Texas, 1854. The editions referenced here were located at The University of North Texas's Portal to Texas History (*https://texashistory.unt.edu/*) using the key words "Alamo Star."
41 Crimmins, M. L. "Colonel J. K. F. Mansfield's Report of the Inspection of the Department of Texas in 1856," *Southwestern Historical Quarterly. Vol. 42, No. 2 (Oct. 1938)*, 129.
42 Crimmins, M. L., "W. G. Freeman's Report on the Eighth Military Department (Continued). *Southwestern Historical Quarterly*. Vol. 51, No. 2 (Oct. 1947), 167.
43 Olmstead, Frederick Law. *A Journey Through Texas: Or, A Saddle Trip on the Southwestern Frontier*. (New York: Dix, Edwards, & Co., 1857), 154-161.
44 Thompson, Jerry, ed., *Texas & New Mexico on the Eve of the Civil War: the Mansfield and Johnston Inspections, 1859-1861*. (Albuquerque: University of New Mexico Press, 2001), 173-76.
45 *Official Records of the War of the Rebellion*. (144 Vols.: Washington, D.C.: Government Printing Office, 1880), Vol. 4, 515, 519-520.
46 Thompson, Jerry D., ed. *From Desert to Bayou The Civil War Journal and Sketches of Morgan Wolfe Merrick*. (El Paso: University of Texas Press at El Paso, 1991), 3, 6, 8.
47 Marks, Paula Mitchell, ed. *When Will the Weary War Be Over? The Civil War Letters of the Maverick Family of San Antonio*. (Dallas: Book Club of Texas, 2008), 36, 126, 133, 144, 152. 164-65.
48 McConnell, H. H. *Five Years a Cavalryman*. (NP: J.N. Rogers & Company, 1888), 47-56.
49 Lanier, Sidney. *Retrospects and Prospects: Descriptions and Historical Essays*. Edited by Mary Day Lanier. (New York: Charles Scribner's Sons, 1890), 84-93.
50 Wright, Mrs. S. J. San Antonio de Béxar: Historical. Traditional. Legendary (Austin: Morgan Publishing, 1916), 115-127. Digital copy located at the following web address: *https://books.google.com/books?printsec=frontcover&dq=san+antonio+de+bexar &newbks=1&newbks_redir=0&id=VvATAAAAYAAJ&output=text*
51 Raines, C. W. Year Book for Texas for 1901. (Austin: Von Boeckmann, Schutze, & Co., 1902), 262-262.
52 Raines, C. W. Year Book for Texas for 1901. (Austin: Von Boeckmann, Schutze, & Co., 1902), 151-52.

Sources Cited

BOOKS

Brickerhoff, Sidney, and Odie B. Faulk. *Lancers for the King: A Study of the Frontier Military System of Northern New Spain, with a translation of the Royal Regulations of 1772.* Phoenix: Arizona Historical Foundation, 1965.

Casteñeda, Carlos, ed. and trans. *The Mexican Side of the Texas Revolution.* Washington, D.C.: Documentary Publications.

Conner, William, ed. *San Antonio de Bexar: A Guide and History.* San Antonio: Bainbridge Press, 1890.

Coues, Elliot, ed. *The Expeditions of Zebulon Montgomery Pike.* 2 Vols.; New York: Dover Publications, Inc., 1987.

Green, Rena M. *The Diary of Mary A. Maverick.* San Antonio: Alamo Printing Co., 1921.

Gregg, Josiah, *Diary & Letters of Josiah Gregg.* Edited by Maurice Garland Fulton. 2 Vols.; Norman: University of Oklahoma Press, 1941.

Jackson, Jack, ed., *Almonte's Texas: Juan N. Almonte's 1834 Inspection Report & Role in the 1836 Campaign.* John Wheat, trans. Austin: Texas State Historical Association, 2003.

Jack Jackson, ed., *Texas by Terán: The Diary Kept by General Manuel de Mier y Terán on His 1828 Inspection of Texas.* Austin: University of Texas Press.

Jenkins, John H., ed. *Papers of the Texas Revolution.* 10 Vol.; Austin: Presidial Press, 1973.

Sanchez Lamego, Ge, Miguel A. *The Second Mexican-Texas War, 1841-1843.* Hillsboro: Hill Junior College, 1972.

Lanier, Sidney. *Retrospects and Prospects: Descriptions and Historical Essays.* Edited by Mary Day Lanier. New York: Charles Scribner's Sons, 1890.

Leutenegger, Fr. Benedict, ed. and trans. *Guidelines for a Texas Mission: Instructions for the Missionary of Mission Concepción in San Antonio, ca. 1760.* San Antonio: Old Spanish Mission Historical Research Library at San José Mission, 1976.

Lundy, Benjamin. *The Life, Travels, and Opinions of Benjamin Lundy*. Philadelphia: William D. Parrish, 1847.

Marks, Paula Mitchell, ed. *When Will the Weary War Be Over? The Civil War Letters of the Maverick Family of San Antonio*. Dallas: Book Club of Texas, 2008.

Matovina, Timothy M., ed. *The Alamo Remembered: Tejano Accounts and Perspectives*. Austin: University of Texas Press, 1995.

McConnell, H. H. *Five Years a Cavalryman*. NP: J.N. Rogers & Company, 1888.

Olmstead, Frederick Law. *A Journey Through Texas: Or, A Saddle Trip on the Southwestern Frontier*. New York: Dix, Edwards, & Co., 1857.

[Page, Frederic Benjamin]. *Prairiedom: Rambles and Scrambles in Texas or New Estrémadura. By A Suthron*. New York: Paine and Burgess, 1845.

Raines, C. W. *Year Book for Texas for 1901*. Austin: Von Boeckmann, Schutze, & Co., 1902.

Roberts, Edith Rydell, ed., *The Mexican War Logbook & Letters of Captain Jefferson Peak*. Richardson: A Publication of the Descendants of Mexican War Veterans, 1996.

Romer, Dr. Ferdinand. *Texas: With Particular Reference to German Immigration and The Physical Appearance of the Country*. Oswald Mueller, trans. and ed. San Antonio: Standard Printing Company, 1935.

Thompson, Jerry D., ed. *From Desert to Bayou The Civil War Journal and Sketches of Morgan Wolfe Merrick*. El Paso: University of Texas Press at El Paso, 1991.

_____. *Texas & New Mexico on the Eve of the Civil War: The Mansfield and Johnston Inspections, 1859-1861*. Albuquerque: University of New Mexico Press, 2001.

Wallace O. Chariton. *100 Days in Texas: The Alamo Letters*. Plano: Wordware Publishing, Inc., 1990.

War Department. *Official Records of the War of the Rebellion*. 144 Vols.: Washington, D.C.: Government Printing Office, 1880.

Wright, Mrs. S. J. *San Antonio de Béxar: Historical. Traditional. Legendary*. Austin: Morgan Publishing, 1916.

ARTICLES

Austin, Stephen F. "Journal of Stephen F. Austin on His First Trip to Texas in 1821," *Quarterly of the Texas State Historical Association*, Vol. 7, No. 4 (April 1904), 286–307.

Castaneda, Carlos E., ed. and trans. "A Trip to Texas in 1828," *Southwestern Historical Quarterly*. Vol. 24, No. 4 (April 1926), 257, 249–288.

Clopper, J. C. "J. C. Clopper's Journal and Book of Memoranda for 1828 for the Province of Texas." *Southwestern Historical Quarterly*. Volume 13; No. 1; (July 1909), 44–88.

Crimmins, M. L. "Colonel J. K. F. Mansfield's Report of the Inspection of the Department of Texas in 1856," *Southwestern Historical Quarterly*. Vol. 42, No. 2 (Oct. 1938), 122–148.

Crimmins, M. L., "W. G. Freeman's Report on the Eighth Military Department (Continued). *Southwestern Historical Quarterly*. Vol. 51, No. 2 (Oct. 1947), 167–174.

Cruz, Gilbert R., ed. "San Antonio City Ordinances, 1829," in *Catholic Southwest: A Journal of History and Culture*. Vol. 20, 2009, 80–100.

Faulk, Odie, ed. "A Description of Texas in 1803: Report of Governor Don Juan Bautista Elguézabal." *Southwestern Historical Quarterly*. Vol. 66, No. 4 (April 1963), 513–515.

Hoffman, Fritz, ed. "The Mezquía Diary of the Alarcon Expedition into Texas, 1718," *Southwestern Historical Quarterly* Vol. 41, No. 4 (April 1938), 312–323.

Hunter, John Warren. "Some Early Tragedies of San Antonio: The Autobiography of Carlos Beltran," *Frontier Times*. Bandera, Texas. Vol. 18, No. 3; 115–141.

Leutenegger, Benedict and Benito Fernández. "Memorial of Father Benito Fernández Concerning the Canary Islanders, 1741," *Southwestern Historical Quarterly*, Vol. 82, No. 3 (January 1979), 265–296.

Leutenegger, Benedict. "Report on San Antonio Mission in 1792," *Southwestern Historical Quarterly*. Vol. 77, No. 4 (April 1974), 487–498.

Magnaghi, Russell M. "Texas as Seen by Governor Winthuysen, 1741-1744," *Southwestern Historical Quarterly*, Vol. 88, No. 2 (October 1984), 167–180.

Nance, Joseph Milton. "Brigadier General Adrian Woll's Report of His Expedition into Texas in 1842." *Southwestern Historical Quarterly*. Vol. 58, No. 4 (April 1955), 523–552.

WEB SITES

Briscoe Center for American History, Bexar Archives, Translation of Croix to Ripperdá, enclosing ordinances and by-laws concerning the government of Texas and the establishment and management of mesteñas fund, January 11, 1778. Digital Archives: *https://www.cah.utexas.edu/projects/bexar/gallery_doc.php?doc=e_bx_002652*.

Portal to Texas History, University of North Texas, *Alamo Star*, San Antonio, Texas, 1854. (*https://texashistory.unt.edu/*)

Sons of Dewitt Colony Texas Web Site. "Account of the Siege and Battle of Bexar From Within Bexar From the Diary of Samuel A. Maverick," *http://www.sonsofdewittcolony.org/dewitt.htm*.

Sons of Dewitt Colony Texas Web Site. " Juan Almonte's Report on Texas, Spring/Summer 1834, Published in 1835," *https://www.sonsofdewittcolony.org/almonterep.htm*.

Texas State Library and Archives, 5th Congress, General Laws, Texas Digital Archives, *https://tsl.access.preservica.com/uncategorized/IO_a7a3e14f-4c48-481e-8cea-00b72fe9f50d/*.

U.S. Quartermaster Records

Index

Adams, William 150
Alcalde 16, 37, 50, 53, 83, 103, 104, 105, 106, 107, 108, 113, 115, 119
Alacrón, Martín de 7
Alamo 2, 3, 62, 66, 72, 73, 74, 75, 77, 86, 89, 91, 107, 108, 126-130, 132, 134, 135, 137, 140-145, 149, 153, 166, 167, 172, 173, 175, 181-183, 192-195, 197, 198, 200, 204, 218, 219, 222, 229-231, 241, 243, 251, 278, 279, 286, 289, 290
Alamo Plaza 252, 272, 280
Alamo Star (newspaper) vi, 1, 196, 205, 287, 291
Almonte, Juan N. 122, 286, 289, 289, 291
Alsbury, Horace 183
Alsbury, Juana Gertrudis Navarro 183
Andrade, Col. Juan José 145
Apache Indians 26, 41, 49
Arroyo de Cibolo 44-47
Arredondo, Gen. Joaquín de 70, 77, 78
Auguyo, Marquíz Miguel de 18
Austin, Moses 83
Austin, Stephen F. 83, 84, 94, 118, 126-131, 134, 247, 286, 290

Battle of Flowers 267, 277, 282
Barragan, Capt. 131
Bejar (alternate spelling) 20, 23, 30, 45, 46, 56, 89, 92, 125, 127, 128, 138, 164,
Beltran, Carlos 71, 286, 291
Berlandier, Louis 85, 86
Bowie, James 127-130, 138, 141, 175, 182, 252, 255
Buenaventura y Olivares. Fray San Antonio 10, 46
Buffalo 63, 90, 173, 174, 177, 262, 275
Burleson, Gen. Edward 136

Casafuerte, Marquíz de 23, 24, 28,
Canary Islanders 18, 22, 23, 26, 43, 102, 285, 291
Casiano, Don José 149, 150, 151, 210
Castroville 269
Catholic Church 11, 161, 162, 193, 194, 220, 259
Cattle 3, 9, 15, 24, 25, 37, 38, 48, 49, 50, 52, 53, 55, 63, 88, 123, 146, 176, 222, 254, 274
Chile 15, 63, 64
Cholera 118, 119, 120, 121, 124, 270
Clopper, Joseph C. 94, 179, 286, 290
Clopper, Nicolas 94,
Chihuahua 71, 179, 193, 253, 268

Civil War 181, 227, 251, 256, 271, 272, 287, 290
Comanche Indians 71, 74, 126, 154, 155, 156, 196, 202, 218, 235
Commerce Street 259, 149, 152, 153, 156, 158, 212, 259, 262, 273, 282
Copano 137, 138
Constitution of 1824 102, 128,
Cordero, Gov. Manuel Antonio de 66, 67, 75
Cos, Gen. Martín Perfecto 125, 126,
Costales, Captain Don Gabriel 24, 33
Council House Fight 154, 155,
Court 27, 56, 123, 155, 156, 166, 180, 191, 208, 215, 222, 276
Crockett, Col. Davy 141, 144, 175, 182, 252, 280
Croix, Teodoro de 49, 50, 54, 55,
Cupples. Dr. George 210, 242, 269, 270

Daughters of the Republic of Texas 1, 9, 19, 35, 100, 104, 170, 180, 188, 199, 212, 225, 236, 246, 248, 258, 260, 261, 268, 271, 274, 275, 279, 282
Delgado, Antonio 73-76
Dogs 112, 152, 197, 198, 204, 248, 264

Fandango 96, 97, 98, 106, 187, 188, 189, 190, 215
Fiesta San Antonio 277
Ford, John S. "Rip" 236, 273
Fort Sam Houston 280, 281
Freeman, W. G. 219, 220, 287, 290

Galveston 150, 226,
Gambling 16, 190, 217
Garza, José de la 133, 134, 136, 160, 181, 221
General Land Office 1

German 187, 198, 203, 204, 208, 210, 224, 226, 259, 260, 263, 264, 267, 269, 270, 271, 282, 287, 290
Goodspeed, John
Gregg, Josiah 94, 179, 287, 289
Gregg, Harmon 94, 179
Gillespie, Robert A. 200, 215,
Gutierrez, Don Bernardo 73-75

Halley's Comet 126
Harrison, Pres. Benjamin 277
Herrera, Blas 75, 76, 145-146
Herrera, Símon de 66, 67, 70, 73, 74, 75
Hidalgo, Father Miguel 70, 181
Horses 8, 20, 25, 42, 44, 46, 48, 49, 52, 53, 63, 64, 72, 74, 76, 87, 88, 97, 100, 129, 131, 141, 167, 170, 177, 184, 189, 201, 206, 216, 243, 268, 276
Houston, Gen. Sam 128, 205, 235, 280
Howard, Capt. Tom 155, 156, 229

Indian (Mission) converts 12, 22, 44

Jacale 86, 180

Kemper, Samuel 73, 74
Knights of the Golden Circle (KGC) 241, 242

La Bahía (Goliad) 46, 57, 62, 63, 72, 92, 116, 126, 136, 137, 138
La Noche Triste 76
La Salle 7
Lamar, Mirabeau B. 163, 235
Lanier, Sidney 256, 287, 289
Léon Creek 8,
Lockhart, Matilda 154, 155

INDEX

López, Fray Francisco 56, 61,
Louisiana Purchase 62,
Los Adaes 41, 47
Lundy, Benjamin 114, 286, 290

Main Plaza 71, 73, 77, 150, 151, 153, 155, 159, 165, 212, 236, 248, 252, 257, 258, 271, 273, 276
Manchaca, Miguel 73, 74
Mansfield, Col. Joseph K. F. 218, 227, 287, 290
Maverick, Albert (child) 245
Maverick, Elizabeth (child) 245
Maverick, Franklin (slave) 247
Maverick, George M. (son) 248, 249
Maverick, Jinny Anderson (slave) 157
Maverick, Lewis (child) 153, 245, 248
Maverick, Mary A. 149, 153, 159, 245, 247, 286, 289
Maverick, Mary, B. (child) 245, 246
Maverick, Samuel A. 125, 149, 150, 151, 157, 161, 220, 236, 237, 238, 245, 246, 272, 273, 286, 291
Maverick, Samuel, Jr. (child) 245,
Maverick, William (child) 247
Medina River 41, 211
Merrick, Morgan Wolfe 241, 244, 287, 290
Méxia, Gen. José Antonio 128, 129,131, 132,
Mexican Independence 98, 181
Mexican War 179, 193, 196, 241, 242, 253, 287, 290
Mier y Terán, Gen. Manuel de 85, 138, 286, 289
Milam, Benjamin Rush 133, 136, 181, 200
Mission Nuestra Señora de la Concepcíon de Acuna 30, 42,
Mission San Antonio de Valero 18, 19 56, 63, 221
Mission San Juan de la Espada 30, 43, 57, 108, 162, 222

Mission San José 261, 30, 57, 58, 89, 108, 127, 151, 153, 154, 162, 172, 222, 261, 285, 289
Mission San Juan Capistrano 30, 43, 57, 58, 153
M'Guire, Father 66, 67
McConnell, H. H. 251, 287, 290
McCulloch, Ben 236, 239, 241
McCulloch, Henry 236,
McKinley, Pres. William 278, 279, 280

Nacogdoches 58, 62, 63, 92, 115, 162
Navarro, José Angel 135, 160
Navarro, José Antonio 70, 160,
Newcomb, James P. 196, 205,
Norther 131, 134, 171, 253
Nuñez, Don Miguel 28

Olmstead, Frederick Law 221, 287, 290
Ordnances (town) 103

Queen of the West 1, 198

Padilla, Jun Antonio 115, 120, 133
Page, Frederic Benjamin 169, 287, 290
Peak, Capt. Jefferson 182, 287, 290
Pike, Zebulon 65, 285, 289
Presidio de Béxar 18, 44,
Presidio regulations 44, 47, 50

Railroad 201, 251, 253, 254, 270, 274, 275, 281,
Ralston, J. H. 195
Reconstruction 196, 251, 273
Rivera, Brigadier Don Pedro 39
Rio Grande 7, 8, 88, 100, 117, 123, 127, 137, 139, 166, 182, 256, 272, 273

Rodriguez, Joseph Antonio 28, 127
Rodriguez. Pablo 74
Rodriguez, Señora 72, 74, 78
Roemer, Dr. Frederick von 187
Rubí, Marquéz de 44
Ruiz, José Francisco 70, 145,
Rusk, Thomas Jefferson 131

Saltillo 18, 19, 63, 113
Salcedo, Gov. Teodoe Manual María 70, 73, 74, 75, 76
Sambrano, José Dario 79
San Antonio River 7, 9, 22, 23, 30, 31, 42, 75, 100, 101, 137, 138, 150, 153, 171, 173, 175, 177, 199, 201, 252, 262
San Antonio de Béxar 2, 42, 62, 70, 102, 122, 123, 125, 137, 150, 170, 173, 176, 179, 180, 195, 264, 267, 277, 285-290
San Antonio de Valero 18, 19, 56, 63, 221,
St. Ana, Fray Benito Fernando de
Santa Anna, Gen. Antonio López de 122, 133, 138, 139, 141, 142, 145, 163, 165, 166, 181, 198, 252
San Pedro River/Creek 42, 252, 257
Sánchez y Tapía, María 85, 89
Second Flying Company of San Carlos de Alamo de Parras 62
Seguín, Erasmo 83, 150, 153, 182, 183
Seguín, Juan N. 130, 145, 146, 167, 183
Sheep 8, 36, 63, 105, 110, 123, 176, 177
Slaves and Slavery 29, 78, 97, 114, 122, 208, 235, 251
Soledad Street 135, 151, 152, 153, 157
Smith, John W. 115, 125, 126, 131, 132, 134, 135, 229
Smithers, Lancelot 150
Spring 8, 9, 10, 120, 131, 142, 152, 170, 171, 172, 174, 177, 192, 203, 223, 224, 230, 240, 242, 244, 253, 262, 270, 272, 286, 291

Sons of the South 249
Stock show 283

Tax 26, 48, 53, 55, 102, 103, 109, 110, 111
Texas Rangers 3
Tobin, William 272, 273
Travis, William Barret 139, 141, 175, 198, 200, 216, 222, 252
Twiggs Surrender 235

Ugartechea, Col. Domingo de 126, 129, 130, 132, 133, 134, 136,
United States Quartermaster Department 161
Urruita, Captain Joseph de 33

Vagabonds 48, 50, 51
Vance, Martha 246,
Vaquez, Rafael 163
Veramendi, Martín de 70, 119,
Viesca, Gov. 113, 133
Villa de Béxar 18
Villa de San Fernando 19, 64, 89, 173

Walker, Samuel H. 200, 216,
Wilcox, John A. 204, 206
Wilkinson, Gen. James 66
Winthuysen. Gov. Tomas Felipe de 41, 44, 285, 291
Wool, Gen. John E. 179, 183, 193

Yorba, Senora Eulalia 140, 141

Zerbin, Dr. 66, 67